TSAR AND PEOPLE

Studies in Russian Myths

TSAR AND PEOPLE

Studies in Russian Myths

by Michael Cherniavsky

New Haven and London:

Yale University Press, 1961

TO MY FATHER

Preface

This book is the outgrowth of my article "Holy Russia: A Study in the History of an Idea," published in the *American Historical Review, 63* (April 1958). Both the article and the present work, which was originally conceived of as a number of separate studies, have their origin in a rather sudden realization that the problems of Russian national and social myths have been almost completely overlooked by historians seeking to understand the history and nature of Russian society. The many Russians who were aware of the content of such epithets as "Holy Russia," the "Russian God," and the "Russian Soul" ended up, in each case that I know of, debating, denying, or justifying the validity, the appropriateness of the particular epithet: Is Russia holy? Is there a Russian God and what is He like? Why is the Russian Soul so unique? The outsiders, the non-Russian scholars, tended to accept the epithets which symbolized Russian myths at their face value, as clichés, to be dismissed as expressions of national arrogance, or as vague abstractions indicating Russian differences from the West. Neither group saw such epithets as reflections of living myths, shifting in emphasis and content in the course of Russian history, reflecting both the aspirations of Russian society and the changing historical reality as felt by the Russian people. The part of this book, then, which deals with the "People" is an attempt to fill these lacunae by describing the origin, history, and development of the main Russian national myth, that of "Holy Russia," from its beginnings in the seventeenth century to its end in 1917.

Different from the historiographic status of the Russian national myth is that of the Russian ruler. Numerous and excellent studies have been made of various aspects of Russian political theory and theology, of the role and function of the Russian ruler in theory and practice. The justification for those sections of the book which deal with the myth of the Russian Tsar lies in the attempt to trace at least one aspect of that myth—that of the saintly ruler —through the peripatetics of Russian history, from the Christianization of Russia in the late tenth century to the late nineteenth century, at which time the myth died.

The technical problem of transliteration into English of Russian words and phrases I have met by using the Library of Congress system, with one major exception: names such as Dostoevsky, Tolstoy, and Gorky are familiar enough that the "ii" and "oi" endings are better transliterated as "y." Hence, for the sake of consistency, all proper names ending in "ii" and "oi" appear here with "y" and "oy" endings, respectively.

My thanks are due to the *American Historical Review* for permission to use, extensively, my article "Holy Russia: A Study in the History of an Idea"; to Macmillan & Co., Ltd., and to Sir Maurice Bowra for permission to quote translations of Russian poems from *Book of Russian Verse* and *A Second Book of Russian Verse;* to Edward

Arnold, Ltd., for permission to quote Oliver Elton's translation of Pushkin, from *Verse from Pushkin and Others;* and to Baroness Moura Budberg for permission to quote from her translation of Gorky's diary, *Fragments from My Diary* (Penguin).

To the many friends and colleagues who have participated in my work, I am grateful. I should like also to acknowledge the debt I owe to the Wesleyan University Research Fund, whose generous financial help underwrote the costs of research, of the preparation of the manuscript and of the illustrations; to the Sterling Library of Yale University, without whose facilities this work could not even have been started; to the Ford Foundation for assistance with the costs of publication; to my student Peter Rosenbaum, who helped me greatly with the index; and to two friends: Ihor Ševčenko of Columbia University, whose very great learning and critical mind were always at my disposal; and Loren Baritz of Wesleyan University who prodded me, encouraged me, listened to me endlessly, and read the manuscript time and again, in parts and as a whole.

MICHAEL CHERNIAVSKY

Middletown, Conn.
September 1960

Contents

Illustrations

(*following page 60*)

1. Ivan IV, fresco in the Novo-Spasskii Monastery, from *Poslaniia Ivana Groznogo*, ed. V. P. Adrianova-Perets (ANSSSR, 1951), 400.

2. Group of clerical saints on the east wall in the Cathedral of the Birth of the Virgin in the Snetogorskii Monastery near Pskov, early fourteenth century. From N. M. Chernyshev, *Iskusstvo Freski v Drevnei Rusi* (Moscow, 1954), pl. 10.

3. Ivan IV, in the Kazanskaia Letopis', from *Poslaniia*, 384.

4. St. Paul, ca. 1500, in the Ferapont Monastery at Belozero; from Chernyshev, pl. 6.

5. St. Paul, fresco by Andrew Rublev, early fifteenth century, in the Cathedral of the Assumption of the Virgin in Zvenigorod; from L. Ouspensky and W. Lossky, *Der Sinn der Ikonen* (Basle, 1952), 113.

6. Portrait of Ivan IV in *Bol'shaia Gosudarstvennaia Kniga* of 1672; from *Portrety, Gerby i Pechati Bol'shoi*

Gosudarstvennoi Knigi 1672g. (St. Petersburg, 1903), 26.

7. Grand Prince Iury Dolgoruky; from *Portrety,* 14.

8. Tsar Alexis; from *Portrety,* 32.

9. Tsar Michael; from *Portrety,* 31.

10. Tsarevich Dimitry of Uglich; from *Portrety,* 28.

11. Peter I, engraving by J. Houbraken, based on a portrait by Karl Moor of 1717; from D. A. Rovinsky, *Podrobnyi Slovar' Russkikh Gravirovannykh Portretov, 3* (St. Petersburg, 1888), col. 1576.

12. Peter I and Ivan V in the "Thesis of Obedovsky," engraving, late seventeenth century; from Rovinsky, *3,* col. 1531.

13. Peter I, engraving by P. Picart, 1717; from Rovinsky, *3,* col. 1616.

14. Ivan IV, by Victor Vasnetsov, 1897; from N. Morgunov, *Viktor Vasnetsov, 38* (Moscow-Leningrad, 1940).

15. Tsar Feodor Ivanovich, cloth, sixteenth century; from *Vrememnik Ivana Timofeeva,* ed. O. A. Derzhavina, *17* (ANSSSR, 1951).

16. *Spas Iaroe Oko* (The Saviour of the Angry Eye), icon, mid-fourteenth century, now in the Tretiakov Gallery in Moscow; from *Istoriia Russkogo Iskusstva,* ed. I. E. Grabar, *3* (Moscow, 1955), 81.

17. Ivan IV, sixteenth-century portrait; from *Poslaniia,* frontispiece.

18. John the Evangelist, Church of the Dormition, at Volotovo near Novgorod, fourteenth century; from Chernyshev, pl. 29.

List of Abbreviations

A.A.E.	*Akty, Sobrannye v bibliote-kakh i Arkhivakh, Arkhe-ograficheskoi Ekspeditsiei*
A.H.R.	*American Historical Review*
A.I.	*Akty Istoricheskie, Sob-rannye i izdannye, Arkhe-ograficheskoi Kommissiei*
ANSSSR	Akademiia Nauk SSSR
Cherepnin	*Dukhovnye i Dogovornye Gramoty Velikikh i Udel'-nykh Kniazei, XIV–XVI vv.*, ed. L. V. Cherepnin (ANSSSR, 1950)
Chteniia	*Chteniia v Imperatorskom Obshchestve Istorii i Drev-nostei Rossiiskikh Pri Mos-kovskom Universitete*

Dostoevsky	All references are to the 10-volume edition of *Sobranie Sochinenii* (Moscow, 1956–1958).
Dostoevsky, *Dnevnik*, I	*Dnevnik Pisatelia za 1873 god* (Paris, n.d.)
Dostoevsky, *Dnevnik*, II	*Dnevnik Pisatelia za 1876 god* (Paris, n.d.)
Dostoevsky, *Dnevnik*, III	*Dnevnik Pisatelia za 1877 god* (Paris, n.d.)
D.R.V.	*Drevneia Rossiiskaia Vivliofika*
H.S.S.	*Harvard Slavic Studies*
I.R.A.O.	*Izvestiia Imperatorskago Arkheologicheskago Obshchestva*
Istoriia	S. M. Soloviev, *Istoriia Rossii s Drevneishikh Vremen*, 24 books in 6 volumes, 3rd edition (St. Petersburg, n.d.)
Karamzin	N. M. Karamzin, *Istoriia Gosudarstva Rossiiskago*, 12 vols. in 6 (St. Petersburg, 1892)
P.D.P.I.	*Pamiatniki Drevnei Pis'mennosti i Iskusstva*, ed. by *Obshchestvo Liubitelei Drevnei Pismennosti*
P.S.R.L.	*Polnoe Sobranie Zakonov Letopisei*
P.S.Z.	*Polnoe Sobranie Zakonov Rossiiskoi Imperii*

R.I.B.	*Russkaia Istoricheskaia Biblioteka*
S.G.G.D.	*Sobranie Gosudarstvennykh Gramot i Dogovorov*
S.R.I.O.	*Sbornik Imperatorskago Russkago Istoricheskago Obshchestva*
T.O.D.R.L.	*Trudy Otdela Drevne-Russkoi Literatury*, Institut Russkoi Literatury, ANSSSR
Z.R.A.O.	*Zapiski Imperatorskago Russkago Arkheologicheskago Obshchestva*

Introduction

Psychologists and anthropologists have shown the universality of most myths, founded as they are on human insecurity, on a universal need to justify and in some sense to explain away reality. But while all societies manifest basic and similar fears and needs, each expresses them in unique form, according to its particular history and circumstances. Inasmuch as myths, which are expressions of human needs both individual and collective, are specific and different, they enter the province of the historian. And insofar as they manifest the desires and anxieties of a particular society, they are within time and space, rather than vague abstractions about humanity at large. Hence the Russian myths about the ruler and the people are not manifestations of inherent and eternal Russian characteristics; they do not reveal the essential and singular "nature" of a Russian. Instead, they indicate popular reaction to the particular conditions of Russian life, the unique circumstances of Russian history.

But these myths, Russian though they were, are not without meaning for those who are not part of Russia and its history. In a conversation with Eckermann about Roman historical legends, Goethe remarked: "If the Romans were great enough to invent such stories, we should at least be great enough to believe them." Goethe was referring to the "heroic" fables about Lucretia and Mucius Scaevola, but his words reveal the power and hint at the danger inherent in all myths, legends, and fables, for in their very essence lies the human impulse to deny reality: "Perhaps it is not so, but it *should* be so." The poet wanted us to believe in these stories because they were edifyingly noble and heroic and thus human in the best sense. It is most unlikely that he would have given the same advice about the Russian myths of Tsar and People, and, in our own "Age of the Irrational," we have learnt too well that, unfortunately, all myths are edifying, all have some followers, no matter how unpalatable or even monstrous the myths may appear to the rest of us. Still, myths have always existed, and not the least among them in fantasy and complexity were the Russian ones. And, if they were not human in the best sense, they were nonetheless profoundly human. Their very power and intensity, their sway over Russians and even non-Russians,[1] can cause repugnance; but Goethe's advice might be modified to recommend a degree of tolerance sufficient to study these myths and to see them as expressions of minds similar to our own.

The myth of the Tsar and the myth of the People have been chosen for this study because they appear to be the most striking of Russian myths. But they were not the only

1. Some of the Russian epithets which symbolized the myths—"Little Father Tsar," "Holy Russia," "Mother Russia," and, most particularly, the "Russian Soul"—have become commonplaces outside Russia as well. So much so that even non-Russians began to believe in them. For some examples of such transference of belief, see my study "Holy Russia: A Study in the History of an Idea," *AHR, 63* (1958), 629, note 56 and 636, note 90; also see William James' conversation with Gorky, *Sobranie Sochinenii, 24* (Moscow, 1955), 136.

ones created by the Russian people, and their history is
not the history of Russian mythologizing. Nor is it an
accurate reflection of Russian intellectual history, for those
who were involved with the myths tended to be more in-
secure, more patriotic, more traditionalist and conservative than the Russians who were indifferent to these myths
or bent on creating others in opposition to them. Finally,
the history of these myths presents a serious methodologi-
cal problem. As myths, the image of the ruler and that of
the people are assumed to have been widely, if not universally, current. This assumption we must make while
studying the medieval period, for both the paucity of
sources and the fact of a comparatively homogeneous society allow us to consider the available evidence as expressing popular beliefs. For the modern period, in which
the educated upper classes had a monopoly of written and
published opinions, the assumption becomes tenuous, to
say the least. What the mass of the Russian people thought
and felt about these myths, we do not really know; but
the people accepted and used the commonplace symbols
of the myths—the particular epithets for ruler and people
—and thereby acknowledged at least the existence of the
ideas behind the symbols, whatever their content may have
been.

Even though it is limited to only two myths, Tsar and
People, this work cannot pretend to comprehensiveness.
National self-consciousness and the worship of power are
areas of human concern too broad to be embraced by a
few symbolic formulas, no matter how flexible. In all
their irrationality and even perversity, however, myths
are created by man in response to challenges and questions posed by the conditions of their lives; thus, myths
reflect reality or, what is the same thing, the history of
a society—even if the reflection is distorted. Incomplete
though it is, describing only a narrow band in the spec-

trum of Russian thought, the history of the myths of Tsar
and of People should then reveal, in some measure, another dimension of Russian history, and, at the same
time, may suggest something about the nature of historical myths.

1. Saintly Princes and Princely Saints

> "Russian history reads like the lives of the Saints."
>
> —K. AKSAKOV

THE assassination of Prime Minister Peter A. Stolypin in September of 1911 had one curious consequence. Metropolitan Pitirim of St. Petersburg, a protégé of Rasputin, suggested that Stolypin be canonized as a martyr for Russia. No new St. Peter was entered in the liturgy of the Russian Orthodox Church, but the reasoning behind the suggestion of the metropolitan is interesting. Clearly, as an extreme reactionary, Pitirim considered the murder of the minister a dreadful crime and saw it as a consequence of Stolypin's labors for Russia; yet labor for one's country and even martyrdom for its sake need not, in canon law, lead to canonization and sainthood. Secular martyrdom, so to say, can result in ecclesiastical recognition for the victim,[1] but not in the extent suggested by the Russian prelate. No matter how radical the individual opinions of Pitirim were, it is proper to inquire whether

1. On the connection between salvation and death for a political or national cause, see E. H. Kantorowicz, "Pro Patria Mori in Medieval Political Thought," *AHR*, *56* (1951), 471f.

5

he was not basing them on a valid and recognizable historical tradition whereby martyrdom for Russia signified one's elevation to sainthood.

The ruler cult in Russia, medieval and modern, has been studied for a long time, with excellent results,[2] but one aspect of it, which appears to have been overlooked, bears on the problem at hand. A list of Russian saints up to the eighteenth century shows that out of some eight hundred, over one hundred were princes or princesses.[3] The figures for the period between the introduction of Christianity in the tenth century and the Mongol conquest are even more striking: out of some 180 saints, a third were rulers. Statistics tell, of course, a very small part of the story; they do reveal a tendency of the Russians and their church to sanctify their princes frequently and, perhaps, rather easily.

Very broadly, the saintly princes can be divided into two groups: those who were regarded as saints for ecclesiastical, canonical reasons, and those who were made saints on what are, in effect, secular grounds. The first group is represented by St. Vladimir the Apostle-like and his grandmother St. Olga, who occupy in Russian hagiography the place equivalent to that of Constantine and Helen in early Christianity;[4] by the prince of Chernigov, St. Michael, who underwent martyrdom at the hands of the

2. Cf. M. A. Diakonov, *Vlast' Moskovskikh Gosudarei* (St. Petersburg, 1889); V. Val'denberg, *Drevnerusskie ucheniia o predelakh tsarskoi vlasti* (Petrograd, 1916); H. Schaeder, *Moskau das Dritte Rom* (Hamburg, 1929); V. Malinin, *Starets Eleasorova monastyria Filofei i ego poslaniia* (Kiev, 1901); A. E. Presniakov, "Samoderzhavie Nikolaia I," *Russkoe Proshloe,* 2 (1923), 3–21, and "Samoderzhavie Aleksandra II," *4* (1923), 3–20.

3. These figures are derived from the catalogue of Archimandrite Leonid, *Sviataia Rus, ili svedeniia o vsekh sviatykh i podvizhnikakh blagochestiia na Rusi, P.D.P.I., 97* (St. Petersburg, 1891).

4. Cf. N. I. Serebriansky, *Drevnerusskiia kniazheskiia zhitiia,* in *Chteniia,* *254* (1915:3), 23f., 47f.

Tatars for the Christian faith; [5] and it included most of the canonized princesses of the ruling dynasty. [6]

The problem of "secular" sanctification begins with the first saints of Russian Christianity, the brothers Boris and Gleb. These two young sons of St. Vladimir were killed by their older brother Sviatopolk in his struggle for the Kiev throne during the weeks following the death of Vladimir. [7] It has been already observed that neither of the young princes fulfilled the traditional requirements for sanctity; [8] they died without attempting to resist their enemies, yet they did not die *for* Christ and their faith, and they wept and pleaded with their murderers for mercy. [9] However, the title the brothers received indicates the nature of their sanctity: Boris and Gleb are called the *Strastoterptsy*—"passion-sufferers." [10] The brothers did not die for Christ but in Christ, imitating Christ and his passion; Boris, shortly before his murder, prayed: "Lord Jesus Christ, You who have deigned to appear on earth in human guise and who have allowed yourself to be nailed to the cross, You who have accepted the passion because of our sins, help me also to accept mine." [11] It is in this sense that the chronicle portrays Boris' understanding of his own

5. Serebriansky, 109f.

6. Cf. N. Barsukov, *Istochniki Russkoi Agiografii*, P.D.P.I., *82* (St. Petersburg, 1882); Leonid, *Sviataia Rus'*.

7. *P.S.R.L.*, *1*, 55f.; on the various redactions, see Serebriansky, 81f.

8. G. P. Fedotov, *Sviatye Drevnei Rusi* (Paris, 1931), 20; I. Kologrivov, *Essai sur La Sainteté en Russie* (Bruges, 1953), 29f.; this last work is mostly a paraphrase, and sometimes simply a translation, of Fedotov.

9. Fedotov, 24f., discusses the tradition of parental authority which the chronicles use to explain the submission of the two brothers. Sviatopolk, as an older brother, acquired the clannish authority of the father after Vladimir's death.

10. On the meaning of this term in its Russian context, cf. Fedotov, 32–33.

11. *P.S.R.L.*, *1*, 58.

martyrdom, and in the presence of the murderers the
prince appeals to Christ: "Deign to allow me, Lord, to imitate the holy martyrs." [12] The veneration for the two saints
was genuinely popular,* and the thaumaturgic powers of
their tombs, which revealed their sanctity, were displayed
a very short time after 1015.[13] The cult of Boris and Gleb
probably preceded that of their great-grandmother, the
"Helen-like" St. Olga, and preceded by centuries the official cult of their father, the "Apostle-like" St. Vladimir.[14]
The psychological nature and meaning of this cult are revealed quite clearly by the chronicle celebrating the en-
tombment of the princely brothers:

"Joined together were their bodies, and far more were
their souls, living with the Master, Tsar of all, in infinite
joy, in unutterable light, granting thaumaturgic gifts to the
Russian land . . . [granting] the lame to walk, sight to
the blind, health to the sick, freedom to the chained, liberation to prisoners, consolation to the sad, escape to the
threatened; they are intercessors for the Russian land,
shining lights, warriors who pray to the Lord for their
people. So we must praise them worthily, passion-sufferers
of Christ, we must pray earnestly to them, saying: Rejoice,
Christ's passion-sufferers of the Russian land, for you heal
those who come to you with faith and love . . . Rejoice
. . . [you] who are like stars illuminating the whole of
the Russian land . . . Rejoice . . . you who reign with
Christ eternally, praying for the new Christian people and
your kinsmen, for the land is blessed by your blood . . .
Rejoice, bright stars, rising at dawn; our Christ-loving
passion-sufferers and intercessors! force the pagans under
the feet of our princes." [15]

* I should like to point out that here and elsewhere throughout this
work, the word "popular" is used in its original sense, "of the people,"
rather than in our present sense of "widely accepted."

12. Fedotov, 26.

13. *P.S.R.L.*, *1*, 59.

14. E. E. Golubinsky, *Istoriia kanonizatsii sviatykh v Russkoi tserkvi,
Chteniia*, 204 (1903:1), 56, 63f.

15. *P.S.R.L.*, *1*, 57–58.

The youth of Boris and Gleb and the dramatic circumstances of their death undoubtedly attracted popular attention,[16] but what focused the cult around the princes was a need for saints, for intercessors for the "new Christian people." Russian society took advantage of the first opportunity to gain a particular and effective advocacy for itself with the new and all-powerful Lord of the Russian people. This need appears to be, in effect, a justification for the murders of the princes; the "Accursed" Sviatopolk fulfilled what was a necessary function,[17] and the princely brothers were offered as a blood sacrifice, the pledge of Russian Christianization. But though the early cult of Boris and Gleb may be partially explained by the psychological need of the society and the convenient drama of the martyrdom, there still remains the problem of the significance of the princely status of the first Russian saints.

If the qualification for sanctity and hence intercession for Russia was to suffer an unjust and cruel death, the number of candidates in late tenth-century and early eleventh-century Russia must have been staggering. The argument from silence is a dangerous one, yet the princely status of Boris and Gleb is clearly emphasized; while the usual iconographic mark of the saint is the martyr's crown or diadem, Boris and Gleb are portrayed with the princely caps of the Russian dynasty.[18] The importance of these princely saints emerges more clearly when we examine

16. The murder by Sviatopolk of a third brother, Sviatoslav, at the same time, apparently made little impression on the people. The chronicle refers to it *en passant*, *P.S.R.L.*, *1*, 60.

17. Boris prayed to God that his own death should not be held against Sviatopolk as a sin, and the chronicle, characterizing the murderers as devils, points out that while angels are sent by God to do good here, devils are sent to do evil (*P.S.R.L.*, *1*, 58). Both are, however, viewed as divine agents.

18. See, for example, E. Benz, *Russische Heiligenlegenden* (Zurich, 1953), 80, pl. 7; P. Mouratow, *L'Ancienne Peinture Russe* (Rome, 1925), fig. 33; L. Küppers, *Göttliche Ikone* (Düsseldorf, 1949), 60.

subsequent sanctifications in the search for a pattern of princely canonization, for in the Kievan period, at least, there are no laic saints *except* for princes.[19] In 1147, after a reign of twelve days, prince Igor' Ol'govich was overthrown by Iziaslav; after some time in prison, where he fell ill, the prince took monastic vows and retired to a monastery. Shortly afterwards the Kievan popular assembly decided to kill Igor', and, despite the efforts of princes and prelates, he was brutally murdered by a mob.[20] Within three years Igor' was acknowledged as a miracle-working saint, and he too was a *strastoterpets,* a sufferer of the passion.[21] Again in this case, while the feeling of guilt was far more pronounced on the part of a repentant mob of former subjects than it was on that of the *bravi* of Sviatopolk concerning Boris and Gleb, the murder was purely political in intent and consequences, and nothing about Igor's life or death reveals the traditional qualities of a Christian saint. The murder of a prince-monk certainly increases the guilt of the murderers but should do nothing to the status of the murdered. A hint of a pattern in the line of princely saints discussed here appears in the words of Igor' when he pleads to be allowed to become a monk: "Allow me, brothers, to take the vows, for I had had this thought already during my reign." [22] Igor' did not wish to be the ruler over Kiev, he had not wanted the throne, yet he was killed because he was a prince, because he had held the supreme power. The princely saints were passion-sufferers because they died for what they were, as Christ had to die for what he was, in order to provide salvation.

19. The one exception was the Bulgarian St. Abraham, who was martyred in Bulgaria and whose body was brought to Russia in 1230; Golubinsky, 62.

20. *P.S.R.L.,* 2, 33–34; 25, 41–42.

21. Igor' was counted among the prince-saints and not among the monks; Fedotov, 86.

22. *P.S.R.L.,* 2, 29.

The image of the political passion-sufferer, indicated by Boris, Gleb, and Igor', is crystallized most clearly and strikingly in the person of Andrew Bogoliubsky, Grand Prince of Suzdal' and Vladimir. The historical significance of Grand Prince Andrew is great, but his character was hardly saintly or even edifying; in 1169, upon acquiring the right to the throne of Kiev as the senior prince of the Riurikid dynasty, Andrew remained in his own patrimony of northeastern Russia and sent his armies to occupy and sack Kiev, the "mother of Russian cities." [23] Chronicles display to us a stern, even cruel and ruthless man, the first of the centralizing despots from the new centers of the northeast, a forerunner of the Moscovite "gatherers of the Russian lands." [24] Andrew's religiosity and piety were of the formal kind, and his chief achievement for the faith was the building of the splendid cathedral of Vladimir.[25] In 1175 a group of his own boiars burst into his bed-chamber and murdered him. The cult of the dead prince, who was hated for good reason in both Kiev and in Novgorod, apparently remained a local one; formal, national recognition came on the orders of Peter the Great in 1702.[26] But the locale which accepted Andrew as a passion-sufferer was the center of the later Moscovite state and tsardom, and it is worthwhile to examine the nature of the prince's sanctity.

Like Boris and Gleb, Andrew, the chronicle tells us, knew of his coming death, of the plans of the murderers, and apparently did nothing about it. When the murderers broke down the door of his room the prince reached for his sword—the sword of St. Boris, his ancestor—but

23. Cf. *Istoriia*, 2, chap. V, VI, for character and activities of Andrew.
24. *P.S.R.L.*, 5, 163f.; *Novgorodskaia Pervaia Letopis'* (ANSSSR, 1950), 31f.; *Karamzin*, 3, chap. I.
25. *P.S.R.L.*, 1, 149; *P.S.R.L.*, 25, 63f.; his piety did not prevent him from looting and desecrating the churches of Kiev.
26. Golubinsky, 134.

it had been hidden by his disloyal chamberlain. The murderers hacked away, while the martyred prince reproached them for their ingratitude, promised divine punishment for their crime, and offered up his soul to God.[27] The body of the dead prince lay naked in the entrance to his church until, on the third day, the clergy came to do it honors.[28] Andrew's demise, symbolically, parallels Christ's passion even more closely and explicitly than that of Boris and Gleb, though personally and politically the Grand Prince was far removed from saintliness. In Andrew's case, for the first time, the chronicle reveals the theological status of political power in order to condemn the murderers the more: "As the apostle Paul says: Every soul obeys the ruler, for the rulers are established by God. In his earthly being, the caesar is like every man, but in his power he has the rank of God, spoke the great Chrysostom; those who oppose the ruler oppose the law of God." [29] In quoting St. Paul and "Chrysostom," the chronicle follows an old tradition of the sanctity of power; [30] the function, so to say, of Andrew's *personal*, human saintliness is revealed in the exhortation to the dead prince: "Worthily, Andrew, you have received the crown of victory from God . . . following your divinely wise brothers [Boris and Gleb], washing in blood your suffering . . . The memory of your murder astonished the heavenly angels, who saw your blood shed for Christ . . . Pray, passion-sufferer, to almighty God to grant peace

27. *P.S.R.L.*, *5*, 165; Andrew acknowledged the similarity between himself and Boris and Gleb by calling his murderers another *Goriaser*, the name of Boris' slayer.

28. Karamzin, *3*, n. 23; that the symbolism was consciously employed is indicated by the fact that some of the chronicles omit this detail or report that Andrew was put in a coffin on the day following his death; *P.S.R.L.*, *25*, 84; *P.S.R.L.*, *1*, 157.

29. *Troitskaia Letopis'*, ed. M. D. Priselkov (ANSSSR, 1950), 254.

30. On the origin of this quotation, see I. Ševčenko, "A Byzantine Source of Muscovite Ideology," *H.S.S.*, 2 (1954), 142.

to the world." After describing the murder itself, the chronicle concludes:

"The apostle teaches us: Whom God loves, he punishes . . . [He] did not fix the sun in one spot . . . to reach out over the universe, but created for it the east and south and west; in the same way, he did not bring his favorite, prince Andrew, to Himself in vain, though having led such a life his [Andrew's] soul would be saved, but [had him] come to Christ united with his brothers Roman and David [the baptismal names of Boris and Gleb], having washed away his sins in his martyred blood . . . Rejoice, Grand Prince Andrew . . . and pray to God to have mercy on our lord Vsevolod, your brother; may God grant him victory over enemies and long life . . . and a peaceful reign and tsardom."

Although the hagiographer emphasized Andrew's devotion to Christ and the faith, demonstrated in his church-building and in his support of monastic foundations, his life was not a saintly one according to the most favorable accounts. His death is stylized and he is made to die like a "sacrificial lamb" just as Boris and Gleb died, but yet in the case of Prince Andrew the emphasis is greater on the central problem. Unlike his saintly predecessors, Andrew was active as prince, and it was this activity which killed him: "no one who is virtuous can avoid having many enemies"; [31] but his princely activity made him a saint when he accepted the consequences of his rulership: Andrew died a saint because he accepted the consequences of being a prince.

The purpose of Andrew's "martyrdom" is also clear. Through his death the prince not only expiated his own sins but, with the other saintly princes, also became an intercessor before Christ, a protector of the Russian land. In this sense, the saintly princes performed the same function after death that they did in life—the protection

31. *Troitskaia Letopis'*, 253–255.

and care of their subjects and lands. They were admitted
to this role, however, only because their death was a result
of their participation in the Christlike passion possible
only for princes; they accept, "voluntarily," the death that
comes to them by virtue of their being princes, and
through this acceptance they are able to remain princes
after death for all time.

This element of sacrifice in the myth of the Christlike
princes is quite explicit in the passion of Grand Prince
Michael of Tver, saint and *strastoterpets*. Michael, as
senior prince, inherited the Grand Principality, which was
then disputed, successfully, by the first Grand Prince of
the Moscow line, Iury Danilovich. Iury was able to claim
the title because of the support he received from the high
officials of the sovereign over all Russia, the Tatar khan.[32]
Michael gave up the title of Grand Prince but claimed his
own principality of Tver. In defense of it he defeated the
Tatar-Moscovite army led by Iury, and was summoned
by the khan for trial at the Golden Horde. Convinced
that the summons was a trap, the family and the boiars of
the prince pleaded with him not to go; the chronicle tells
us Michael's answer: "You see, my children, the tsar does
not demand you . . . nor anyone else, but only me, for
he wants my head; if I will decline [to go] my patrimony
will be captured and many Christians will be killed; so,
if it is necessary for me to die, it is better for me to give
up my soul for many others." [33] Michael went on to the
khan's headquarters, underwent a trial at the hands of
his great enemy, the Tatar general Kavgadyi, and, after
much suffering and many humiliations, was murdered on
order of the khan. The fact that the martyrdom of Michael
took place because of the Tatars, during the period when
the Tatar yoke was imposed on northeastern Russia, allows

32. *Istoriia, 3,* 901f.
33. *P.S.R.L., 5,* 210.

other strands to be woven into the pattern of the passion-suffering prince. Michael died, in his own words, for the *patria,* thus emphasizing the distinction between the Christian Russians and the idolatrous Tatars; [34] but despite the claims of the chronicle, Michael did not die for the faith, as did his namesake, St. Michael of Chernigov.[35] Nor did he really die for the Russian *patria* at the hands of its enemies; it was Iury of Moscow who contrived his death for the sake of the Grand Principality, and when the khan granted permission for the murder, Iury's men did the job in a particularly brutal way. Michael's supposed great enemy and villain, Kavgadyi, upon seeing the naked and torn body of the dead prince, "spoke with fury to Grand Prince Iury, saying: 'Was he not your eldest brother, like your father, then why does his body lie there naked?'" [36]

Michael died in the same way and for the same reasons as his saintly kinsmen, in a political struggle, because he was a prince; and, like his predecessors, Michael suffered his passion—more voluntarily, one must admit, than did the others. As one of his tortures, Michael had a heavy wooden board or yoke tied onto his shoulders; in his last confrontation with Kavgadyi, the latter, mocking Michael, promised him the khan's pardon and suggested to Michael's retinue that they relieve the prince by holding up the wooden yoke. None of them was willing to do so, until finally one man, nameless, stepped forth and helped

34. The image which Michael used is an interesting one. He compared himself to St. Demetrius of Thessalonica, who, according to the Russian prince, was also willing to die for his city, which was his *"otechestvo,"* his fatherland.

35. Michael of Chernigov refused to undergo a purification ceremony at the Khan's court which involved the use of Tatar pagan idols. Cf. Fedotov, 84–85; Serebriansky, 109f.

36. The prince was apparently kicked to death. There is no mention of weapons used or blood shed, which may have been due to the Tatar custom forbidding the shedding of royal blood; *P.S.R.L., 5,* 214.

Michael [37] (as Simon of Cyrene helped Christ). This similarity of detail was symbolic of the true nature of the passion suffered by the *strastoterpets,* who joined his brothers Boris and Gleb before God.

Despite Michael's greater consciousness of the political significance of his sacrifice, the chief element in his sanctification was the passion. It was as a passion-sufferer that he was counted with Boris and Gleb, and it was the passion which defined this particular strand within the myth of the saintly prince. The significance of Michael's suffering-and-death lay in its voluntary inevitability. The sacrifice was voluntary, by definition, and, equally by definition, inevitable. It would be as unreasonable to postulate the Grand Prince's avoidance of his passion as to question the inevitability of Christ's. Jesus as the Christ had to undergo willingly his sacrifice and Michael (or Boris, or Gleb), as prince, had to accept his own sacrificial role.

The element of sacrifice also dominates the story of the last passion-sufferer, who was, as well, the last of the saintly princes—tsarevich Dimitry, son of Ivan the Terrible, with whose murder in 1591 the Riurikid dynasty came to an end. The canonization of the boy prince was initiated by the government of tsar Vasily Shuisky both as an attack against the dead tsar Boris Godunov who was popularly accused of the murder, and as a weapon against the numerous false Dimitrys of the Time of Troubles.[38] The popular cult of the child-martyr, however, anticipated even the prompt official recognition. This last offspring of the imperial line was venerated as a national saint, an intercessor for the whole Russian land.[39] While the volun-

37. *P.S.R.L.,* 5, 212.

38. S. F. Platonov, *Ocherki po Istorii Smuty* (St. Petersburg, 1899), 314f.; Golubinsky, 120–21.

39. S. F. Platonov, *Drevnerusskiia Skazaniia i Povesti o Smutnom Vremeni* (St. Petersburg, 1888), 40f., 283f.; cf. Barsukov, 153–55.

tary nature of the sacrifice necessarily had to be underplayed, considering that the saint was a little boy, murdered while playing with his friends, one can argue that
the inevitable nature of the sacrifice was more evident:
What more fitting end to the dynasty of saintly princes
could be found than the sacrificial death of its last and
most innocent member?

The passion-suffering saintly princes of Russia expressed
in the most dramatic way the sanctity of power in Christian society. What takes place within the myth is not so
much the identity of prince and Christ; it is, rather, the
translation of Christ and his passion into the prince and
his suffering. Many Russian princes were saints in the
spiritual sense, but the princes who died for princely
reasons expressed most clearly their princely status and
thereby came closest to being an image of Christ.

While the passion-suffering princes attained their saintliness through their mere being, even through a necessary
passivity at the end, another thread in the fabric of the
myth of holy princes was woven by the active rulers, the
warrior-princes, defenders of the Russian lands. The first
of these, Prince Mstislav the Brave of Novgorod (d. 1180),
is presented by the chronicle as a gay and dashing warrior,
whose mind was occupied only by "great deeds," who
spent his life in fighting for Russia, and who at his death
was mourned by all the land. His knightly qualities even
gained him the love and respect of the Turkic nomads,
eternal enemies of the Russian princes. Mstislav did not
meet death in battle for Russia, but while he was planning
a campaign against Livonia, after he had returned from a
victory over the Estonians. The warrior prince died in a
church, where he had himself carried in order to receive
the sacrament. The reason for his sanctification is given
by the chronicle: "He was always eager to die for the
Russian land and spoke thus to his men: 'Brothers! have

no fear; for if we die for the Christian [folk] then we shall be cleansed of our sins, and God will join our blood with that of the martyrs." [40] As a warrior-saint Mstislav is purely secular, and there were no attempts to add pietistic stylization to his life by the chroniclers. On the contrary, his war-like, princely qualities were emphasized, for it was because of them that he was a saint, gaining his own reward in heaven for fulfilling himself, and extending his beneficence over his people beyond death.

The image of the saint *pro patria* is most clearly and positively defined in the *vitae* of the most famous of the "defenders of the Russian land," Grand Prince Alexander Nevsky (d. 1263).[41] The great prince divided his time between beating back enemies in the west (the Swedes on the Neva river, the Teutonic knights on Lake Chud) and placating the Tatar sovereign of Russia in the east, and he emerges as the secular holy prince par excellence. What are the lineaments of such a prince? He was born, the *vita* tells us:

"to the merciful, men-loving and gentle Grand Prince Iaroslav and [princess] Theodosia. As says the prophet Isaiah, thus speaks the Lord: 'I institute the prince, and he is holy, and I lead him' (Isaiah XIII, 3). In truth without out divine ordinance he could not reign and his countenance is like no man's, and his voice is like a trumpet among the people, while his face is like that of Joseph, whom the Egyptian tsar had placed as a second tsar in Egypt; his strength is of the strength of Samson; and God gave him the wisdom of Solomon, while his courage was like that of the Roman tsar Vespasian . . . Thus, prince Alexander always conquered and was never defeated."

Alexander is shown here as the foreordained, divinely guided *minister Dei,* victorious because of qualities which

40. Karamzin, *3,* n. 54.

41. For *vitae,* see Serebriansky, 151f.; V. Mansikka, *Zhitie Aleksandra Nevskago* (St. Petersburg, 1913), *P.D.P.I., 180.*

were given to him by God for the purpose of victory. Always victorious, "shining over the Russian land," the prince never forgot the nature of his glory. Hearing of the coming Swedish invasion and of the boastful speeches of the Swedish envoy,

"[Alexander's] heart was set on fire and he entered the church of the Holy Sophia [in Novgorod] and kneeling before the altar began to pray to God, tearfully: 'Praiseworthy God, just and great God, almighty and eternal God, Who has created the earth and set the limits to the nations, who has ordered [men] to live without transgressing into foreign parts. Accept the song of the prophet which says: Judge, O Lord, those who injure me, assail my opponents; accept my sword and shield and be my aid.' (Ps. XXXIV, 1–2.) After finishing his prayer, he rose and bowed before the archbishop. [The archbishop], who was at that time Spiridon, blessed him and sent him on his way. He, emerging from the church, wiped away his tears and cheered up his men, saying: 'God is not with force but with the right; let us remember the Psalmist who says: some are in their armor and some on horseback, but we shall call on the name of our God.' Having said this [Alexander] advanced against the enemy with a small army, without waiting for his full forces, but relying upon the holy Trinity."

The first reaction of the angered prince was to hurry to church. He prayed to God, weeping in his humility, and it was his humility which insured his victory; of this he was so certain that he rushed to battle with only a part of his army.

God's help and guidance for Alexander, however, did not remain a vague and impersonal divine beneficence. A chieftain from Izhora, watching on the seashore all night for the invading Swedes, with dawn "heard a terrifying noise from the sea, and saw a single ship being rowed over the sea; in the middle of the ship stood the holy martyrs Boris and Gleb . . . Boris spoke: 'Brother Gleb, give orders to row and let us help our kinsman, prince Alexander.'" Alexander received divine help both as God's elect, a second Joshua, and as a saintly kinsman of princely saints. Reiterated here is the myth of the saintly blood, the sanctity of the Russian princely line, as well as the personal saintliness of the Grand Prince.

Despite the implications of this episode, Alexander was not primarily the warrior-saint. He was a "martyr for the Russian land" and as such received the help of the martyred passion-sufferers as well as of the heavenly hosts. As much as his victories the *vita* emphasizes his deeds of martyrdom—Alexander's voyages to khan Batu the conqueror of Russia, to intercede for Russian towns and peoples who had earned the anger of the sovereign. The *vita* presents the encounter between prince and khan in dramatic and epic terms:

"At that time there was a mighty Eastern tsar, to whom God had submitted many peoples, from the east to the west; the tsar, hearing of the bravery and glory of Alexander, sent a messenger with the words: 'Alexander, as you know, God has submitted to me many peoples; you alone do not wish to submit; but if you want to preserve your lands then come to me and gaze upon the glory of my tsardom.' Meanwhile prince Alexander had come to Vladimir after the death of his father, in great force; awesome was his coming and the news of it spread to the mouth of the Volga. And the Moabite women began to frighten their children, saying: 'Alexander is coming' . . . Seeing him, tsar Batu was amazed and said to his nobles: 'You have told me the truth for there is no one like this prince,' and after honoring him [Batu] let him go." [42]

The awe-inspiring prince had to submit to the pagan tsar and here again fulfilled the task of defending Russian lands at whatever cost in personal suffering. A late and

42. *Pskovskie Letopisi*, ed. A. N. Nasonov (ANSSSR, 1955), 2, 11–14. The Moabite women refers to the non-Russian tribes of the Volga region, victims of the Russian colonizing drive.

very popular redaction of the *vita* emphasizes this point. According to it, Alexander was asked to undergo the same ritual of purification that Prince Michael of Chernigov was faced with—to pass between lines of fires and idols before being admitted to the khan's presence.[43] While Michael was martyred for his refusal and joined the ranks of the passion-sufferers, Alexander's firm stand gained him the respect of the khan.[44] Unlike Michael, who in many ways is an exception among the saintly princes,[45] Alexander remains a secular saint-prince, and it was a secular martyrdom that Alexander really underwent:

"Grand Prince Alexander wanted to go to the tsar in the Horde, in order to plead for his people [*otmolil daby liudi ot bed*] . . . At that time (1263) Grand Prince Alexander went to the Horde, to Tsar Berkai and the tsar held him back so that he wintered in the Horde where he fell ill . . . having reached Gorodets he felt very ill and, taking the vows, on the 14th of the month of November, that same night he died . . . [about this] Metropolitan Cyril spoke to the people: 'my dear children, know that the sun of the Russian land has set,' [so that] priests and deacons and monks, rich and poor and all kinds of men cried out 'we are lost now.' His holy body was taken to the city of Vladimir . . . [to] the church of the Conception of the Holy Virgin, [on] the 23rd day of November . . . A

43. Serebriansky, 215–17.

44. Redaction of Vasily of Pskov, Serebriansky, appendix, 133–34.

45. For good reasons if one is to believe the *vitae* as to what men, determined to stay faithful to their God, had to undergo. One cannot envisage many Russian princes willing to submit to the kind of tortures inflicted, for example, on prince Roman of Riazan' in 1270 for refusing to deny his faith; cf. *Kniga glagolemaia opisanie o Rossiiskikh sviatykh,* ed. M. V. Tolstoy, *Chteniia* (1887:4), 239. The description of the martyrdom, however, was probably borrowed from traditional earlier Christian hagiography. Considering the religious tolerance of the Tatars, the most likely reason for the lack of many martyrs for the faith, particularly among the princes, was the fact that the Tatars did not persecute for religious reasons. In Tatar eyes, Michael of Chernigov had committed a political offense rather than a religious one.

great miracle happened at that time, worthy of memory: when the holy body was placed in the coffin the monk Sebastian . . . came up and wanted to open its hand so that the metropolitan could place in it the charter of forgiveness; he [Alexander] then, as if alive, stretched out his hand and took the charter from the metropolitan . . . thus has God glorified his favorite, who had labored hard for the Russian land and for Novgorod and for Pskov, having given his life for the whole Grand Principality and for the orthodox faith." [46]

Alexander is holy as the sun of Russia, a sun which lighted up and warmed the Russian land; the sun is an imperial image rather than a saintly one, radiating splendor and glory rather than humility and piety.[47]

The justification for dwelling in such detail upon the story of Alexander Nevsky does not lie only in the fact that his *vitae* are more detailed, popular, and available than those of other princely saints; nor in the fact that Alexander became the patron saint of the St. Petersburg, imperial, period of Russian history.[48] Alexander Nevsky was, for Russia, the *typos,* the exemplary of the saintly prince, and the *vitae* in their various redactions try to embrace all the ideal aspects of this image. In terms of political theology, Alexander represented a different aspect of Christ's image than the passion-suffering princes. As the passion-sufferers in a symbolic way emulated Christ by their passivity and submission, the active warrior-princes, such as Alexander imitated Christ by fulfilling the highest potential of their imperial status. As the passion-sufferers were princely saints, saints who suffered because they were princes, so the active warrior-princes were

46. *P.S.R.L., 5,* 190–91.

47. On the ruler as sun, see H. P. L'Orange, "Sol Invictus Imperator," *Symbolae Osloensis, 14* (1935), 86–114; O. Treitinger, *Die Oströmische Kaiser- und Reichsidee* (Jena, 1938), 112ff.

48. Cf. below, chap. 3, n. 29.

saintly princes, princes who ruled gloriously because they were saints.

These last, for whom Alexander Nevsky serves as an ideal model, are to be found time and again in periods or areas of political stress or crisis. The son-in-law of Alexander himself provides one of the clearest examples of this type of sanctity. Dovmont-Timofei of Pskov, a pagan Lithuanian converted to Christianity, spent his life fighting against his former compatriots and kinsmen. He died during a plague in Pskov (1299), and he, too, had "given his life for the people and the orthodox faith." [49] The largest single group of saintly princes occurs at the time of the Tatar invasion, 1237–40; virtually every prince killed in battle while fighting the Tatars is to be found in the list of martyr-saints of Russia.[50] In their cases, according to the brief *vitae* which are, in effect, just a register of their deaths, sanctity is simply *pro patria*. They all died in defeat, and there is no image of their activity as princes, either in peace or in war. Death for the fatherland meant, for them, not only salvation but saintliness— a saintliness which was, however, limited to princes. To die for the fatherland and the faith should mean equal martyrdom for all, according to the words of the saint-prince Mstislav, but this was not the case, and we return again to the myth of the holy ruler. What seems to be involved is the conception that death *pro patria* for the prince is a sacrifice because of its uniquely voluntary nature; voluntary in the sense that it is a consequence of the acceptance, by the prince, of his own nature and status. The corollary of this, of course, is that for the others, the mass, the voluntary nature of the sacrifice is different.

49. *Pskovskie Letopisi*, 2, 18.
50. Cf. the catalogues of Leonid, Tolstoy, Golubinsky, Barsukov, referred to *supra*.

While they die for their country and thus also for their prince, he dies for his country and thus also, through faith, for Christ. The exceptional laic hero-saints serve to emphasize this principle: Ilya Muromets was an epic hero, moving in a world beyond time, personifying the eternal struggle against the nomad from the steppes; [51] Osliabia and Peresvet, who died in 1380 on the field of Kulikovo in the first great Russian victory against the Tatars, were monks, sent to Dimitry Donskoi by the great saint, Abbot Sergius of Radonezh, and they served to symbolize the unity of church and state in the national effort of resistance; [52] Prince Michael Skopin-Shuisky, the popular hero during the Time of Troubles (1606–1610), was a nephew of the "boiar" tsar Vasily Shuisky and symbolized the heroic leader at a time when no image of a legitimate and sanctified tsar existed to overshadow him.[53]

Insofar as the saintly prince depended for his saintliness on his princely nature and status, no sharp difference could be drawn between the saintly prince and the princely saint. There were not two sharply differing ways of attaining sanctity. Rather, either of two aspects of the princely personality led to sanctity, and these aspects may be assigned in a general way to categories of "being" and "doing." The chronicles, for example, distorted the facts in order to present some of the princes killed in the Tatar invasion as escaping death in battle, being captured by the Tatars, and then martyred for their refusal to renounce the Christian faith,[54] making them passive saints

51. A type was probably St. Mercury of Smolensk, supposedly of the thirteenth century. The earliest information about him, however, dates from the early seventeenth century; see Golubinsky, 141, no. 64.

52. Barsukov, 430.

53. Cf. A. N. Popov, *Izbornik*, 379–388, in Platonov, *Drevnerusskie Skazaniia*, 277, n. 2.

54. See, for example, on prince Oleg Krasnyi of Riazan', Golubinsky, 364; on prince Vasil'ko of Rostov, 141.

rather than active ones. The element of unity for the two types of saintliness was provided by the Christian faith. Death for country and death for Christ were equivalent for Andrew Bogoliubsky, Michael of Chernigov, Alexander Nevsky, and Vasil'ko of Rostov.[55] A prince, Christlike in his nature by virtue of being a prince, in his sacrifice for Christ, country, and Christians performed a commensurate role in the economy of salvation. The personal salvation of a prince was utilized for the benefit of his country when the prince was "put to work" after death.

The desire to equate and interweave the two types of saintliness is nowhere more apparent than in the case of a hero-saint who was not officially canonized—Dimitry Donskoi, victor over the Tatars in 1380 on the field of Kulikovo.[56] The *vita* follows the pattern set by that of Alexander Nevsky, but with greater emphasis on the saintly line from which Dimitry was descended. He was born, of course, to noble, great and pious parents, but he also was "of the holy root . . . of tsar Vladimir the new Constantine . . . and he [Dimitry] was kinsman to the new miracle-workers Boris and Gleb." [57] The battle of Kulikovo itself is set by the *vita* within the framework of princely saintliness. The Tatar Mamai is called a second Sviatopolk [58] (the accursed murderer of Boris and Gleb), and Dimitry is seen as a second Iaroslav the Wise, avenger

55. Cf. note 64.

56. Cf. Golubinsky, 353; while the Grand Prince is entered in the lists of the saints, Golubinsky tells us, his cult had apparently died out. On the *vitae*, see V. P. Adrianova-Perets, "Slovo o zhitii i o prestavlenii velikogo kniazia Dmitriia Ivanovicha, tsaria Russkago," *T.O.D.R.L.*, 5 (1947), 73f.

57. *P.S.R.L.*, 6, 104.

58. Mamai could be castigated in this way and worse, for he was not the Khan, i.e. not the legitimate ruler of Russia but an usurper; cf. my study, "Khan or Basileus: An Aspect of Russian Mediaeval Political Theory," *Journal of the History of Ideas*, 20 (1959), 465 and note 20.

of his brothers; little wonder that Boris and Gleb, as well as a heavenly host, aid Grand Prince Dimitry during the battle. As princely saintliness was a measure for the supreme political good, so supreme political evil was delineated by the crimes which produced the first Russian princely saints.

Dimitry's victories brought him a glory similar to that of St. Vladimir, the first Tsar of the Russian land, to whom Dimitry is comparable in title as well as deeds. The glory of the Grand Prince is balanced, or rather integrated, with his piety and saintliness, however. Hearing of the approaching attack by Mamai, Dimitry prayed to the Virgin: "O most holy Mistress . . . pray to your son for me, a sinner, that I may be worthy to lay down my head and life for your Son's name and for yours, for I have no other help except yourself . . . gain for me . . . help and strength from the holy dwelling of your Son and my God, against my evil enemy . . . glorify the Christian name over the foul pagans." The prince is the servant and tool of Christ, and only Christ can help him; Dimitry stands alone before the enemy, and to defeat the Tatars is his task—his alone with the help of Christ. The responsibility and the status of the prince are acknowledged in the answer of the Russian nobility to the exhortation of the Grand Prince to die for the orthodox faith and gain martyrdom.[59] "The Russian princes and nobles answered him [Dimitry]: 'Lord Russian tsar! we have promised to lay down our lives serving you; and now, for your sake, we will shed our blood and with it gain a second baptism.' "[60] The nobles and army of the Grand Prince of Moscow die, not *pro patria* or *pro fide* but for

59. *P.S.R.L.*, *6*, 104–105; the same kind of exhortation that was made by Alexander Nevsky and Mstislav.
60. *P.S.R.L.*, *6*, 105.

the prince, and through that sacrifice hope to gain the second baptism signifying salvation. In the death for the fatherland which, as we saw, was equated with death for the faith, the prince stands as mediator between men and Christ; he dies for Christ as they die for him. And the prince, mediator between man and God in life as a prince, remains a mediator, and intercessor, after his death as a saint.

As mediator, Grand Prince Dimitry revealed the tension between the face he showed to men and the one he turned to his God. It was this tension that the *vita* tried to resolve when it balanced the image of the "first Russian Tsar," saint *per gloriam* in his princely acts, with the image of the saintly man, saint *per naturam:* "Possessing imperial rank [he] lived like an angel, in fast and prayer, standing all night through, hardly sleeping, praying from the earliest hour . . . ruling the Russian land, sitting on the imperial throne . . . wearing the imperial purple and diadem, [he] desired all his days to put on the monk's raiment . . . he was, in truth, an earthly angel or a heavenly man." [61] The ideal of the angelic ruler, the saintly prince, is translated into the concrete image of the monk-tsar, the synthesis of glory and humility; in his glory Dimitry wishes to be humble, and through his humility before God he gains the tsarlike glorious victories. The dialectic of the heavenly and the earthly in the image of the prince is further emphasized when the *vita* describes the death of Dimitry and summarizes his achievements: "The air was troubled and the earth shook upon the death of the Grand Prince; the people, we are told, cried out: 'Woe to us, brothers! the king of kings is dead, the lord of the sovereigns, the sun has darkened, the moon is obscured by a cloud, the shining star goes down in the

61. *P.S.R.L., 6,* 106–07.

west.' " [62] The hagiographer goes on then to compare Dimitry to the great biblical figures, including Adam; he begins by addressing the dead prince: "Shall I call you an angel? but in your body you have lived like an angel. [Shall I call you] a man? but you have done deeds which are beyond human capacity and essence." [63]

In his great work, Ernst Kantorowicz shows that the Christian ruler as mediator between God and men shared with Christ the attribute of a dual nature.[64] Weak, fallible, and mortal as all men in his humanity, the ruler, at the same time, as the *christus domini*, possessed the divine attributes of his princely nature. As Christ, whose image

62. *P.S.R.L.*, *6*, 109. This expression of grief was modeled on Byzantine epitaphia for a dead ruler; cf. the *Byzantine History* of Nicephoras Gregoras, bk. X, ch. 1, in *Corpus Script. Hist. Byz.* (Bonn, 1829–55), *34*, 465–72, especially 466.

63. *P.S.R.L.*, *6*, 110; the hagiographer goes on, seeking to find worthy comparisons, and failing every time: "Shall I call you the First-created [Adam]? But he had received God's law and broken it; you, however, had kept the faith since your holy baptism. Shall I call you Joseph? But, because of his wisdom, men called him God; you, however, remaining pure, are a slave of God, and, holding God's throne, appear as the lord of the Russian land. . . ." After finding that even Moses did not do enough honor to Dimitry, the writer shifted ground: "The Roman land praises Peter and Paul, the Asian [*Asiiskaia*] John the Evangelist, India [praises] the apostle Thomas, [the land of] Jerusalem the brother of the Lord, Jacob; Andrew the First-called [is praised] by the Pomor'e [the Black Sea coast], and tsar Constantine by the Greek land, while Vladimir [is praised] by Kiev and its neighboring towns; you, however, Grand Prince Dimitry Ivanovich, are praised by the whole Russian land." Taking over the famous praise by the metropolitan Ilarion of St. Vladimir, in which Ilarion used the Christianization of Russia to equate St. Vladimir with the apostles and the apostle-like, *isapostolos*, Constantine the Great, our writer simply adds Dimitry to the list, even if he had to do it at the expense of Vladimir. Dimitry and his victory thus signified a second baptism for Russia, even though the hagiographer must have known that not all Russia sided with Dimitry in his struggle with the Tatars, and certainly knew that Dimitry was forced to reacknowledge the suzerainty of the Tatar Khan shortly after his own victory. The desire to find superlatives, to raise the Grand Prince to a new level, led him beyond all reason and meaning.

64. E. H. Kantorowicz, *The King's Two Bodies* (Princeton, 1957).

he is, the king is both god and man; he is man in his being, and a god in his function. The dual nature of the prince in Western medieval Europe created a tension in his image which was finally resolved by the separation of the person and the office of the prince. However, without touching here upon the nature of this dualism and the process of this separation in the West, one can note a significant difference in the image of the saintly prince in Russia. In the West, the tension was between two unequal entities, one higher and one lower, a divine nature and a human one. In Russia, the tension was between the divine nature of princely power and the saintly nature of the prince as a man. While in the West it was possible, in the twelfth century, before the secularization of the state, to distinguish between the king as man, mortal and sinful, and the king as King, the anointed of God, who was to be regarded and obeyed as was God,[65] this distinction would be meaningless in Russia; the prince as the vice-gerunt of God was contrasted with the man who was a saint, and as such, again, the image of Christ, possessed of eternal life. The tension could not be resolved—or, if one prefers, the balance was maintained—in the myth of the prince in whose nature the two aspects, princely and human, were equally deified.

G. Fedotov, who was the first to my knowledge to raise the problem of Russian princely saintliness, is quite correct in pointing out that the Russians, in sanctifying their princes, were not following the example of their Byzantine teachers.[66] While sanctification was not for purely political reasons and achievements, he argues, it was on the one hand a recognition of both the personal saintliness and

65. *The King's Two Bodies*, 42f.
66. Fedotov, 78. For Byzantine imperial saints, few in number, cf. R. Salaville, "Pour un repertoire des néo-saints de l'église Orientale," *Byzantion*, 20 (1950), 223–37.

the social service (an expression of the commandment to love one's neighbor) of the prince, and on the other hand, an expression of pagan ancestor-worship.[67] The "why?" of the Russian saint-princes is not at issue here, but Fedotov is right when he writes that surprisingly little distinction sometimes was made between princes recognized as saints, in some manner or other, and those who were not. In 1571, during the attack of the Crimean khan Devlet-Girei on Moscow, the monk Anthony of the Rozhdestvenskii monastery in Vladimir recorded a vision he had, which was included in the later redactions of the *vita* of Alexander Nevsky: he saw the saints Boris and Gleb as knights, entering his church and awakening Alexander. The three princes then galloped off to raise their kinsmen Andrew Bogoliubsky and the Grand Princes Vsevolod, Iury, and Iaroslav.[68] Among this heavenly host of princes, Grand Princes Vsevolod (III) and Iaroslav (father of Nevsky) were certainly never canonized.[69]

Fedotov, however, does not push the point far enough. If Russian princes were sanctified, in some form or other, as symbols and foci for nascent national feeling, the question arises on what basis were the princes actually sanctified chosen? Certainly the personal qualities and life of these saintly princes never worried the writers of their *vitae*. Actually, of the princely group that the monk Anthony managed to see, Grand Prince Iaroslav was counted among the saints at least since the seventeenth century, even though he was never canonized by the Church.[70] This brings us to the crux of the problem: the myth of the saintly princes and princely saints was sufficiently comprehensive so that one would expect to find

67. Fedotov, 92f.
68. Mansikka, appendix, 112f.
69. Fedotov, 100.
70. Tolstoy, p. 218, no. 400.

virtually all Russian princes sheltered under its wings. And, in fact, when we turn to all the available lists of saints, canonized or not, we find that our expectations come very close to being fulfilled. A catalogue and a statistical analysis of the saint-princes would be super-fluous, but one example can serve to illustrate the situa-tion. It is the case of the Moscow dynasty of Riurikid princes, which from the early fourteenth century emerges as the holder of the Grand Principality and the ruling family of northeast Russia. Starting with the late thir-teenth century there were twelve rulers of Moscow, ruling for over three centuries. Seven of them were recognized as saints: Daniel, Iury, Ivan I, Dimitry Donskoi, Vasily III, Ivan IV, and Feodor.[71] The list is an interesting one; while Fedotov is right in pointing out that sanctification of princes stopped, generally, in the fifteenth century, the last three saints of the Moscovite line ruled in the six-teenth century. More interesting is the lack of any ap-parent principle of selection: Daniel's claim to distinction lay in his being the founder of the Moscow dynasty; Iury, after having disposed of a number of rivals, was himself murdered through Russian intrigues during a visit to the Horde; Ivan I was renowned for his stinginess; the harshness and ruthlessness of Vasily III were surpassed only by that of his son, Ivan IV the Terrible, and Tsar Feodor, Ivan's son, was extremely pious and feeble-minded. The selection appears to be, in fact, so haphazard as to raise the suspicion that no selection was involved at all. Of the saints of the Moscow dynasty only one, Daniel, was canonized, and then only in the eighteenth century.[72] The names of the others have come down to us in a few

71. Cf. Golubinsky, 190, 353, 358, 349, 355, 369; Leonid, nos. 500, 502, 503; Barsukov, 145, 152, 245–46, 586; *P.S.R.L.*, *3*, 73. This does not include tsarevich Dimitry, or any of the saint-princes of the Moscow dynasty who had not ruled as Grand Princes or Tsars.

72. Golubinsky, 190.

scattered notices. In other words, the casual nature
of the list suggests two alternative conclusions: either
princely sanctity was not very meaningful in medieval
Russia, or the list is not complete; that is, those princes
whose names are not to be found among the saints in
late catalogues had received popular acknowledgment of
their saintly status which has not come down in the few
sources available to us.[73] The proportion of saint-princes
in the Moscow line is high enough, but if anything, it
was declining in comparison to earlier times; of the four-
teen princes of Kiev in the two centuries from St. Vladimir
to St. Andrew Bogoliubsky, ten are listed as saints, and
there again the inclusions and the omissions seem to be
equally accidental.[74] The two alternatives suggested above
are not mutually exclusive. The meaninglessness of
princely saintliness as an explanation for the nature of
the saintly lists that we have can also be applied to the
argument that is advanced here: that, basically, in Russian popular tradition and in Russian political theology,
all princes were seen as saints, through actions or in their
being, mediators between God and their people in life
and in death, and in that sense true images of Christ.

To ask "why?" about any historical fact is not very
profitable nor particularly meaningful, for the answer is
usually wrong and always incomplete. But to conjecture
is tempting, and a possible answer is suggested by the
material we have been examining. What we see in the
princely *vitae* is a constant identification of Russia and
Christianity. Whatever forms the state took in pre-Chris-

73. The alternatives are not, of course, mutually exclusive; considering
the paucity of the sources, however, the second one is more likely.

74. Vladimir (Golubinsky, 63); Iaroslav (Golubinsky, 351); Iziaslav
(Leonid, no. 8); Sviatoslav (Leonid, no. 153); Vladimir Monomakhos (Leonid,
no. 10); Mstislav (Golubinsky, 58); Iaropolk (Leonid, no. 9); Igor' Ol'govich
(Golubinsky, 58); Rostislav (Leonid, no. 12); Andrew Bogoliubsky (Golubinsky, 134).

tian Russia, the theory of the State, the very concept of State was introduced into Russia as part of the Christian ethos. In other words, there was no concept of a secular state in Russia, no concept outside Christianity and its purposes; Kievan Russia received and assimilated Christianity but not the antique concept of secular society and state which antedated the new religion. If, however, the State and Christian faith were synonymous, the prince, the expression of civil, laic action fighting and working for the State, thereby became a fighter and worker for Christ and entered legitimately the ranks of the saints of Christ.

The holy prince as an expression of the Christian translation of the antique ruler-cult was not a uniquely Russian contribution to the deification of power; the French kings certainly benefited by having the blood of St. Louis in their veins,[75] and the cult of the Hohenstaufen *Stupor Mundi,* Frederick II, was a cult of his person as well as that of his office.[76] Despite the constitutional abstractions that were developed and elaborated for centuries, even in the West the prince as "body natural" could not be envisaged as just an ordinary man. In Russia the person of the prince received such enormous emphasis because it, and the faith, were the main if not the only concrete expressions of the Russian State and its continuity both during the Kievan and the Tatar periods.

As medieval Russia expressed its ruler-cult in the Christianized form of the saint-prince, this form was necessarily reflected in the myth of the prince. The image of

75. Cf. P. E. Schramm, *Der König von Frankreich* (Weimar, 1939); M. Bloch, *Les rois thaumaturges* (Strasbourg, 1924). On the type of saintly kings in the West, cf. R. Folz, "Zur Frage der heiligen Könige: Heiligkeit und Nachleben in der Geschichte des Burgundischen Königtums," *Deutsches Archiv, 14* (1958), 317–45.

76. E. H. Kantorowicz, *Frederick the Second* (London, 1931); see also his *King's Two Bodies*, 97f.

the saint-prince implied an emphasis on and an exaltation of the person of the ruler which merged it with his divine power and office. What one could call a political Nestorianism of the West, the splitting apart of the two natures of the prince, the human and the divine, his person and his functions, could not apply, at least in theory, to the Russian prince, who in his person was as much an image of Christ as he was in his office and function. The duality of the nature and function of the prince was expressed, as in the case of Dimitry Donskoi, in a mystical dialectic wherein as a glorious Tsar Dimitry sought monkish humility, and this humility in turn exemplified and explained the glory of his rulership. The role of the ruler-monk was the material equivalent of the image of the prince-saint in the *vita* of Dimitry Donskoi, and it is worthwhile to see whether this conception prevailed in the cases of the other Grand Princes and Tsars of Russia. In fact, in the case of the Moscow dynasty we find an interesting custom: eight of the twelve Moscovite rulers, beginning with Grand Prince Daniel, before their death took the monastic vows and died as monks.[77] Both the duality and the unity within the image of the prince-saint were symbolized by the ritual introduced into the ceremonies of Russian rulership. As the glory of the prince indicated the divine nature of his office, so his voluntary vows indicated his spiritual status as an angelic being.[78] That the myth of the holy ruler thus entered princely

77. Daniil (*Troitskaia Letopis'*, 351); Ivan I (*ibid.*, 364); Simeon (A. V. Exempliarsky, *Velikie i Udel'nye Kniazia Severnoi Rusi* [St. Petersburg, 1889], *1*, 87); Ivan II (*Troitskaia Letopis'*, 376); Vasily III (*P.S.R.L.*, *6*, 292); Ivan IV (Karamzin, *9*, n. 758); Feodor (Karamzin, *10*, n. 372); Boris Godunov ("Inoe Skazanie." *R.I.B.*, *13*, 39). That the custom was not restricted to the Moscow dynasty we have already seen to be the case; cf. *P.S.R.L.*, *25*, 144 for Alexander Nevsky.

78. On monks as angelic beings, cf. *Catholic Encyclopedia* (New York, 1911), *10*, 468.

ritual can be argued because the statistics given above are deceptive. Of the princes who apparently did not take the vows before their death, Iury was murdered; curiously enough, Dimitry Donskoi himself, the model of the monk-prince, apparently died a layman; [79] concerning Vasily I (d. 1425) the chronicles are silent on this point, and the same is true for Ivan III (d. 1505).[80] Only in the case of Vasily II (1425–62) are we told something definite. Describing the illness and death of the Grand Prince, the chronicler wrote: "At this time his wounds became infected and he fell gravely ill and desired to take the monastic vows, but he was not allowed to [do so] [*ne dasha emu voli*] and because of that illness he died on the 27th day of March." [81] The statement is cryptic enough; who was it that forbade the dying Grand Prince to perform the usual ritual, and why? That the attempt, if that is what it was, to abolish this particular ceremony was not successful in the long run can be seen from the case of the princes of the sixteenth century, Vasily III, Ivan IV, and Feodor. Yet the injunction is significant, for it tried to abolish the most striking ritual in the image of the saintly prince.

It is possible to conjecture who it was that persuaded (a more accurate rendering, historically, of the way in which the injunction took place) Vasily II to abstain from the traditional act. The power to grant monkhood lay in the hands of the Church; in the case of the Grand Prince, undoubtedly in the hands of the highest clergy, the metropolitan and the bishops.[82] But if the Church was respon-

79. *P.S.R.L.*, *25*, 216f., though see below, p. 47, for 16th-century evidence.

80. For Vasily I, see *P.S.R.L.*, *4*, 120; *5*, 25, 263; for Ivan III, cf. *P.S.R.L.*, *4*, 136, 281; *5*, 261.

81. *P.S.R.L.*, *25*, 278. Cf. Exempliarsky, *1*, 187.

82. One can assume that this was the general rule even though there were exceptions; in the case of Alexander Nevsky, none of the higher clergy seem to have been with him at the time of his vows and death; cf. *P.S.R.L.*, *25*, 144.

sible for the attempt to change the princely myth, the chronicle gives us no reasons for such an attempt. Yet it is possible to suggest an answer to this question also. The church, in medieval Russia, was the main if not the only source of political thought, and in our argument we shall have to turn to the important events in the reign of Vasily II which formulated or affected that thought.

Briefly, these events were civil war within the Moscovite Grand Principality, which, in effect, secured the throne for the senior line of the Moscow dynasty; the virtual unification of northeastern Russia by Moscow; [83] the attempt at the union of the Latin and Greek churches at the Council of Florence; and the fall of Constantinople, the New or Second Rome, to the Turks in 1453. The internal events marked the emergence of the early Russian absolutist, centralized state. The Russian reaction to the external events determined the main current of political theory for the new state. Again, to summarize this reaction, Russian rejection of any union or compromise with "latinity" as a betrayal of the faith and of God, left the Russians, in their own eyes, as the only true and orthodox Christians in the world.[84] The fall of Constantinople, of the Roman empire, Christian and universal by definition, was seen by them as a consequence of Byzantine betrayal of God at Florence, which left an impossible void in a world seeking salvation; a void which was filled, through a *translatio imperii,* by Moscow—the Third Rome.[85] What is significant for us is the general tenor or mood of this idea which in the course of the century that followed the fall of Byzantium transferred the attributes, privileges, status, and functions of

83. A. E. Presniakov, *Obrazovanie veliko-russkago gosudarstva* (Petrograd, 1918); *Istoriia, 4,* chap. 2, 3.

84. Cf. my study, "The Reception of the Council of Florence in Moscow," *Church History,* 24 (1955), 347–60.

85. On Moscow, the Third Rome, cf. literature listed in note 2 above.

the Byzantine Christian Roman emperor to Moscow and its ruler, the Grand Prince.

The prince remained as the focus in Russian writings on the attempt to betray the faith and thus the salvation of the Russian people. It was he who uncovered the Latin plot, conducted the struggle against the apostate head of the Russian Church, metropolitan Isidore, and finally restored Russia to orthodoxy.[86] Summarizing Vasily II's achievement, the pamphletist expressed it dramatically:

Rejoice oh pious Grand Prince Vasily, for you have confirmed The Russian land in faith; truly you have placed on your head the crown of holy baptism.

Rejoice, Orthodox Prince Vasily, for you have confirmed all your priests; they who were naked, you have confirmed . . .

Rejoice, Orthodox Prince Vasily, you have stifled the Latin heresy and would not let it grow amongst Orthodox Christians . . .

Rejoice, Orthodox Prince Vasily, the confirmer of Orthodoxy and of all the Russian land . . . the joy and happiness of the Divine Church and of all Orthodox Christians . . .

Rejoice, Orthodox Grand Prince Vasily Vasilievich, beautified by the crown of the Orthodox Greek faith, and with you rejoice all the Orthodox princes of the Russian land . . .

Rejoice, Prince Vasily, for you are renowned in all the Western Lands and in Rome itself; you have glorified the Orthodox Faith and the whole land of Russia.[87]

The Grand Prince saved and confirmed Russia through his own piety and efforts. But if the credit for Russian salvation was due Vasily II, it was due him for his function as prince. Russia was saved because Vasily II ruled it as Grand Prince; his personal piety, his love of God are significant insofar as Russia is involved, rather than as

86. "The Reception of the Council of Florence," 352f.
87. Malinin, appendix, 99–100.

personal characteristics. It was as prince that Vasily II glorified himself before the West and thereby glorified the "whole Russian land." The emphasis in this hymn of praise is on Vasily II as prince, rather than on the prince as a person, a "body natural."

The most complete expression of the new status of Moscow and its ruler is to be found in the famous letter of the monk Philotheos to Grand Prince Vasily III, early in the sixteenth century:

"[I write] to you, the Most bright and most highly-throning Sovereign, Grand Prince, orthodox Christian tsar and lord of all, rein-holder of the Holy oecumenical and Apostolic Church of God of the Most Holy Virgin . . . which is shining gloriously instead of the Roman or Constantinopolitan [one]. For the Old Rome fell because of its church's lack of faith, the Apollinarian heresy; and of the second Rome, the city of Constantine, the pagans broke down the doors of the churches with their axes . . . And now there is the Holy synodal Apostolic church of the reigning third Rome, of your tsardom, which shines like the sun in its orthodox Christian faith throughout the whole universe. And that is your realm, pious tsar, as all the empires [tsardoms] of the orthodox Christian faith have gathered into your single empire . . . you are the only tsar for Christians in the whole world. . . .

Do not break, O tsar, the commandments laid by your ancestors, the Great Constantine and the blessed Vladimir, and the God-chosen Iaroslav, and the other blessed saints, of which root you are. . . .

Listen and attend, pious tsar, that all Christian empires are gathered in your single one, that two Romes have fallen, and the third one stands, and a fourth one there shall not be; your empire will not fall to others, according to the great Evangelist." [88]

What we see then, in the period following the critical events of the mid-fifteenth century, is a new aspect to the

88. Malinin, appendix, 51–56.

image of the ruler, contained in a new conception of the state. The Byzantine elements of this conception, however, emphasized the central role of the new basileus-tsar; the emphasis was on the new functions of the Russian prince, functions which increased his glory and made him a "tsar," a basileus. These functions, in return, affected the image of the Russian saint-prince.

Vasily III is a glorious Tsar, according to Philotheos, because of his new and overwhelming responsibility before the world of safeguarding the Russian Church and State. Because, ever since the Council of Florence, orthodoxy and thereby salvation are identical with Russia, the concept of Russia, vague and indeterminate, acquires a luster and prominence expressed by the imperial image of Moscow, the Third Rome; because Russia's new status was established by its ruler and depended on him, his image acquires additional glory and greater scope, expressed by the title of "tsar." In other words, while "Moscow, The Third Rome," expressed the idea of a state, it was defined by an ecclesiastic hierarchy and political boundaries which were established by the Russian ruler.[89] Hence, neither Church nor State were independent abstractions, having their own existence and imposing their own limitations on Russian society; both depended, by definition, on the image of the Russian prince, for both received their legitimacy, and thus their reality, from him.

The imperial and solar imagery applied to Vasily III, while describing his status, had an old tradition behind it. Vladimir the Apostle-like, Alexander Nevsky, Dimitry Donskoi were sun-like and tsars in essence. All of them had saved Russia or made her salvation possible. The

89. Beyond the frontiers, as in southern Russia or Russian Lithuania, orthodoxy was not preserved and salvation not assured. Hence, while the Russian ruler retained the title, "Grand Prince of all Russia" (*vseia Rusi*), salvation was confined to the Third Rome, the actual domain of the Moscovite dynasty.

emphasis, necessarily, was on their actions, on their fulfillment of princely function. Though the tradition was
well established, in the sixteenth century it received a
new impetus, for now not only the fate of Russia but the
fate of the world depended upon the activities of the
Russian prince. In other words, there was a change of
emphasis from the person to the function of the prince.
This is not to say that the image of the ruler became ab-
stracted or depersonalized; on the contrary, the personal
qualities of the prince—his orthodoxy, his piety, even his
saintliness—determined, as in the case of Vasily II, his
actions. The change from saintly prince to pious tsar
meant the raising of his functions to a higher, apocalyptic
level; his person could not be made more exalted in any
case.

Hence, to return to the problem of the supposed ecclesiastical objection to the monachization of Vasily II,
an explanation can be suggested which does not require
a discussion of the various lines of Russian political and
ecclesiastical thought from the middle of the fifteenth century. The myth of the ruler's person, of the saint-prince, was
well established. What the Russians sought was material
for the image of the new and glorious Tsar. Byzantine imperial ritual did not include the taking of monastic vows
before death; and since the Russians sought to imitate
this ritual,[90] they may have tried to omit ceremonies which
were not to be found in it.[91]

90. Byzantine court offices and ritual began to be adopted at the very
end of the fifteenth century; cf. V. Prokhorov, *Khristianskie i russkie
drevnosti i arkheologia* (St. Petersburg, 1872).

91. While a number of Byzantine Emperors of the late period did take
monastic vows before death (as did many laics in general) death-bed
monachization was not part of the imperial ritual of dying. Cf. R. Guilland,
"Οἱ Βυζαντινοὶ αὐτοκράτορες καὶ τὸ θέλγητρον τοῦ μοναστηρίου," Ἐπετηρὶς
Ἑταιρεις Βυζαντινῶν Σπουδῶν, *21* (1951), 215–234. On the idea of the king-
monk in the medieval West, cf. Hellmut Kämpf, *Das Reich im Mittelalter*
(Stuttgart, 1950), 29f.

The ceremonial aspect, of course, was only a manifestation of a much more complex problem. If one accepts the evidence of the chronicles that Ivan III, the first of the "Terrible" (*Groznyi*) rulers, had also omitted the old ceremony of monachization, then the period of omission, from the middle of the fifteenth century till the death of Ivan III's son, Vasily III, in 1535, was also the period during which the new conceptions of the ruler were being formulated and refined. The works of Philotheos, Abbot Joseph Sanin, and many others emphasized the absolute and divine nature of princely power.[92] This power, though it depended upon the personal qualities of the prince, was not derived from them. The Russian prince had been saintly for a long time. His new powers, however, were those of a "Tsar," ruling over a tsardom, which Russia had not been in the past. What was necessary, therefore, were new and other justifications for this power which were not available in the myth of the saint-prince.

The well-known "History of the Princes of Vladimir," written in the first quarter of the sixteenth century, advanced the legend that Russian princes were descended from emperor Augustus through his brother, Prus, the ruler of Prussia.[93] The focus of the account was a double one. By their birth, through the legendary Prus and through his direct descendant Riurik, the Russian princes were the heirs of the legitimate Roman emperors; through their power and glory, however, the Kievan ancestors of the Moscovite princes acquired imperial rank from the legitimate emperors of the Second Rome, Constantinople. So the *Skazanie* develops also the legend of the "gifts of Monomakhos," the regalia sent to Vladimir Monomakhos

92. On the political theories of the time, see I. U. Budovnits, *Russkaia Publitsistika XVI Veka* (ANSSSR, 1947); Ševčenko, *H.S.S.*, 2.

93. R. P. Dimitrieva, *Skazanie O Kniaziakh Vladimirskikh* (ANSSSR, 1955), 175, hereafter referred to as *Skazanie;* for the history and analysis of the work, see the commentaries in this edition.

from Constantinople in recognition of his status as a Tsar.[94] The whole story emphasized, time and again, the idea of the continuity and, therefore, the legitimacy of the Russian ruler and the Russian State. What emerges before our eyes is not a line of saintly princes but of glorious *basileis*-tsars. The Russian princes were heirs of the two Romes not only spiritually or eschatologically, as they were for the monk Philotheos, but historically, virtually dynastically. Still the Orthodox rulers of the only Orthodox people, they received what was in effect a secular justification as well.[95]

The emergence of an independent centralized Russian State, due both to the unification of Russian lands and to the liberation from the Tatar yoke, forced Russian thought to develop new concepts of the ruler and the State to account for the new conditions. Byzantine sources, as all sources can, lent themselves to the creation of these new conceptions or myths, in which the emphasis shifted from the prince as person to the prince as power, as the personification of the State. This change was reflected in

94. *Skazanie,* 177; the emperor Constantine Monomakhos is said to have sent the regalia with the following message: "Receive from us, oh God-loving and pious prince, these worthy gifts, due your birth and ancestry . . . for your glory and honor and for your enthronement over your free and autocratic [*samoderzhavnago*] tsardom. About this you will be begged by our envoys, for we request of Your Honor peace and love; thus the Church of God will be trouble-free, and all orthodoxy will be at peace under the power of our tsardom and your free autocracy of Great Russia; for you shall be called, henceforth, the God-crowned tsar, crowned with this imperial diadem by the hand of the most holy metropolitan, the Lord Neofit with his bishops." For a discussion of the "gifts," see D. I. Prozorovsky, "Ob utvariakh pripisyvaemykh Vladimiru Monomakhu," *Z.R.A.O., 3* (1882), 1–64.

95. Cf. *Skazanie,* 110f.; there is another element which the *Skazanie* brings out: the rights of the Russian rulers are established not only through their imperial descent, but also by the right of conquest, for the "History" emphasizes the foreign origin of the Russian dynasty. For a discussion of the significance of this theory of conquest, see my "Khan or Basileus," 475.

the symbols of princely status. The Grand Princely seals of the Moscow House are an interesting instance of this change. Those of the Moscow Grand Princes from Ivan I till Vasily II bear in all cases the image of the personal name-saint of the ruler.[96] The seals of Vasily II, reflecting the changing conceptions of the ruler, attempted to convey the impersonal or suprapersonal nature of his status.[97] The process continued with Ivan III when, shortly after 1480, the seal of the Grand Prince bore the new, impersonal, state symbol—the two-headed eagle—which remained the Russian State symbol until 1917.[98]

96. Ivan I: John the Baptist; Simeon: St. Simeon the Persian; Ivan II: St. John, patriarch of Jerusalem; Dimitry Donskoi: St. Demetrius of Thessalonica; Vasily I: St. Basil of Caesarea; Cherepnin, 567f.

97. One of the seals shows a horseman with a lance, the beginning of the well-known symbol, the "Moscow horseman," which eventually developed into the image of St. George and the dragon, part of Russian imperial iconography until 1917; cf. Cherepnin, 569, no. 24. Another of Vasily II's seals shows a female head with a radiate crown, Cherepnin, 570, no. 35/1; yet another displays a lion killing a snake, Cherepnin, 572, no. 61a/1; S.G.G.D., I, 320; for other seals attributed to Vasily II, see Cherepnin, no. 44/1, 52/1. None of them, however, show the image of the personal saint of the Grand Prince.

98. Cherepnin, 575, no. 85/1; S.G.G.D., I, 333; for earlier seals of Ivan III, cf. Cherepnin, nos. 63/1, 64a/1, 65/1, 69/1; on the question of dating the seal, cf. S.G.G.D., I, seal no. 125, and "Khan or Basileus," p. 470, n. 48.

2. *The Most-Gentle Tsar*

"Without the Tsar the land is a widow; without the Tsar the people is an orphan."

—RUSSIAN PROVERB

THE problem of the duality of the ruler's nature was common to all Europe: the conception of a sharp distinction between the person and office of the prince, between King and Crown, was attained by the sixteenth century, at the earliest, and then only in England.[1] The question, then, for Russia is not why the Russians did not develop the concept of the abstract State to counterbalance the prince, but rather how the traditional image of the saint-prince and the new image of the glorious Tsar of the Third Rome influenced each other in the developing Russian myth of the ruler. One should expect to find the interplay of these two strands within the myth correspond to the period of development, roughly in the age of Ivan IV the Terrible (1533–1585), the culminating figure of Moscovite Russia.

In his article, I. Ševčenko shows conclusively that the chief sources for Russian political theory in the sixteenth

1. Cf. Kantorowicz, *The King's Two Bodies*, 7f.

century were the writings of the sixth-century Byzantine, Agapetus.[2] He sees, in effect, Russian political thought moving within the framework of the equation set up by Agapetus for the problem of the dual nature of the ruler.[3] The clearest expression of this equation is Agapetus' chapter 21:

"Though an emperor in body be like all other, yet in power of his office he is like God, Master of all men. For on earth, he has no peer. Therefore as God, be he never chafed or angry; as man, be he never proud. For though he be like God in face, yet for all that he is but dust, which thing teaches him to be equal to every man." [4]

It is exactly the movement within the framework *divine-human* that concerns us here. As Ševčenko points out, Agapetus was not describing, in his detailed program, an emperor, but rather the ideal of an emperor.[5] Accepting Agapetus' definition for the dualism within the prince, Russian writers, describing the Russian prince, had a great range of possibilities open to them. Any epithet or image, from God to miserable sinner, would be legitimate within the formula with which they chose to work.[6]

Both the chief exponents of the new "imperial" ideology, Joseph Sanin and Philotheos of Pskov, emphasized constantly and exclusively the divine nature of the new Tsar.[7]

2. Ševčenko, *H.S.S.;* also see V. E. Val'denberg, "Nastavlenie pisatelia VI veka, Agapita v russkoi pis'mennosti," *Vizantiiskii Vremennik,* 24 (1923–26), 27–34.

3. Ševčenko, 173f.

4. Ševčenko, 147 and n. 29.

5. Cf. Val'denberg, *Drevnerusskie Ucheniia,* 6of.

6. Both the choice and the range of possibilities were, of course, largely theoretical, considering the nature of the problem and the sources available.

7. Sanin certainly had good reasons for his position, in his concern with the question of church property and with the problem of the new heresies; cf. Budovnits, 66f.; A. A. Zimin, "O politicheskoi doktrine Iosifa Volotskogo," *T.O.D.R.L.,* 9 (1953), 159–177; Philotheos' motivation may

For Philotheos, the world can only be saved by the exercise
of divine functions on the part of Vasily III. For Joseph,
only the supreme ruler, Grand Prince and Tsar, obeyed
like God, can achieve the purposes in which the abbot of
the Volokolamsk monastery was interested—persecution
of heresy and preservation of church property.

The "Thanks and Praise for . . . the birth . . . of the
God-crowned tsar and Grand Prince Ivan [IV]" [8] in the
posthumous praise of Vasily III described the Tsar:

"Such must be moreover the soul of the tsar which has
so many cares [*mnogopopechitel'naia*], which, like a mirror
is ever cleansed and continually shines with divine rays
(*viny oblistaema*) so that it learns the judgment of things,
as it is written: "In his physical being the tsar is like all
men; in the power of his majesty he is like unto God, Who
is above all; [he] has no one superior to him on earth;
[he is] unapproachable by men due to the loftiness of his
earthly tsardom and is approachable for the sake of the
heavenly Tsardom." . . . Verily are you called a tsar for
you reign over passions . . . you are crowned with the
diadem of chastity and arrayed in the purple robe [*porfiroi*]
of justice. Such was also the pious Tsar of Tsars, Grand
Prince Vasilii." [9]

Ševčenko has shown in detail how the passages of Agapetus
were juggled rather skilfully in order to produce "more
stress on the ruler's lofty station." [10] The aim of this jug-
gling is clear in the last sentence of the quotation; what is
presented is not the ideal of the ruler but a portrait of

---

be ascribed to the general position the church, and particularly the
monasteries, held in support of the ruler; cf. V. Sokol'sky, *Uchastie russkago
dukhovenstva i monashestva v razvitii edinoderzhaviia i samoderzhaviia*,
(Kiev, 1902). Ševčenko's suggestion (161) that one understand Philotheos
as a Pskovian Quisling is not too convincing.

8. In *P.S.R.L., 21: 2*, 605–615; for its dating and importance, cf. Ševčenko,
159–60.

9. *P.S.R.L., 21:2*, 610–11.

10. Ševčenko, 162–63.

Vasily III. But if the purpose of the eulogy was to emphasize Vasily's status and nature as the ruler, the tension
between the ruler's two natures was not ignored, for the
description of Vasily III continued: "Above all he was
concerned for his soul, trying hard to imitate the divinely-
wise life of his saintly and righteous ancestor, the praiseworthy Grand Prince Dimitry Ivanovich Donskoi; [who]
sitting on the tsar's throne and ruling the Russian land,
had in his heart the desire for a cave; wearing the imperial purple and diadem, always desired to wear the
monk's robe, which [desire] he attained." [11] The tension
of the dual nature remains, but it is interiorized within the
prince. In fact the two natures of the prince are transformed into his two functions; he desires to be humble,
a monk, as he desires to be a good and great ruler, and
both of these aspects of the prince are reflections of Christ.
If in his glory the prince is like God, in humility he becomes a monk, an angelic being. The eulogy conveys
Vasily's obsessive desire during his last illness to become
a monk. Finally, the day before his death,

"[He] ordered the holy ecclesiastical synod to consecrate
and anoint him with holy oil in the name of the Lord.
And after this [he] called to himself Daniel, the metropolitan of all Russia, and his brothers and his chosen boiars
. . . and ordered them to write his testament . . . [Mean-
while] he was undeviating in his desire to take on the
monastic form. He bound the metropolitan with an oath,
saying: 'I know that no one wants that I should be a
monk. You, father, be ashamed before no one, but make
me, according to the will of God, a monk, according to
my promise, for I am sinful.' " [12]

Vasily's insistence was justified, for we are told that his
brother Andrew and the boiars tried at the last moment

11. *P.S.R.L.*, 21:2, 611
12. *P.S.R.L.*, 21:2, 612.

to prevent the monachization and had to be threatened by
the metropolitan himself, before Grand Prince Vasily III
could die as the monk Varlaam.[13] We are told clearly who
it was that opposed the old ritual, but the reasons for this
opposition are no clearer in the case of Vasily III than
they were in the case of his grandfather. We do learn, however, that the issue of the ritual, of the prince becoming
a monk, was an important one; sufficiently so for the dying
Vasily III to take such strong notice of it and for his own
brother and the boiars to come out in open opposition
to the will of their stern and terrifying ruler.[14]

It is tempting to conjecture that Prince Andrew and the
"chosen boiars" in this case manifested that aristocratic,
boiar opposition to the new autocracy of the Russian
Grand Princes which, beginning with the late fifteenth
century, continued until the end of the Time of Troubles,
in 1613.[15] To substantiate such a conjecture, it is necessary to return to the ceremony at issue, for what this ceremony accomplished was the destruction of the tension between the prince's two natures. The prince who became a
monk on his deathbed was the prince who, all his life,
was both Tsar and angel-like monk. No matter how human in nature the prince might be, his monastic state was
a guarantee of salvation and more, for the monk was, as
an idea, not just human but a being intermediate between
man and God. In other words, the human nature of the
prince was ritualized just as his divine nature was ritualized
in all the imperial ceremonial, and thus also deified but
not depersonalized. The ceremony expressed the personal

13. *P.S.R.L.*, *21:2*, 614.

14. Cf. Baron Sigismund Herberstein, *Zapiski o moskovitskikh delakh*,
A. I. Malein, trans. (St. Petersburg, 1908), 73f.

15. Andrew's son Vladimir Staritsky was the candidate of the boiars
who refused to support Ivan's infant son at the time of Ivan's near-fatal
illness in 1553. Cf. V. O. Kliuchevsky, *Boiarskaia Duma Drevnei Rusi*
(Moscow, 1883), 240f., on the nature of boiar opposition.

humility and thus the sanctity of each particular prince. The insecurity of the period of transition was apparently conquered, and the Russian ruler could benefit by the older myth of the saint-prince as well as by the new imperial one. The visible ceremony symbolized the complete interiorization of the tension, making this tension meaningless for political theory. The result of Vasily III's pious insistence is indicated by the eulogy. Hours before his death, the Grand Prince fixed his eyes on an icon of the martyr St. Catherine; thereupon, with a joyous face, he exclaimed thrice: "Oh my mistress, great martyr Catherine! The time has come for us to reign [tsarstvovati]," [16] and, after his death, we learn that "instead of a stench from the sore on his foot, the church was filled with [the smell of] perfume." [17]

Though the prince is godlike in his power, in his human nature he also does not appear as a simple mortal, but as another, more humble aspect of Christ. The age of Ivan the Terrible does witness attempts to reinforce the tension of two disparate natures. The metropolitan Philip, murdered on Ivan's orders and sainted for his martyrdom, addressed the Tsar in public in the cathedral of the Dormition: "Have you forgotten that you too are made up of earthly dust, and require absolution for [your] sins?" [18] St. Philip gained his martyrdom for this reminder, but it is doubtful whether the tsar or anyone else in the cathedral would have accepted the argument of the metropolitan. Ivan IV died as a monk, and hence the absolution of his sins was as automatic a consequence of his being a man as his power was of his being Tsar. A striking

16. *P.S.R.L.*, *21:2*, 614.

17. *P.S.R.L.*, *21:2*, 614.

18. "ili zabyl, chto i sam ty prichasten persti zemnoi i proshcheniia grekhov trebuesh?"; G. P. Fedotov, *Sviatoi Filipp Mitropolit Moskovskii* (Paris, 1928), 147; cf. Ševčenko, n. 93 and 166f. on the *vita* of Philip and its reliability.

example of St. Philip's reasoning is found in the famous correspondence between Ivan IV and Prince Andrew Kurbsky, renowned for his friendship with his Tsar and for his betrayal of Ivan and flight to Lithuania. Here it was the terrible Tsar who dwelt on the human nature of the prince: "although We wear the purple robe, beautified with gold and pearls, nevertheless We are mortal and weighed down with human infirmities." [19] Not only did Ivan admit his own humanity, but he pleaded it as an excuse for his "small sins," for "I, too, am a man; and no man is without sins, only God is sinless." [20] He accused Kurbsky of heresy for "requiring man to be above human nature." [21]

Tsar Ivan's evocation of his humanity, however, does not have the ring of either Shakespeare's Henry V or of Tacitus' Tiberius.[22] And his human nature, whose sins in any case are caused by Kurbsky and other evil counselors, cannot be separated from his divine function.[23] In Ivan's eyes his own humanity is fully absorbed by his godlike office. He points out to the rebellious prince that any attempt to oppose him as a man necessarily leads to opposing God.[24] Even if he were unjust, in the end Kurbsky's duty would be to suffer piously, in accordance with God's will.[25] But Kurbsky really is not in a position to judge the actions of the Tsar, who is, at all times, the instrument of God; for what may appear to be sinful for a man to do is part of the duty of a pious ruler.[26] In other words, while

19. *Poslaniia Ivana Groznogo*, eds. D. S. Likhachev, Ia. S. Lur'ie, V. P. Adrianova-Perets (ANSSSR, 1951), 45–46; cf. Ševčenko, 165.

20. *Poslaniia*, 14.

21. *Poslaniia*, 15; cf. Ševčenko, 165 and n. 85.

22. *King Henry V*, IV, i, 259f.; *Annals*, Bk. IV, ch. 38.

23. *Poslaniia*, 14.

24. *Poslaniia*, 11.

25. *Poslaniia*, 12.

26. *Poslaniia*, 18–19; "How can you not understand that the ruler must neither act like a beast nor submit silently? . . . Even during the times of the most pious tsars one can find many cases of the most cruel punish-

Ivan admits to human frailty, his human sins are a personal matter affecting only himself and his personal salvation.[27] How completely Ivan removed the tension between Tsar and man from the consideration of mortals is shown by his view of the relation between Tsar and subject. Kurbsky, he argues, by his betrayal lost not only his own immortal soul "but also damned the souls of his ancestors, for they were given, by God's will, to our grandfather, the great sovereign, to labor, and they [the ancestors], having given their souls, served until death and had ordered you, their children, to serve the children and grandchildren of our grandfather." [28] The tsar's humanity was certainly beyond the concern of political theories in a situation where the tsar owned not just the bodies of his subjects but their souls as well.

In the history of the saintly princes, then, the age of Ivan IV the Terrible was an age of transition. The early tradition of the prince as a complete *mimesis* of Christ, saintly by nature as man and saintly by action as prince, was modified by the new conception of the State. The myth shifted from the saintly princes of Russia to the imperial rulers of Rome, Constantinople, and Kiev as the models and justification of the Moscovite Tsar. In the first Russian Church councils, 1547–49, held under the presidency of the young Tsar, the official list of national canonized saints included only two of the great princely saints—St.

ments. Are you really capable, in your unreason, to suppose that the tsar must always act the same way, irrespective of time and circumstances? . . . Remember the greatest of tsars, Constantine; how he killed, for the sake of the empire, his own son! And prince Feodor Rostislavich, your ancestor, how much blood he spilled, at Easter, in Smolensk! Yet they are counted among the saints . . . Tsars always must be circumspect; sometimes gentle, sometimes cruel, merciful and gentle to the good, while the evil ones get cruel punishments. If this is not the case, [there is] no tsar."

27. Actually, one can argue that his personal salvation is really threatened when he fails in his functions as tsar.

28. *Poslaniia*, 13.

Michael of Tver and Alexander Nevsky.[29] Yet, if the official
cult of the saint-princes was underplayed, it continued
sufficiently in the popular imagination for Ivan IV, his
father, and his son to be subsequently listed among the
saints, and this tradition in turn was reflected in the de-
liberate resumption of the ritual of monachization for all
the three rulers. Or, to turn the problem around, the myth
of the saintly princes was absorbed into the new myth of
the Tsar. This absorption destroyed the tension between
the twin but unequal natures of the Agapetan ruler and
hence could lead to an emphasis on the "body politic,"
the godlike office, of the new Tsar, without denigrating
the "body natural." The twin natures of the ruler were
neither sundered nor abolished, but merged, for the human nature of the prince was as exalted as his divine
office. Thus, a disciple of Joseph Sanin, the monk Zinovy
Ottensky, wrote on the proper attitude towards a representation of the Tsar: "We see the image of a man who is
more just and higher than all who obey him . . . From
this we know that, as compared to the image of the Tsar,
all serene and great and honorable ranks, [including]
episcopal ones . . . are far inferior; the image of the Tsar
as man is the supreme one of all." [30] The iconography of
Tsar Ivan supports the feelings of Zinovy and reveals the
various strands of the ruler myth. The portrait of the Tsar
with his regalia is impersonal; the face is not individualized
and the whole squat, impassive figure serves only to carry
and wear the attributes of power (Fig. 6). No more human,
however, does Ivan appear in the fresco of the Novo-
Spasskii monastery, where the Tsar gazes out in the garb
and with the appearance of an early Russian prelate-saint
(Fig. 1),[31] or on the page of the Kazan' Chronicle, where

29. Golubinsky, 99f.
30. "Istiny Pokazanie," in Sokol'sky, 192–93.
31. Cf. Fig. 2.

the young Tsar, on horseback, spearing and trampling the prostrate khan of conquered Kazan', appears in the guise of the popular warrior-saint, St. Demetrius of Thessalonica (Fig. 3).[32] Most striking is what is probably the most accurate representation of Ivan, now in Copenhagen (Fig. 17). The Tsar is portrayed in the manner of the apostles and great church fathers; [33] what we see is a saint, but a saint of such power and human passion as to be more than human.

The myth of the saint-prince received its ideological baptism and its first test in the sixteenth century with the rise of the centralized state and its consequent ideology. It had to undergo an equally severe testing soon afterwards in the shattering political crisis known as the Time of Troubles. In the few years between 1598 and 1613, Russia experienced the end of a seven-hundred-year-old dynasty, a succession of three Tsars of whom one was the successful pretender to being the son of Ivan IV, Dimitry (d. 1591), and an anarchic civil war conducted by innumerable pretenders to and claimants of the Russian throne. That such a crisis should be reflected in the political literature of the time is not surprising.[34] Numerous memoirs and histories tried to solve problems which were new to Russian political consciousness: how to assign the cause or causes of such catastrophic misfortunes; how to distinguish between a legitimate, true Tsar and a false one who is nevertheless crowned and consecrated.[35]

The various writers tended to agree in their analysis and conclusions, but among them the clerk Ivan Timofeev stands out both in literary talent and in depth of historical

32. Cf. e.g., Mouratow, *Peinture*, fig. 58.
33. Cf. Figs. 18, 4, 5, and also 15 for Ivan's son Feodor.
34. On the writings of the time, see Platonov, *Drevnerusskie Skazaniia.*
35. Cf. Val'denberg, *Drevnerusskie Ucheniia*, 357f.; for the texts, see *Pamiatniki Drevnei Russkoi Pismennosti otnosiashchiesia k Smutnomu Vremeni, R.I.B., 13.*

perception.[36] Like the others, Timofeev wrote his *Vremennik* after the troubled times were over, under the first Romanov Tsar, Michael, when both the state and the monarchy had been restored and the Russian Tsar occupied his accustomed place in his traditional fullness of power.[37] Russia was restored to normality as far as Timofeev and the other writers were concerned, and the Time of Troubles served, in effect, as an example in negation for what was right and normal.

The learned clerk knew and accepted the formula of Agapetus.[38] But it is not surprising to find that he emphasized the divine nature of the ruler's office. Time and again Timofeev pointed out that the Tsar stands above human judgment, that the sins of the individual holder of the scepter do not affect the nature and hence the status of the office.[39] Timofeev rejected both the person and activities of Tsar Vasily Shuisky, yet he denied his contemporaries the right to overthrow the Tsar.[40] For Timofeev, the Tsar and the State were one; the Tsar was the living head of Russia, without which it could not exist, and during the last chaotic years of the Time of Troubles, Russia is portrayed allegorically, in two long parables, as a widow who, without her rightful husband, is preyed upon by strangers and servants both.[41] If Timofeev, then, accepted the sacredness and immutability of the tsar's office, he faced the problem of legitimacy. Could any tsar be removed or not accepted as tsar? In the case of Dimitry, the False Pretender, there was little difficulty for the political theorists.

36. *Vremennik Ivana Timofeeva*, eds. O. A. Derzhavina, V. P. Adrianova-Perets (ANSSSR, 1951).

37. On the attempts to limit the tsar's power permanently during the Time of Troubles, cf. Kliuchevsky, *Duma*, 353f.

38. *Vremennik*, 107; cf. Ševčenko, 178 n. 126.

39. *Vremennik*, 198, 279, 281.

40. *Vremennik*, 108; cf. commentary, p. 369.

41. *Vremennik*, 155f., 159f.

The Pretender was a servant of Satan, and he revealed himself by his denigration of Orthodoxy.[42] In other words, he had to expose himself, for, as the tool of the devil, he had to attack the Orthodox faith. But if the standard of personal and official orthodoxy of the Russian tsar was an easy test to apply for the False Dimitry, the problem was more complicated in the case of Boris Godunov. Timofeev accepts all the traditional legends about Boris and accuses him not only of the murder of the young prince Dimitry of Uglich but also of the murders of Ivan IV and his son Tsar Feodor.[43] The murders are logically, however, only post-facto justification for Timofeev's condemnation of the "false" tsar. His opposition to Godunov centers around the Tsar's person in a rather curious way. He recognizes the high qualities of Boris as a ruler—his intelligence, his kindness, his genuine desire to rule well. Yet in describing Boris' reign Timofeev attacks all the actions and orders of the Tsar, and in the most violent terms. What he attacks, however, are not the actions of the tsar as such; all of them are quite proper for a tsar to perform. The point, for Timofeev, is that Boris was not a tsar; hence everything Godunov did was, by definition, as improper as all the actions of a true tsar are, by definition, proper. Boris was a "slave," like everyone else, and his real crime was in trying to be a tsar.[44]

If Timofeev's purpose was to provide some guidance in distinguishing between true and false tsars, he surely failed, as so many political thinkers had failed before him. He argues in a circle, where the judgment of the ruler's actions is determined by the ruler's true or false nature, which, in turn, is revealed by his actions. Nevertheless,

42. *Vremennik*, 84f.; "Plach o Plenenii i o Konechnom Razorenii Moskovskago Gosudarstva," *R.I.B.*, *13*, 225f.

43. *Vremennik*, 15f., 28f.

44. *Vremennik*, chap. 3, "Borise zhe tsare," 72f.

though our clerk admits, in effect, that there is no concrete solution to the problem, he considers the obedience offered to the false tsars as one of the great sins of the Russian people.[45] Only because they were sinful were the people unable to discriminate between true and false rulers, for there is a difference between them, a difference in their natures, not as tsars but as men. The application by Timofeev of the old principle, *Quod licet Jovi, non licet bovi,* to Boris Godunov, leads both to an emphasis on the person of the tsar and to the merging of the person with the office. The same action which would have been proper for a true tsar was evil when performed by Boris because the latter was acting for human reasons, out of a human motivation. If human motivation is evil, however, no matter what it may be, then the "body natural" of a true tsar is as mystical and as exalted as his office.

Timofeev's views on this problem are most clear as he attempts to discuss the causes of Russia's misfortunes. The false Tsar Boris, he recognizes, followed the policies of his old master Ivan the Terrible. But what could be attacked as evil and sinful in Boris should not even be mentioned in writing about a true and legitimate Tsar.[46] Yet Timofeev felt that Ivan IV, through his cruelties and destruction, created much of the spiritual and physical disorganization which was the cause of the troubles that followed.[47] In fact, many of the disasters were caused directly by the sins of the wrathful Tsar, and still Timofeev provides a solution to the problem imposed by his views on the ruler. Describing the Tatar (Crimean) raid of 1571, which resulted in the complete destruction of Moscow except for the Kremlin, Timofeev wrote that it all had happened "because of the

45. "We had less fear of heaven than of earthly [power], we have adored a slave more than [we had adored] a Lord; certainly through this we have called upon ourselves all the evil." *Vremennik,* 69.

46. *Vremennik,* 16f.; 33f.

47. *Vremennik,* 13f.

diversion into sin of the head of all—the tsar himself." [48]
Rather suddenly, we find, this allows our writer to compare
Ivan to King David, who too had sinned, and had chosen
a particular punishment from God. Thus, Timofeev is
able to praise Ivan, who, like David, submitted to his
punishment "humbly and silently." [49] Timofeev's argument that the sins of the Tsar were expiated by his Christian acceptance of the retribution which, on the face of it,
was visited mainly on his innocent subjects, can be explained not only by the identification the writer makes
between the person and the office of the prince but also
by his view of the prince's nature. Timofeev does not accept the view that the Tsar, by nature, is just a man, and
Ivan's sins and suffering are consequently not just human.
Describing the suffering of the Tsaritsa, Maria Nagaia, at
the death of her son, the saintly martyr Dimitry of Uglich,
Timofeev warns us: "Let no one in his simplicity think
and imagine that it was the same sorrow as we, the lowly,
would have, according to our nature; no, it [our nature]
is as incomparable [to Maria's]—in sorrow as in joy—as
a droplet of rain [is incomparable] with the whole great
depth of the sea." [50]

The mysterious and mystical element by which the
tsar's nature differs from that of ordinary men is not
captured by Timofeev. But there is one concrete manifestation of the nature of a true tsar—and here we are
reminded of the False Dimitry—his personal piety. Ivan
the Terrible is descended from the Roman Emperor Augustus, with all the nobility that implies, but

"more than through ancestry he must be accounted with
his noble predecessors through piety [blagochestie]; pious
of the pious, sons of their fathers, they [the Russian princes]

48. *Vremennik*, 14.
49. Ibid.
50. *Vremennik*, 33.

descended legitimately and in a holy manner [*sviatolepno*] down to the present day. Such was always the family of my autocrats and they have never angered God too much; their possessions, spreading to the four corners of the earth, remain unshaken till the present." [51]

That the piety, the faith is a personal characteristic we are shown in the case of Ivan's son, Tsar Feodor, for whom Timofeev evokes the traditional image of the tsar-monk.[52] And again the personal nature of Ivan's piety and its cosmic significance are stated clearly by Timofeev:

"He [Ivan] kept the right faith . . . from his ancestors till his death, like a shepherd, unshakeable and inviolable. And [here is] what is marvelous! He terrified everyone so much that if he would have wanted to show the weakness of their faith in some . . . he could have, with the terror of his power, exposed their lack of firmness . . . We know that even among the clergy there could be found some who could not have resisted their fear . . . He, our tsar, was such a faithful servant [of God] who kept everyone in such terror, that for his pillar-like steadfastness in the faith and for his confirmation of others [in it] he should be crowned [*sc.* with praise]." [53]

The echoes of Philotheos of Pskov can be heard clearly, but the dramatic quality of Ivan the Terrible's reign enables Timofeev to underline the personal responsibility of the tsar. While for Philotheos the Orthodoxy of the tsar is the central part of his function, for Timofeev it is the

---

51. *Vremennik*, 77.

52. Timofeev compares Feodor to the Indian saintly tsar Iosaf: "The latter [Iosaf] in the desert, Feodor on the throne [showed their qualities]; the latter [Iosaf] displayed the imperial diadem through the intensity of his monastic heroism, while the former [Feodor] performed secretly, in his soul, monastic deeds, hidden by the diadem. Monkhood he combined with tsardom, without separating them, the one embellishing the other." *Vremennik*, 25; on Iosaf, from the legend of "Varlaam and Iosaf," a Christianization of a legend about Buddha, cf. *Vremennik* commentary, p. 466, n. 67.

53. *Vremennik*, 16–17.

personal piety of the tsar on which the fate of Russia, and thereby the world, depends.

For Timofeev, then, reflecting on recent Russian history, the myth of the ruler contained two aspects. The Time of Troubles drove home the fact that a Russian state, a Russia, widowed or not, did exist. The effect of this was to identify the tsar with the State; thereby the Tsar is all power and glory, far above humanity and its judgment. The saint-prince, however, was not forgotten. He emerged in the intent to eliminate any tension between the human and the divine in the ruler. As the ruler is identified with the State, so his human nature is raised to the level of his function. It was a natural reaction to a period of anarchy to overemphasize the absolute and sacred character of the tsar's office. What accompanied it, though, was the emphasis on the prince as person; his autocracy was justified and had to be justified not only from above, by God, but also from below, by his exalted humanity.

How accurately did Timofeev reflect the seventeenth-century image of the tsar? In 1671–72 Tsar Alexis ordered the best painters available in Russia to participate in the composition of the so-called "Great State Book," or "Titulatory." [54] The main part of the book was an official and brief history of Russian rulers deriving their descent from Augustus; each biography was accompanied by a richly ornamented and colored portrait. The portraits, of course, bear no relation to the originals, but in their stylization they can be divided into three groups. The portraits of the pre-Christian Riurik, Oleg, and Sviatoslav, forming the first group, are simply ludicrous. The second group is made up of the images of all the Grand Princes, from St. Vladi-

---

54. For the text, see *D.R.V.*, *16*, 86f.; for reproductions, cf. *Portrety Gerby i Pechati Bol'shoi Gosudarstvennoi Knigi 1672g.*, ed. by St. Peterburgskii Arkheologicheskii Institut (1903), hereafter referred to as *Gos. Kniga.*

mir to Vasily III. Whether the artists had any early portraits to go by is uncertain but in this instance also irrelevant; all the Grand Princes are portrayed in the same
manner, in the iconographic tradition of representing the
apostles, and all of them are haloed as saints.[55] The last
group begins with the portrait of Ivan IV, the first Tsar,[56]
and ends with that of the reigning prince, Tsar Alexis. As
might be expected, the False Dimitry was omitted from the
list, but both Godunov and Shuisky are included, and
between Tsar Feodor and Boris Godunov we find the portrait of the prince St. Dimitry of Uglich. Even in the case
of these virtually contemporary princes we cannot speak
of lifelike representation. Their individuality is expressed
at best by beards and moustaches. All of them are portrayed
as Tsars, in full and virtually identical regalia, in the same
pose and with the same expression of impassiveness. Even
Tsar Feodor, popularly accepted as a saint and considered
one by Timofeev and the other historians of the seventeenth century, is shown as a tsar and only a tsar.[57] Only
the Tsarevich Dimitry, saint and prince but not tsar, is
depicted as a saint, with the crown of martyrdom (Fig. 10);
in all the others, the rulers, the tsar overwhelms the man.

A change, then, took place in the myth of the ruler,
which was reflected in the iconography of Russian princes.
With the imperial coronation of Ivan IV, the saint-prince
was transformed into the Pious and Orthodox Tsar. If the

55. For a particularly fantastic representation, that of the stern warrior
prince, Iury, Dolgoruky, see Fig. 7; that the princely halo was not an imita-
tion of Byzantine iconographic tradition is seen from the fact that the
Russian tsars, from Ivan IV on, are shown without one. On the halo of the
Byzantine emperor, see A. Alföldi, "Insignien und Tracht der römischen
Kaiser," *Mitteilungen des deutschen archäologischen Instituts: Römische
Abteilung*, 50 (1935), 139ff.

56. See Fig. 6.

57. See Figs. 6, 8, 9 and *Gos. Kniga*, 27. For changes in regalia, see E. V.
Barsov, *Drevne-russkie pamiatniki Sviashchennago Venchaniia Tsarei na*,
in *Chteniia* (1883:1), 132f.

1. Ivan IV, fresco in the Novo-Spasskii Monastery

2. Fresco in the Cathedral of the Birth of the Virgin in the Snetogorskii
Monastery

3. Ivan IV, miniature from the Kazanskaia Chronicle

4. St. Paul, in the Ferapont Monastery at Belozero

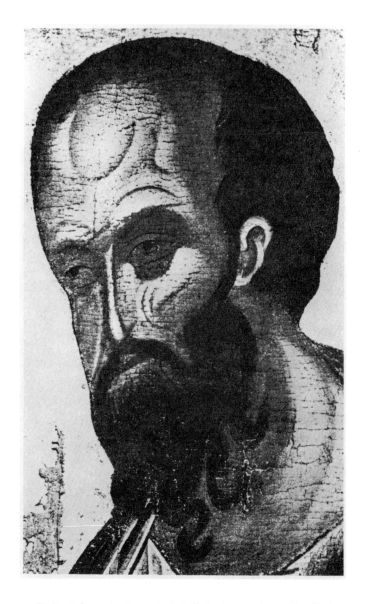

5. St. Paul, fresco in the Cathedral of the Assumption of the Virgin in Zvenigorod

6. Ivan IV, from the *Great State Book* of 1672

ВЕЛИКІЙ КНЗЬ

ЮРЬЙ ВЛАД
РОВІЧЬ ДОГОРУ

7. Grand Prince Iury Dolgoruky, from the *Great State Book* of 1672

8. Tsar Alexis, from the *Great State Book* of 1672

ЦРЬ [I]ВЕЛИКІИ КНЗ
МИХАИЛ ѲЕѠРО
ВІЧЬ ВСЕА ВЕЛИКИ
РОСІИ САМО
ДЕРЖЕЦЬ

9. Tsar Michael, from the *Great State Book* of 1672

ЦРВИЧЬ ДИМΙΤΡΙΙ ΙΟΑΝΝΟΒΙЧЬ

10. Tsarevich Dimitry of Uglich, from the *Great State Book* of 1672

PETRUS PRIMUS
RUSSORUM IMPERATOR

11. Peter I, engraving by J. Houbraken

12. The "Thesis of Obedovsky," engraving, late 17th century

13. Peter I, engraving by P. Picart

14. Ivan IV, by V. Vasnetsov, 1897

15. Tsar Feodor Ivanovich, cloth, 16th century

16. The icon *Spas Iaroe Oko*, from the Tretiakov Gallery

17. Ivan IV, 16th-century portrait

18. John the Evangelist, Church of the Dormition in Volotovo

19. M. V. Nesterov, "Sviataia Rus" (Holy Russia)

20. M. V. Nesterov, "Na Rusi" (Russia)

tsar was no longer a saint, however, what was he as a man? The histories of the Time of Troubles and the iconography give us some additional hints. From the former we learn that the political pupil of Ivan IV, Boris Godunov, was the last tsar to take monastic vows on his deathbed.[58] The tsar-portraits of the "Great State Book" show that there was an interesting innovation in the regalia of the Romanov Tsars, Michael and Alexis; both of them are shown wearing a golden pectoral cross, which was part of the ancient regalia of the Russian rulers but which the earlier tsars apparently did not wear.[59]

For the clearest image of the seventeenth-century tsar we must turn to the reign of Tsar Alexis (1645–1676), the son of Michael Romanov and father of Peter the Great. This does not mean that the Tsar as myth is easy to discern. Overlaying it are the real personal qualities of Alexis, in the words of one historian "the most appealing phenomenon ever seen on the throne of the Moscovite tsars." [60] Blurring the outlines of the image too was the whole complex of Russian court ritual and customs. While Europeans visiting Moscow were amazed at the constant and familiar presence of the boiars around the Tsar, one is equally amazed by his perpetual ceremonious isolation without any of the moments of relaxation practiced even by a Louis XIV.[61] Through these curtains there is visible the image of the *tishaishii*—most gentle—tsar. The epithet,

58. "Inoe Skazanie," *R.I.B.*, *13*, 39. The other tsars of the Time of Troubles, of course, did not have the opportunity to practice this ritual; the False Dimitry was killed, and Vasily Shuisky was forced to abdicate and retire to a monastery.

59. On the golden pectoral cross, cf. Prozorovsky, "Ob utvariakh"; Cherepnin, the Testaments of the Grand Princes, nos. 1, 3, 4, 8, 12, 20, 61, 89, 100.

60. *Istoriia*, *12*, 606.

61. Kliuchevsky, *Duma* 318f.; Gregory Kotoshikhin, *O Rossii v Tsarstvovanie Alekseia Mikhailovicha* (St. Petersburg, 1884), this last a contemporary account.

which did not form a part of official diplomatic titulature, was a translation of the Byzantine *Galenotetos*.[62] Curiously enough, historians apparently accept it as a characterization of Alexis as a person—the kind, gentle, and humane tsar, certainly an unusual phenomenon on the Russian throne.[63] That *tishaishii* tried to convey a personal quality of the tsar is more than probable; but the epithet is found in a context which gives it more than a casual status. In the fascinating account, *Journey of the Patriarch Makarios of Antioch to Russia,* written by his son, archdeacon Paul of Aleppo, we are told that the tsar was prayed for at the end of each church service: "[We] pray for our tsar, the Christ-loving, pious, God-crowned, most-gentle [*tishaishii*] prince Aleksei Mikhailovich." [64] That the epithet is not to be taken literally seems clear. Kind and humane Tsar Alexis was, but he was the autocrat and Tsar, and many instances have been preserved of his very explosive temper.[65] The meaning of *tishaishii* is indicated by its setting in the prayer for the tsar and even more by its setting in the acclamation which followed the prayer: "God grant long life to the tsar, most-gentle, crowned,

62. Cf. Agapetus (Migne, *Patrologia Graeca, 86,* i, col. 1163–86), chapters 50, 52. The epithet, however, was not part of the official titulature; cf. F. Dölger, "Die Entwicklung der Byzantinischen Kaiser titulatur," *Byzantinische Diplomatik* (Munich, 1956). The epithet was, most probably, a translation of the Latin "Serenissimus," which the Russians, in turn, translated, in the seventeenth century, as *Presvetleishii* (Most-illumined); cf. *D.R.V., 16,* 86f.

63. E.g., *Istoriia, 12,* 606; Kliuchevsky, *Kurs Russkoi Istorii 3* (Moscow, 1957), 320f.; N. F. Kapterev, *Patriarkh Nikon i Tsar Aleksei Mikhailovich, 1* (Moscow, 1909), 35f.

64. *Puteshestvie Antiokhskago patriarkha Makariia v Rossiiu v polovine XVII veka, opisannoe ego synom, arkhidiakonom Pavlom Aleppskim,* trans. G. Murkos, in *Chteniia* (1897:4), 158.

65. *Istoriia, 12,* 605f.; Kotoshikhin mentions that everyone assumed that Alexis was "tikhii," quiet, implying that the assumption was not quite correct, *O Rossii,* 141–42.

guarded by God, greatest of tsars." [66] Together with "Christ-loving" and "pious," *tishaishii* referred to the Tsar's person, in distinction from the other epithets which applied to the office. "God-crowned," "Autocrat," "Guarded by God," described the status of the Tsar, if not of a tsar; the personal epithets described the human nature of the ruler, the Tsar as man.

If these epithets were personal, they were, however, not really individual. The tsar as man was pious, Christ-loving, *tishaishii*, but it was impossible to imagine a tsar who, as a man, was not all these things; he simply could not be a true Tsar. The proof for this lies in the ritualization of these very same personal characteristics. The view of an outside observer such as the archdeacon Paul is particularly valuable. The daily life of the Tsar resolved itself into a virtually nightmarish religiosity. His every action necessitated a religious ceremony, and every religious occasion required his personal participation. Time and again the eastern patriarch and his suite felt that they were at the point of a physical collapse, that they could not bear yet another all-night service; yet through all these vigils moved the figure of the Tsar—praying, giving his hand to bishops to kiss and in turn kissing their hands, listening to army reports, and praying again.[67] The Tsar's travels are marked and defined by his monasteries and again the liturgies, the prayers, the blessings, the Tsar served by the monks and the Tsar serving the monks personally at table.[68] There is little doubt that Alexis was a very religious man; not more so, however, than was Ivan the Terrible. But the ritualization of this piety was not a consequence of the

66. *Puteshestvie, Chteniia* (1897:4), 158.

67. For Makarios' and Paul's reaction, cf. *Puteshestvie, Chteniia* (1898:4), 95f. *et passim*.

68. *Puteshestvie, Chteniia* (1898:4), 122. Also see I. E. Zabelin, *Domashnyi Byt Russkago Naroda* (Moscow, 1872; 2 vols.), especially Vol. 1, *Domashnyi Byt Russkikh tsarei v XVI i XVII st.*

personal piety of Alexis. It appears more complete for Alexis because the sources are more available and because the ceremonial manifestations of the tsar's human nature become more focused. The halo and the deathbed monk's cowl were translated into the golden pectoral cross.

The translation of the saint-prince into the pious Tsar involved what one may call a certain distanciation between Christ and the prince. The tsar possessed the human qualities which define a saint, but the transcendental consequence of being the complete image of Christ was no longer drawn. One reason for this, as has been shown, derived from the new concept of the state. The ruler was identified with the state, an abstraction permeated with Byzantine imperial ideology, which was interposed between the prince and Christ as the God-man.[69] Another reason lay in a new institution of seventeenth-century Russia—the patriarchate. Historical accidents do play a role in the development of historical myths, and the importance of the patriarchate was founded, to a large degree, upon accident. Established in 1589 in order to complete the formal ideological structure of the new, Third Rome, it lasted only a little over a century.[70] Its importance came during the worst of the Time of Troubles when, in the absence of a tsar, the patriarch provided the chief visible symbol of the Christian society.[71] It became greater still when the

69. Or, to put it into theological terms, the immanent and epiphanic Christ as the model of the prince was replaced by the more abstract image of God the Father, a process which also occurred in the West, in the shift from the medieval to the absolutist state. Cf. Kantorowicz, *The King's Two Bodies,* 159f.; M. Maccarrone, *Vicarius Christi: storia del titolo papale* (Rome, 1952).

70. On the establishment of the patriarchate in the reign of Tsar Feodor, cf. Kapterev, *Kharakter otnoshenii Rossii k pravoslavnomu vostoku v XVI i XVII stoletiakh* (St. Petersburg, 1914), 42f. Established in 1589, the patriarchate was abolished by Peter I formally by the institution of the Holy Synod in 1721; the last patriarch, Adrian, died in 1700.

71. On the role of the patriarch St. Germogen and his martyrdom, cf. Platonov, *Ocherki,* 476f.

young, shy, and not very able Tsar Michael had as patriarch his own father, Filaret Romanov.[72] Not only did
Filaret rule the state behind the scenes, but he received
many imperial regalia and privileges, including the title
of "Sovereign." [73] The close personal friendship between
Alexis and patriarch Nikon enabled this new tradition to
continue, as an expression of the generosity, love, and
piety of the tsar.[74]

We have no evidence of specific instances of patriarchal
interference in the ruler-cult for the purpose of limiting
it, but there can be little doubt that from the time of
St. Germogen during the Time of Troubles till Nikon, the
patriarch provided a new and a second focus of spiritual
and ceremonial authority. The best proof for this is the
famous controversy between Nikon and Alexis, between
Patriarch and Tsar.[75] In the course of the long-drawn-out
argument it was the patriarch, Nikon, who attacked by
developing a new concept of the ruler. Basically his argument was a curiously anachronistic evocation of the theories of popes Gregory VII and Innocent III.[76] The tsar's
office, dealing only with men's bodies, was in essence lower
than that of the priest, who held the power over men's
souls and salvation. The lesser is blessed by the greater,
and it is the priest who blesses the ruler and not the other
way around.[77] Moving from his original position of the

72. Filaret became patriarch in 1619, immediately following his return
from Polish captivity; *A.A.E.*, *3*, 327f.

73. On the role of Filaret, see *Istoriia*, *9*, 1159f.

74. On Nikon and the tsar, cf. Kapterev, *Patriarkh Nikon*, *I*, 40f., 394f.;
II, 122f.

75. On the controversy cf. Kapterev, *Patriarkh Nikon;* also see the
monumental work of W. Palmer, *The Patriarch and the Tsar* (6 vols.
London, 1871–76), particularly *1* and *3*.

76. On the similarities between Nikon and Innocent III, see Val'denberg, *Drevnerusskie Ucheniia*, 373f.

77. "Vozrazhenie sviateishago Nikona patriarkha," *Z.R.A.O.*, *2* (1861),
470f.; cf. Val'denberg, 375.

equality of the two powers, Nikon went further still: the
tsar is also subject to the priest as a man, having to confess
his own sins and requiring absolution, while the patriarch
is "the living and animate image of Christ." [78] The practi-
cal consequences of these theories for the radical patriarch
were the inadmissibility of any interference on the part of
the tsar in any church matters and the right of the patriarch to pass final judgment on all State actions and
measures.[79]

Nikon's case was finally settled at a church council in
Moscow graced by the presence of two eastern patriarchs.
The latter, in response to the Tsar's queries, went much
further than the *Epanogogia* in delineating the rights and
power of the ruler: the Tsar is supreme in all things,
spiritual or physical, and no one can disobey any of his
commands; every thing that he "wishes is thereby the rule
and the law." [80] What is interesting here is the fact that
a significant number of the higher clergy supported Nikon
in many of his theories, particularly those concerning the
freedom of the Church from the Tsar,[81] and this was reflected in the final decision of the council, a compromise
statement according to which both the authorities were to
be independent in their respective spheres.[82] But what is
still more interesting is that neither in practice nor in
theory did Nikon's views have any effect. While the controversy was a logical culmination to the existence of such
an exalted authority as the patriarch, it served mainly to
illustrate the power of the ruler myth. Both before and

78. "Vozrazhenie," *Z.R.A.O.*, 2, 481; for the Byzantine origin of this idea,
cf. G. Vernadsky, "Die Kirchlich-Politische Lehre der Epanagoge und
Einfluss auf das Russiche Leben in XVII Jahrhundert," *Byz.-Neugriechische
Jahrbücher, 6* (1928). I owe this reference to Professor Vernadsky.

79. "Vozrazhenie," *Z.R.A.O.*, 2, 481; cf. Val'denberg, 382.

80. *S.G.G.D., 4,* 91.

81. Val'denberg, 395f.

82. Val'denberg, 396.

after Nikon, the tsar ruled the Church as completely as he ruled the State, and ruled it without any opposition. In practice, then, the views of the eastern patriarchs, and Russian tradition, fully prevailed.

In trying to examine the possible reasons for such a complete victory of the Tsar one is struck by a curious fact, correctly pointed out by Val'denberg: the same Russian prelates who supported Nikon and argued for ecclesiastical independence, nowhere formulate their own conception of the tsar and his power.[83] The reason may lie in the conception of the pious, the *tishaishii* tsar. One could argue for a theoretical separation of ecclesiastic and lay authority, but how meaningful would such a separation be in the case of the pious tsar, of the tsar whose saintliness of personal character complemented his office and duty? Some testimony on the role of the *tishaishii* tsar in the Church comes from a good source—Tsar Alexis himself. In 1652 the Tsar learned of the numerous scandals created in his favorite monastery of St. Sabbas by the treasurer, Nikita. He ordered that the guilty monk be placed under arrest and that the Tsar's letter be read to him in a public ceremony:

"From the tsar and Grand Prince Aleksei Mikhailovich of All Russia, to God's enemy . . . and Christ-betrayer . . . the treasurer Nikita. You have become like . . . Judas, for, as he had sold Christ for thirty pieces of silver, you have exchanged . . . the house of the Miracle-worker [St. Sabbas] and my sinful advice for your own clever and evil drunkenness . . . Who has asked you . . . to reign over the house of the Miracle-worker and over me, the sinner? [84] . . . Remember the words of the Gospel: anyone who has pride in his heart is impure before God . . . And you . . . write to your friends and calculate your dishonor, that

83. Val'denberg, 396.
84. All this is in reference to some peasants from an estate of the tsar who were beaten up by the drunken Nikita.

guards [*streltsy*] are placed at your cell . . . [There have been those] better than you and more honorable, including metropolitans, who were guarded by the *streltsy* on our orders . . . And should I fear your threats? Do you know that, except for God and His Mother . . . and the Miracle-worker Sabbas, I have no other joy, no other hope? . . . And know, angel of Satan, that your honor here [on earth] is only valuable to you and to your father the devil . . . As for me, a sinner, my honor and rank here are like dust . . . Know that I shall plead tearfully with the Miracle-worker for mercy and for defense against you . . . And for your arrogant muttering I will disgrace you in a way you have never known . . . for you did not wish to obey God and the Miracle-worker and myself . . . And I also announce to you that if you will repent before the Miracle-worker and submit to me insincerely . . . you will be expelled and rejected and excommunicated by our God Jesus Christ and his Most Pure Mother and the Miracle-worker Sabbas and myself a sinner." [85]

The letter conveys not only the human charm, sincerity, and passion of the Tsar, but also his logic. As tsar, Alexis finds it quite proper to imprison and punish the acting head of a monastery; [86] his impulse and his right to do so come, however, from being a sinner and recognizing that fact. In other words, it is his piety, expressed in extreme personal humility, which allows him to manage and rule the Church, for it is his piety and humility which allows him to equate, in a jumble, Christ, the Virgin, the patron saint of the monastery, and himself. If Alexis as tsar can punish the guilty treasurer-monk, Tsar Alexis has the right to judge him because, in his humanity, the Tsar transcends the tsardom.

The image of the pious tsar was used to justify not only

85. *Z.R.A.O.*, 2 (1861), 687–89.

86. Since all the immediate authorities were away (*Z.R.A.O.*, 2, 689f.); cf. a similar type of letter, but much more humble and restrained, by Ivan the Terrible, D. S. Likhachev, "Poslanie Groznogo v Kirillo-Belozerskii monastyr, 1573g.," *T.O.D.R.L.*, 8 (1951), 252–86.

the tsar's rule over the Church. In 1672–73 Tsar Alexis wrote a furious letter to prince Gregory Romodanovsky, who was slow in sending up reinforcements to one of his *voevoda* colleagues. The Tsar made clear his reasons for calling the tardy commander an enemy of Christ and a Judas. Through his disobedience Romodanovsky was responsible for the death and misery of Christians; this, in turn, made him an enemy of Christ. The Tsar becomes, in this context, a defender of Christ.[87] In other words, the Tsar once again punishes not so much because his prerogatives have been infringed, but because their infringement is an attack on Christ; his piety, a personal characteristic defining his "body natural," motivates his actions.

The element of piety in the tsar as a personal quality, though ritualized, found a curious reflection in the thought of the archpope Avaakum, fierce enemy of Nikon, leader of the great church schism of the so-called "Old Believers." [88] Avaakum was scornfully amused by the Byzantinized epithet Nikon employed toward the Tsar—"the holy tsar" (*sviatoi tsar*).[89] The Tsar, Avaakum pointed out with irony, is beginning to believe that he actually is holier than anyone else. Yet the archpope himself, in his struggle and in his petitions to Alexis, relied upon the personal piety of the Tsar.[90] Alexis' piety should have enabled him to see the diabolic inspiration of Nikon, and when the Tsar failed to reject Nikon's reform movement, Avaakum (shortly before his own death on the bonfire) attacked not

87. *Z.R.A.O.*, 2, 770–75.

88. On Avaakum and his group of clergy in opposition to the reforms of Nikon, see Kapterev, *Patriarkh Nikon, 1*, 270ff.; edition of Avaakum's writings. *R.I.B.*, *39* (1917).

89. N. Subbotin, *Materialy dlia istorii raskola* (St. Petersburg, 1875–87), 5, 229f. Avaakum objected to the use of this epithet towards someone still alive, though this was part of the official titulature of the patriarch; Nikon used it in the Byzantine sense of "sacred" rather than "saintly."

90. Cf. *R.I.B.*, *39* (1917), particularly 723f.; Kapterev, *Patriarkh Nikon, 1*, 308f.

the competence of the Tsar in the Church but the Tsar's person.[91] For Avaakum, as for Alexis himself, the man and the power in the ruler were indissolubly bound together. The natures of the twin bodies of the prince were mutually reflected in their actions.

In the seventeenth century, as we have seen, the cult of the saint-prince was translated into an exaltation of the "body natural," the person of the tsar, to the level of his "body corporate," his divine nature as ruler. But if in a sense the tsar as man was absorbed by the divine nature of the Tsar, emerging in effect as an hereditary secular saint, a reverse process also took place. If the tsar was, as man, pious, most gentle, saintly, then the tsar in his actions —as the State—shared the personal qualities of the ruler. What one may call the tsar-centeredness of Russian popular uprisings has been noted many times in historical literature. Nearly all the peasant rebellions during the interregnum of the Time of Troubles advanced under the banner of the Tsar, utilizing for that purpose the most unlikely pretenders to the throne.[92] The next great rebellion, that of Stepan Razin, took place during the reign of the Most-Gentle Tsar Alexis, in 1667–71. Led by cossacks, the rebellion was an expression of class war, with all the appurtenances of a Jacquerie. At all times the rebels distinguished between the Tsar and the administration. The boiars were massacred because they were traitors to the Tsar, before whose mercy the rebels offered to submit after every reverse.[93] Unable to claim the person of the Tsar in their camp, Razin and his followers claimed that the Tsarevich Alexis, eldest son of the Tsar and heir to the

91. Kapterev, *Patriarkh Nikon, I,* 357f.; some of his more extremist adherents saw the tsar not as serving Antichrist, but as Antichrist himself; cf. *Istoriia, 15,* 1371.

92. For the innumerable false Dimitrys, cf. Platonov, *Ocherki,* 298f. *et passim.*

93. *Istoriia, 11,* 300f.

throne, was marching with them up the Volga, and the rumor was apparently quite successful.[94] To attack the tsar's
actions was impossible for the cossacks because he was
the pious, Orthodox tsar in person, just as it was impossible
for Timofeev to attack the person of the tsar because of
his divine office.

The myth of the pious ruler drew its strength from the
eschatology of Russian political theory. From its beginning
around 1500, the Third Rome, Moscow, was the chief fact
in the economy of salvation. Upon the orthodoxy and personal piety of the tsar depended the salvation of Russia as
a state and thereby the salvation of the whole world. As
the saint-prince insured the individual salvation of his
people, so the pious tsar guaranteed the salvation of the
individual and of the new abstraction of the community—
the State which was based on an eschatological *raison
d'être*. It was this eschatological foundation for the myth
of the ruler which was undercut by Peter the Great.

94. Even though the tsarevich died in 1670; cf. *Krestianskaia Voina pod
predvoditel'stvom Stepana Razina, Sbornik Dokumentov* (ANSSSR, 1957),
2:1, 75, 101, 141f. *et passim*.

3. The Sovereign Emperor

"The Russian tsar must be terrible and fierce!"
—M. GORKY

IN the kaleidoscope of Peter's reforms one can pick out those which imply a new stage of secularization of the state: abolition of the patriarchate, the establishment of the Governing Synod of the Church under a lay bureaucrat, the law permitting members of the reigning dynasty to marry foreign princesses who are not converted to the Orthodox faith.[1] All this was symbolized by the new title—*Imperator*—which the Senate, established by Peter himself, offered to the Tsar upon the conclusion of the victorious war with Sweden. It was perhaps equally well symbolized by the consequent elimination of the epithet "*tishaishii*," the "most-gentle," from the liturgy.[2]

The change, of course, was not instantaneous. Peter himself, and those around him, necessarily employed traditional formulas and expressions for traditional actions and

1. Cf. *Istoriia*, *16*, 275f.; *18*, 751f.; Kliuchevsky, *Kurs*, *4*, 200f.; N. G. Ustrialov, *Istoriia tsarstvovaniia Petra Velikago* (St. Petersburg, 1858–63), *6*, passim.

2. *P.S.Z.*, no. 3840; cf. *Istoriia*, *17*, 626; *18*, 846.

habits, even when trying to express their new conceptions and ideas. In his memoirs I. I. Nepluiev describes a scene between himself and Peter. Nepluiev had come to thank the emperor for his appointment as resident to Constantinople; the new ambassador fell at Peter's feet, whereupon the emperor raised him up and said:

"Don't bow, brother; I am placed here [to supervise] by God, and my duty is to see to it that anyone unworthy is not rewarded, and anyone worthy is not deprived; if you will be good [effective]—you will be doing good not to me but more to yourself and your fatherland; and if you will be bad—I shall be the claimant, for God demands from me that I should not allow the stupid and the evil any opportunity . . . Serve with faith and truth! at first God, and following Him, I will have to support you." [3]

This could have been said by Peter's father, Tsar Alexis, as an expression of theocratic humility; and Nepluiev's action, his *proskynesis,* embracing the feet of his Tsar, was as traditional as Peter's words.

Nor is this the unique example. Nepluiev's colleague, Nartov, recorded that on one occasion Peter had said, "What is the difference between God and the tsar if both are offered the same respect?" [4] and on another occasion, again to encourage a servitor, the emperor said, "Even . . . though God is high [up], and the tsar is far [away], nevertheless a prayer to the former and service for the latter will not be in vain." [5] Peter's use of the Russian proverb of the seventeenth century [6] indicate his purpose: to main-

3. *Zapiski Ivana Ivanovicha Nepluieva* (St. Petersburg, 1893), 110.

4. *Raszkazy Nartova o Petre Velikom,* ed. L. N. Maikov (St. Petersburg, 1891), 17.

5. *Raszkazy Nartova,* 33–34; "Khotia . . . Bog vysoko a tsar daleko, odnako u pervogo molitva, a u drugogo sluzhba ne propadaet."

6. *Do Boga vysoko, do tsaria daleko;* "It is too high to God, too far to the tsar." One can safely date the proverb because of the title of "tsar"; it seems to belong to the growing body of material indicating the popular awareness of the gulf between the tsar and the people.

tain the association of God and the tsar, but also to point
out the distinction between the two, conveyed in the
difference between prayer and duty. If anything, these
statements reveal a greater humility on the part of Peter
than on the part of his predecessors, expressed in a desire
to diminish the gulf between the ruler and his subjects,
which would be very much in character for the traditional
image of Peter, with his dislike for ritual, pomp, and
ceremony. That a change in Russian conceptions did take
place, nevertheless, a change which necessitates interpreting Peter's words by other than seventeenth-century standards, is shown rather symbolically in the records of the
same two men, Peter's loyal followers. While at his post
in Constantinople, Nepluiev heard of the death of his
emperor; he concluded his praise of his master with the
following words: "And may the Lord put his soul, which
worked so much for the common good, among the righteous." [7] For Nepluiev there was no question, any longer,
of the saint-prince, saintly in function and in essence; the
best he can hope for is a place among the righteous for
Peter, the first emperor from whom everything in Russia
derived.[8] Nartov, too, reacted to Peter's death; his conclusion was a different one: "While Peter the Great is no
longer with us, yet his spirit lives in our souls and we, who
have had the happiness of being with the monarch, will
die faithful to him and will carry to the grave our passion-
ate love for the god on earth [*zemnomu bogu*]." [9]

For Nartov also, there was no question of the saint-
prince, of the pious orthodox tsar; what he sees is the *deus
terrenus,* not the image of God, but a god himself. Neither
of the two men seem to have thought within the framework of the myths we have studied, for both of which the
keystone was the equation *God-Prince.*

7. *Zapiski Nepluieva,* 122–23.
8. Ibid.
9. *Raszkazy Nartova,* 69.

The denial of the theocratic foundation of the ruler-myth under Peter, the disappearance of the "Pious and Most-Gentle Tsar" could have two alternative consequences within the old Russian tradition of the saint-prince: the rejection of a tsar who no longer corresponded, in his personal attributes, to the ideal image, or a new and possibly greater exaltation of the tsar on a different ideological foundation. The first alternative was reflected in popular reaction to the Tsar, which, although heterogeneous, can be ordered in a psychological if not chronological pattern. A conversation about the Tsar's observance of fasting-days took place in 1701 between the priest Paul and the architect Tarasy: in answer to the priest's claim that "the Great Sovereign could not do such a thing as to eat meat during the Great Fast [at Easter] for only the Germans do that [*sc.* eat meat]," the architect said that "He, the Great Sovereign, is himself the son of a German." [10] The meaning of this remark becomes clear when we consider the events of that time. In 1699, while Peter was abroad in Europe, the infantry regiments founded by Ivan the Terrible and stationed in Moscow, the *streltsy,* revolted. While the rebellion was put down with incredible brutality, by 1705 the regiments were restless again. This time they tried to gain the support of the cossacks. Their emissaries informed the cossacks that the Tsar was a changeling, substituted at birth for a daughter born to Tsaritsa Nataliia, or (a more convincing rumor) that the young Tsar had died or had been killed on his European journeys, and that a German changeling ruled over Russia with the purpose of damning all of her souls to perdition.[11]

The conclusion to be drawn from this is evident: an evil tsar could not be a true tsar, and evil was measured (particularly since the seventeenth century) in the myth

10. Ustrialov, *4,* 204.
11. *Istoriia, 15,* 1378 *et passim;* Ustrialov, *4,* 424–25.

of the ruler by the degree of his impiety, as an implicit
antithesis to the piety which was the supreme expression
of the tsar's personal goodness. The emphasis remained
on the person of the tsar. The popular opposition to Peter
did not envisage removing the Tsar for his sins and
malfeasance; it simply did not admit the possibility of the
tsar ever having such vices, and introduced the changeling
legend in order to account for the existing conditions.
The historical logic of this reaction is quite clear: the
Russian prince, saintly in his person, became, with the
rise of the State, the guardian of orthodoxy and thereby
the guarantor of salvation for each Russian; hence the
saintliness of the ruler, expressed in his piety, was of direct concern to each Russian, for it determined not only
the existence of the tsar, but of Russia as well. The im-
pious tsar could not be a true tsar, but what did this mean
for the fate of Russia? Time and again the answer is
given to us by the many men who claimed, in private
and in public, that Peter was the Anti-Christ.[12] In terms

12. *Istoriia, 16,* 25; this view of Peter was held overwhelmingly by the
Old Believers who had already suspected his father, Alexis, of being Antichrist (*Istoriia, 15,* 1371); for sources and literature cf. N. Subbotin, *Materialy dlia istorii raskola* (St. Petersburg, 1875–87), particularly 5; V. V.
Andreev, *Raskol i ego znachenie v narodnoi russkoi zhizni* (St. Petersburg,
1870), 73f.; N. B. Golikova, *Politicheskie protsesy pri Petre I* (Moscow,
1957); P. I. Mel'nikov-Pechersky, *Polnoe Sobranie Sochinenii, 6* (St. Petersburg, 1909), 203f.; M. E. Semevsky, *Slovo i Delo! 1700–1725* (St. Petersburg,
1884), 107f.; G. Esipov, *Raskol'nichie Dela XVIII Stoletiia* (2 vols. St. Petersburg, 1861–63). For the general reaction to Peter, see E. F. Shmurlo, "Petr
velikii v otsenke sovremennikov i potomstva," *Zhurnal Ministerstva Narodnago Prosveshcheniia, 35* (1911), 315–40; *36* (1911), 1–37, 201–73; *39* (1912),
1–40, 193–259. On representations of Peter as Antichrist, cf. A. N. Pypin,
Istoriia Russkoi Literatury, 3 (St. Petersburg, 1902), 309; the manuscripts
to which Pypin refers remain, to my knowledge, unpublished. One of the
Old Believers tracts on Peter adduced a curious argument to prove that
the emperor was Antichrist: Peter had taken on the title of "Father of
the Fatherland," which was a patriarchal title. This showed his desire to
usurp not only imperial but also ecclesiastical, and in fact divine, authority.
To trace the origin of such an idea would take us too far afield, but it

of the theory of Moscow the Third Rome, and of the role assigned in it to the tsar, the logic of this claim is unassailable. The Anti-Christ heralded the end of the world, which was to follow the fall of the Third Rome, and hence of orthodoxy. The final logical step was taken by the thousands of the schismatic Old Believers who immolated themselves in their forest communities at the approach of the tsar's officials or soldiers.

In a recent and stimulating article on the Three Romes, Robert L. Wolff, discussing the power of the ideology of autocracy, wrote: "If a state rests on generally accepted assumptions, it is almost impossible to challenge those assumptions without damaging the structure of the state." [13] This seems a rather idealistic interpretation of history. It is doubtful whether the *streltsy,* the cossacks, or even the Old Believers rebelled because of Peter's impiety; the power of the myth is revealed rather by the fact that the opposition, rebellion, and self-immolation were considered justified by this impiety. In other words, those in opposition to Peter translated their grievances into the language of the myth. Insofar as they justified their actions by denying the further validity of the myth of the ruler, the popular uprisings denied the validity or even the reality of the state.

But if some in Russia were led, by the abolition of the eschatological, religious tradition, to an apocalyptic conclusion, others found a different solution to the problem

---

certainly can serve as an illustration of how deep a gulf existed between the new monarchy and the masses; *Pater patriae, Otets otechestva,* did not, apparently, ring very familiarly in the ears of a Russian peasant. The image of Peter as Antichrist persisted until quite recently, and in fact some of the Old Believers, already in the twentieth century, considered that all the emperors were Antichrists—a strange extension of the Apocalypse in time; cf. M. M. Prishvin, *V Kraiu Nepuganykh Ptits, Sobranie Sochinenii,* 2 (Moscow, 1956), 151.

13. Robert L. Wolff, "The Three Romes: The Migration of an Ideology and the Making of an Autocrat," *Daedalus* (Spring 1959) 306.

of the different image of the tsar. Rejecting, or perhaps indifferent to the theocratic justification, Nartov concluded that Peter the Emperor was god on earth. Here, too, the argument was consistent. The saintly prince, Christlike in his being, became the godlike Tsar in order to lead Russia and the world to salvation; the end of the eschatological focus meant the existence of the state for its own sake and meant that the tsar, godlike for the sake of Christ, was now god for his own and the State's sake. Or, to parody the famous claim of the medieval French kings—*Rex Franciae imperator est in regno suo*—one could say of Peter, *Imperator Rossiae deus est in imperio suo.* Nartov, of course, is rather extreme; but the Russian myth of the Christlike prince, saintly in his person, was, in a sense, strengthened when Christ became irrelevant to the secularized prince, and when therefore the divinity of the prince lost any outside referent or control. In this sense Peter, in secularizing the image of the Russian tsar, created true absolutism, for the myth of the person of the prince remained, but without any standard of judgment to be applied to it. That some of those close to Peter were aware of the possibilities of the Tsar's new image is indicated in the testimony offered under torture by Tsarevich Alexis, Peter's son, at his trial for treason in 1719. Tsarevich Alexis said that his teacher Viazemsky had told him that: "Stepan Beliaev and the church choir sing in front of your father—'Whenever God wills it is the state of nature conquered,' and other such verses; they sing all this, tempting your father; and he is so pleased that they equate him with God." [14]

Both the reactions to Peter presented here were extreme ones. The majority of the Russians, one can argue, were not aware of such a revolutionary change in the image of the tsar. In folksongs and tales Peter, frequently

14. *Istoriia, 17,* 487.

confused with Ivan the Terrible, represents, like his predecessor, the forceful, violently active, ruthless but just Russian tsar.[15] Yet it is difficult to avoid the conclusion that, if there was not a revolutionary change in the ruler-myth, there was at the beginning of the eighteenth century a process of crystallization, of increasing explicitness consequent on the establishment of the secular state. In other words, the change in the tsar's image was not caused by Peter; rather, he spelled out the necessary implications of the process in the Russian state and society.

To illustrate this change, we may be permitted a short digression at this point, for nowhere is it more strikingly manifested than in the realm of iconography. The portrait of Peter (Fig. 11),[16] contrasted with that of his father, speaks for itself: instead of the pectoral cross, the crown, and the *barmy*, we see Western armor; instead of the orb and scepter, two decorations showing a naval battle (on the left) and the plan of St. Petersburg (on the right); instead of the traditional, awesome, ringing titles, the inscription —not even in Russian—PETRUS PRIMUS RUSSORUM IMPERATOR.

If the emperor's portrait, however, can be explained away as a personal preference on Peter's part—his westernized idea of himself as emperor—more convincing evidence is presented by two engravings, both executed during Peter's lifetime. The first one (Fig. 12), done in 1691, summarized in the most fantastic way all the aspects and nuances of the ruler-myth: [17] it shows in the foreground

15. Cf. *Pesni sobrannye P. V. Kireevskim* (Moscow, 1863–79) *6*, 194, 212; *8*, 1f.

16. For the identification and history of the engraving, see D. A. Rovinsky, *Podrobnyi Slovar' Russkikh Gravirovanykh Portretov, 3* (St. Petersburg, 1886–88), 1572f.

17. The engraving was done in Kiev by Innocentius Szczyrski, on order, apparently, of the Theological Academy; the cartouche on the right reads: "Conclusiones Philosophicae: Praesidentibq d[o]m[inus] R[evere]nd[issim]o

the two co-tsars, Peter and his older half-brother Ivan V;
behind them, receding into the background, are two other
pairs of co-rulers, the Byzantine emperors Basil and Constantine, Arcadius, and Honorius. Above them, under the
medallion with the image of St. George, is the inscription:
"God, Lord of heaven and of earth, one and triune, is
well disposed towards the triunely reigning pairs, Arcadius
and Honorius who ruled as one, Basil and Constantine;
and now Ivan and Peter." [18] Poised above them is the
double-headed eagle, symbol both of Byzantium and of
Russia. In the center of his body is a medallion with the
image of St. Vladimir, and along his wings are the names
of nine Russian rulers.[19] Under the right head of the eagle
is St. Alexis, "creature of God," [20] and under the left head
is the image of Tsarevich St. Dimitry of Uglich. The eagle

Sacrae Theologiae Professore Egumeno Canobis Eremitici S. Thaumaturgi
Nicolai ac R[evere]nd[issim]o Patre Sylvano Ozierski Philosophiae Pro-
fessore Praefecto Scholarum." The left cartouche reads: "Conclusiones
Theologicae. Defendita publico in Almo Collegio Serenissimae Orthodox-
orum Rosicae Imperatoru[m] Maiestatis a Theologis et Philosophis
Atheneti Ejusdem (Kiiowienski). Anno Dei et Hominis Christi 1691 . . ."
The origin of the engraving would explain the enormous complexity of
iconographic symbolism to which Moscow had not attained as yet. Cf.
Rovinsky, 3, 1523f.

18. The empty medallions led Rovinsky (3, 1530f.) to conjecture that at
least one of them contained a portrait of Tsarevna Sophia, older sister of
the young tsars and regent, 1683–89. This would also explain, he argued,
the strange association of the trinity with a pair; after Sophia was overthrown by Peter, her image was probably scratched out. While it is more
than likely that the empty spaces had had something drawn in them,
Rovinsky's hypothesis is not very convincing; the Byzantine co-emperors
did not have sisters ruling with them, in this case there are two empty
spaces to explain, and, finally, if one accepts the dating provided by the
academicians, the engraving was done two years after Sophia was imprisoned in a monastery.

19. The Grand Princes Vsevolod Iaroslavich, Vladimir Monomakh,
Iziaslav, Sviatoslav, Iaroslav, the Tsars Ivan IV, Feodor, Vasily Shuisky
and Michael.

20. *Sviatoi Aleksei, bozhii chelovek:* the term was used to denote a kind
of holy fool, child-like and half-witted, belonging to God.

is being handed a sword by the princely passion-sufferer, St. Gleb, while his brother, St. Boris, hands the eagle a lance entwined with olive. To either side of them are medallions of Tsar Feodor Alexeevich and Tsar Alexis, respectively. The heads of the eagle are crowned by John the Baptist and St. Peter the apostle, backed up by two saints each. Above the central, large crown is the Virgin, holding a book with the words "Through Me Tsars reign" inscribed on it. The Virgin herself is being crowned by the three persons of the Trinity, with God the Father and Christ holding up the crown.

The painting demonstrates what could be accomplished when Russian myths were treated in a symbolic fashion by the sophisticated and westernized theologians and philosophers of the Kiev Academy of the seventeenth century. In a rather large space there was represented the image of Russian tsardom: Byzantium, St. Vladimir, Tsars, Grand Princes, saints and martyrs, and above them all the Trinity, symbolized, below, by the two young Tsars.

The second of our engravings was done only twenty-six years later (Fig. 13).[21] At the top we see Peter, wearing armor with an ermine cloak over it, a sword at his side and a field marshal's baton in his right hand. Above his head, in the rays of a radiant sun, two cupids bear the new imperial crown. Behind him is a chain made up of medallions with the ground-plans of fortresses captured by the Tsar. To his right is a painting of the combined Russian fleet, and to his left is a representation of the naval victory at Greinham. He stands at the base of an inverted pyramid; the nine steps that compose it are nine victories won by Peter. Serving as background to the central image of Peter and his victories are portraits of thirty-three Russian rulers beginning with Riurik, who is shown at the very peak of the pyramid. A comparison with the *Great State*

21. For identification and history, see Rovinsky, *3*, 1616f.

Book would show that at least in one respect the portraits differ, for none of the princes or tsars are wearing a halo. But such a comparison would be meaningless, for we learn that all the thirty-three portraits were based by the artist on a similar dynastic group portrait of the Dukes of Brandenburg.[22]

Iconographic evidence is certainly not conclusive. But it is suggestive of at least a certain mood. The road from the theocratic tsar to the sovereign emperor was traveled rather quickly by the court circles, the writers, the official ideologues.[23] The ancestors, whether Brandenburgian or Russian, serve as a background in a literal sense; the saints and martyrs are replaced by the victories, and at the head of it all, replacing the Trinity, stands the tsar, the new god on earth.

Peter's own conception of the state and his role within it would fit clearly within the ideology of enlightened absolutism, where the ruler was the first servant of the abstract and depersonalized State which all men served. Again and again he expressed his ultimate purpose as the service of Russia, who was the enduring and the absolute, and who, manifested by the Ruling Senate (*Pravitel'-stvuischii Senat*), crowned him for his labors with the

22. Rovinsky, *3*, 1622.

23. For example, the long and involved eulogy of Peter, appended to the bottom of the engraving, was written by archbishop Feofan Prokopovich, primate of the Russian church; Rovinsky, *3*, 1622. An additional iconographic manifestation of the changed image of the ruler is provided by numismatic evidence: Throughout the sixteenth and seventeenth centuries, the Moscovite coins bore the representation of St. George. At the same time, the image of the saint was modified by an imperial radiate crown and by being a portrait of the reigning tsar; i.e., the "Moscow rider" of Moscovite coinage was, simultaneously St. George and the Tsar (cf. Fig. 3). With Peter, the tsar gives way to the saint and the coins were not regarded as portraits of the tsar-saint; by the end of Peter's reign even the saintly symbol loses its significance and a decree of 1724 refers to the representation simply as "rider with spear." Cf. I. G. Spassky, "Denezhnoe obrashchenie v Moskovskom Gosudarstve," *Materialy i Issledovaniia po Arkheologii SSSR, 44* (1955), 266–67.

triumphant title of emperor.[24] What this meant was the evolution of an abstract, impersonal image of the ruler. The new title, unfamiliar and strange-sounding, symbolized pure political power.[25] In this sense it was an antithesis to the "body natural" tsar, an antithesis indicated in the contrasting appellations of the ruler, *"Batiushka Tsar'"* (little father tsar) and *"Gosudar' Imperator"* (sovereign emperor), epithets which remained in use until 1917. The contrast is even sharper if one remembers that, along with the imperial title, Peter also received from his Senate the title of *"Otets Otechestva."* [26] *"Batiushka Tsar,"* widely used in the seventeenth century, remains the popular epithet, emphasizing the person of the tsar and his relation as a person to his subjects, as against the official and depersonalized sovereign.[27] The symbolism inherent in the antithesis

24. Cf. *Istoriia, 18,* 848f.; Kliuchevsky, *Kurs, 4,* 200ff., 356f.; for literally hundreds of instances of Peter's views, see the incredible anecdotal compilation by I. I. Golikov, *Deianiia Petra Velikago* (30 vols. Moscow, 1778–1798).

25. M. I. Semevsky, *Slovo,* 18–19; the case of a peasant, Danilo Belokonnik, who was having a drink with a grenadier. When the latter drank to the health of the emperor, Danilo got furious and announced that he only knew one ruler, his pious sovereign, and had never heard of the emperor. Danilo managed to get back to his family after four months in prison and a flogging. Nevertheless, whatever the punishments, even the word "emperor," *imperator,* sounded unfamiliar to the Russian masses until 1917.

26. The antithesis is particularly striking considering the fact that, logically and historically, the *Batiushka Tsar* and *Pater patriae* express the same idea. In the Prologue of the Bavarian *Landrecht* of 1346, Emperor Louis of Bavaria is called: ". . . vaeterlein kayser Ludweigen von Rom. . . ." Hermann Krause, *Kaiserrecht und Rezeption,* Abh.d. Heidelberg. Akad., 1952, abh. *1,* 57, n. 247; this reference I owe to Professor Kantorowicz. It is quite likely, as Professor Kantorowicz has suggested, that the Bavarian usage derived out of the epithets *Pater patriae* and *pater subiectorum;* on the origins of these ideas, cf. Andreas Alföldi, "Die Geburt der kaiserlichen Bildsymbolik," *Museum Helveticum, 9* (1952), 204–43; *10* (1953), 103–24; *11* (1954), 133–69; on these titles in the Middle Ages, cf. Kantorowicz, *The King's Two Bodies,* 92, n. 18; 214, n. 59; 305, n. 75.

27. While Ivan IV, as the first tsar, is also referred to as *Batiushka Tsar,* any references prior to the seventeenth century are unreliable; they can-

can be carried further, however. Timofeev, describing the
Time of Troubles, portrayed Russia as a widow, for her
husband the true tsar had died. The tsar was Russia's
bridegroom as Christ was the bridegroom of the Church,
and *"Batiushka Tsar"* was paralleled, until 1917, by the
commonest epithet for Russia, *Matushka Rus',* "Mother
Russia." [28] Hence the image of the saint-prince and later
pious tsar, the emphasis on the person of the prince, implied a distinction between the tsar and Russia at the same
time that it emphasized the indissoluble bond between
them. The husband-tsar carried the burdens of Russia on
his shoulders, acting because of his personal qualities as
mediator between his children and God as his model,
Christ, had done. The emperor, however, was the father of
his country and, to remove even the possibility of inces-
tuous relations, *otechestvo* (fatherland) is neuter, while
Matushka Rus' is feminine.

A distinction between the *Imperator* and the *Rossiiskaia
Imperia* was lacking, however, despite Peter's efforts to
endow the image of "Rossiia" with life. An interesting illustration of these efforts is Peter's treatment of the feast
day of St. Alexander Nevsky. The relics of the saint were
transported from Vladimir to St. Petersburg in 1723, and
the feast day was changed from November 14th, the day of
Nevsky's death, to November 23, the day of the saint's
burial in Vladimir. Peter, however, ordered yet another
change, to August 30, the anniversary of the victorious
peace treaty with Sweden, on which occasion Russia became an empire.[29] The saint-prince was put to work not
for the salvation of Russian souls but for the glory of the

---

not be substantiated as evidence, for the manuscripts of popular songs and
tales do not go further back than the seventeenth century.

28. For Western use of the marriage image, cf. Kantorowicz, *The King's
Two Bodies,* 214, n. 59.

29. On this, and on further political shufflings of Nevsky's feast-day, see
Golubinsky, 65–66.

imperial state and its new capital, St. Petersburg, whose patron he became. The separation between the emperor and the state which Peter sought did not, however, come about; in Russia (as elsewhere) the line between the ruler's "I am the first servant of the State" and "L'état c'est moi" could not be perceived.

The explanation for this is not very hard to find, at least in terms of political theology. The Petrine reforms were the culminating point for the evolution of the secular state; for that very reason many of them were designed to eliminate the outworn symbols and rituals of the former eschatologically oriented Christian society and therefore tended to emphasize sharply the ideological difference between past and present. Hence, for many Russians, the Russian empire appeared as something quite different and new, created *ex nihilo*. But, at the same time, the emperor carried with him the whole tradition of the ruler, Christlike in person and in power, a tradition which, when Christ became irrelevant, made of the emperor a god on earth. When the contemporary and admirer of Peter I, P. N. Krekshin, wrote: "Our father, Peter the Great! You have led us from nonexistence to existence . . . you have enlightened us and glorified us . . . The drops of sweat of your labors was our aromatic myrrh which perfumed the glory of Russia to the ends of the world," he was pointing out the fact that the new Russia was formed and defined by the emperor, that it was contained in him.[30] That Krekshin himself was aware of the implications of his statement he showed when he continued in his "Notes," "If those who possess blessed papers [*dela*] of Peter the Great or had been eye-witnesses of great deeds will not

30. "Kratkoe Opisanie Blazhennykh Del Velikago Gosudaria, Imperatora Petra Velikago, Samoderzhstsa Vserossiiskago," *Zapiski Russkikh Liudei. Sobytiia Vremen Petra Velikago*, ed. N. Sakharov (St. Petersburg, 1841), 4.

desire to submit [all this information] for the collection
and glorification of true and most-glorious deeds of Peter
the Great, they shall be ungrateful servants [*raby*], they
shall be called those who have concealed the talent of their
Lord [*Gospoda*], and not the sons of the fatherland. Then
our enemies will mock us and will proclaim: 'While the
Sovereign is worthy of such a State, the people are unworthy of such a Sovereign.' " [31]

Into this brief statement Krekshin managed to pack the
tangle of strands which made up the myth of the Sovereign
Emperor. Peter the Creator is reinforced here by the ambiguity in the application of the parable of the talents.
For Russians, not as Christians but as "sons of the fatherland," the emperor is the true "Lord." His thoughts and
his deeds motivate and determine the newly-created paradise, Russia, and the people must be worthy of entrance
into it. A distinction is drawn between the Russian people
and the State, a political abstraction, created by and contained in the emperor.

And in fact, whatever his personal motivations and
qualities or vices, Peter himself demonstrated the identity
of the Tsar and the State, the submergence of the feeble
idea of the secular Russia in the old and powerful myth of
the Russian tsar. Nowhere in the whole complicated bureaucratic structure established by the emperor do we find
anything that can be called an institution: a "Governing
Senate" or a "Most Holy Synod" ordered about and dis-
ciplined by noncommissioned officers of the Guards could
hardly be called institutions, but rather were executive
extensions of Peter's personal will. Despite all his formal

31. "Kratkoe Opisanie," 6. A similar theological ambiguity was evoked
by the bishop of Riazan', Gavriil Buzhinsky, in his sermon on the first
anniversary of Peter's death: "Peter the Great is alive: I am the resurrection and the life . . . and whoever believes in me will live forever. This
knowlege should be a salve to your heart's wound, Russia." Shmurlo,
Zh.M.N.P., *36, 205*.

attempts, the emperor ruled by means of persons, not institutions, and the original appellation, "The Lords Senate" (*Gospoda Senat*), changed to "The Lords Senators"
(*Gospoda Senaty*).[32] The identification of the emperor's
will and the State in this case was so complete that it could
not tolerate the intrusion of an abstraction represented by
an institution.

The nature of this problem is most clearly revealed in
Russian law, a subject deserving of a whole study unto itself, but which will be used here only for the purpose of
illustration. Despite the ever-growing complexity of the
Russian law codes, culminating with the *Ulozhenie* of
Tsar Alexis in 1649, there does not seem to be any theory
or conception of positive law. There was only the absolute,
over-arching Natural Law, the Divine Order, absolute justice, of which the tsar was a manifestation: the "Animate
Law." [33] The reasons for this must be sought in the concrete complexities of Russian history, and the problem is
made the more difficult by the fact that one finds no speculations and discussions about the nature of law. Yet a
partial explanation, which bears on our problem, was provided by the same metropolitan Pitirim who wished to
canonize Stolypin. To justify the chaotic administrative
decrees of the various ministers, the metropolitan proclaimed in 1915 that they too, as well as the tsar, have the
Holy Ghost upon them. Reporting this, the Russian
poetess, Zinaida Gippius, ironically drew the right conclusion: "Grace is above laws." [34] That this principle prevailed in seventeenth-century Russia can be seen in the
judiciary role of the tsar. In effect the tsar did not really
legislate; each case that reached his presence was decided

32. *Istoriia, 18,* 852f.

33. On this term, see A. Steinwenter, *"Nómos Ἔμψυχος; Zur Geschichte
einer politischen Theorie,"* *Anzeiger d. Akad. d. Wissensch. in Wien,*
phil.-hist. Kl., *83* (1946).

34. Zinaida Gippius, *Siniia Kniga* (Belgrade, 1929) 40, 73.

separately, on its own merits, even if the decision was based on precedent.[35] The significance of this principle was that it placed the tsar outside the framework of legal thought. In the medieval West the problem of the *princeps legibus solutus est* was solved by positing the prince as both above and below the Law; above it in his power to make law, below it in his princely moral will which led him to accept the Law voluntarily.[36] In Russia, however, the saint-prince stood completely above the Law, and the assurance of justice was provided by his personal sanctity rather than by his relation to justice. So, too, it was the piety of the "Most-Gentle and Pious Tsars" which guaranteed justice; i.e., the personal qualities of the tsar as man rather than his princely functions.

Inner piety is a quality difficult to measure, however, and only its outward manifestation, adherence to ritual, customs, and traditions, limited the former tsars in their exercise of judicial power. The evolution of the secular state at the time of Peter I, by its abolition of old customs and traditions in the tsarist ritual, abolished the standard by which the person of the ruler could be judged and thereby abolished the distinction between the emperor's personal will and Law or law. To put it another way, Law in Russia did not serve as a middle term between the tsar and the people, but, identified with the *person* of the Tsar, served to emphasize the identity of the ruler and the State. In this case the rejection of the tsar as a person, the denial of his piety or sanctity, should have led to the rejection of all his laws, and of the Russian state as such, and this was the position taken by the more extreme opponents of Peter I. The Old Believers, rejecting Peter I as a changeling or as Antichrist, fled the State physically, and refused

35. Kliuchevsky, *Duma*, 399f.
36. Kantorowicz, *The King's Two Bodies*, 87ff.

to acknowledge or obey the most innocuous decrees or
regulations.

The secular, absolutist state in Russia, as elsewhere,
was symbolized by the final step in the evolution of the
ruler-myth: for, if the rationale in the case of the saint-
princes was the sanctification of power by the person, and
in the case of the pious tsars the sanctification of the person by power, now power sanctified power. In a strange and
ironic way the state of Peter I marked, in the Russian context, a reversion to an older form or conception. One
could argue that Peter's Russia signified the victory of the
khan over the basileus; the tsar-emperor ruled Russia as
his private property, for which he was responsible to no
one; the source of his power lay in itself, in its ability to
conquer, rather than in any unique quality or myth of
Russia itself. One instance of such a view is found in the
law of succession promulgated by Peter in 1722.[37] During
two centuries the Grand Princes of Moscow tried to establish the principle of primogeniture for the Grand Principality as against the right of the Khan to invest whom-
ever he pleased with the throne of All Russia. The sixteenth and seventeenth centuries saw the full acceptance
of this principle, and the end of the Riurikid dynasty in
1598 appeared to Russian society as a catastrophe. Yet
Peter's law of 1722 gave the reigning emperor the right
and power to nominate his successor as he chose, without
any specified limitations. The issue, of course, does not lie
in the political circumstances, in Peter's desire to exclude
from the throne the progeny of his son Alexis; as it turned
out, the emperor had not nominated anyone before his
death. But the form in which Peter clothed his political
considerations indicates both the degree of abstraction and
absolutism that the image of the ruler had reached and

37. *P.S.Z.*, no. 3893.

the persistence of an old tradition, reaching back to the
time before the concept of the state really existed, and
Russia was regarded as the private property of her
princes.[38] The vitality of this tradition was revealed in a
rather paradoxical way as late as 1905: opposing the intention of Nicholas II to grant the Constitution of 1905,
one of the Grand Dukes argued that Nicholas had no right
to do this, i.e. to give up part of his power, for "la Russie
appartient à toute notre famille."[39]

The final symbolic step in the evolution of the autocratic ruler, truly secular and truly absolute in the sense
of owing nothing to anything outside of himself and limited by nothing outside of himself, took place in 1742.
Beginning with the coronation of Elizabeth, the Russian
rulers crowned themselves in the ceremony performed in
the Cathedral of the Dormition in the Kremlin; the senior
archbishop only handed the crown to the emperor (or
empress), who then placed it on his own head.[40] We find
no hints as to the possible reason for this change in the
coronation ritual; the three preceding imperial corona-
tions of 1724, 1727, and 1730 show no changes or indica-

38. The Riurikid clan ruling Russia as a family and having a monopoly
on power was certainly the conception in the Kievan period. Primogeniture was established by the Moscow dynasty, in effect, against the prerog-
ative of the Khan. This was attacked in principle, significantly enough,
by Ivan III, the Grand Prince who in a sense replaced the Tatar khan as
ruler of Russia (cf. "Khan or Basileus," 470f.). Defending his right to
name his grandson Dimitry as co-ruler, the grand prince argued that
Russia was his to dispose of as he pleased. Cf. Karamzin, 6, n. 466. Another instance, perhaps, of the power of the Tatar tradition and ideology
which even reached Peter I.

39. Presniakov, "Samoderzhavie Nikolaia I," Russkoe Proshloe, 2 (1923),
4–5.

40. The ruler also placed the imperial mantle, the barmy, over his
shoulders himself; V. I. Zhmakin, "Koronatsii Russkikh Imperatorov i
Imperatrits 1724–1856gg.," Russkaia Starina, 37 (1883), 522 et passim;
Paul I, at his coronation in 1796, gave himself communion as well, but
the instance was not repeated; cf. Igor Smolitsch, "Die Stellung des rus-

tions of change.[41] Yet the self-crowning, which began in 1742, reflected more accurately the new myth of the ruler than did the traditional ceremonies during the first part of the century. The Sovereign Emperor was emperor *sui generis,* containing within himself all power and the source of all power, completely secular, or, what is the same thing, deified. And, ironically enough, the history of the eighteenth century in Russia substantiated the new image of the sovereign first revealed by Peter I. The male line of the Romanovs ended five years after Peter's death, in 1730, with his grandson Peter II; the rest of the century saw three empresses, one of them (Catherine II) a German princess quite unrelated to the Russian dynasty, and an emperor (Peter III), a Duke of Holstein, related by blood and not at all by culture or ideology. All of these were playthings of the Russian gentry which made up the Guards regiments stationed in the capital. Certainly, if our chronicler of the Time of Troubles, Ivan Timofeev, could see this pageant of rulers, he would have had to give up his standard of suitability. How to determine the proper and natural Tsar, not a "slave-tsar," when none of the old categories would apply? There was not really a dynasty one could identify, no sanctity one could feel, no piety one could admire. The Sovereign Emperor was such an abstraction that a German woman could fill the position.

This is not to say that the traditional forms of the ruler-myth were abandoned. Archbishop Feofan Prokopovich, the ideologist of the Petrine state, in his formal exhortation at the coronation of Peter II in 1727, spoke of the emperor as God's vicar, the elect of God; for his Christian virtues the emperor will be associated in heaven with the

---

sischer Kaisers zur Orthodoxen Kirche in Russland vom 18. bis 20 Jh.," *Forschungen zur Osteuropäischen Geschichte* (Ost Europa Institut an der Freien Univ. Berlin), 2 (1955), 148.

41. Zhmakin, "Koronatsii," 500f.

saintly tsars, his ancestors.[42] And, praising Peter I, Feofan still called him Christ. Yet it is significant that in the chief work of the new ideology, *Pravda Voli Monarshei* (The Justice of the Monarch's Will), written in 1722, the archbishop only referred to the "Christian Sovereign" or "Christian Monarch," never to the Orthodox one.[43] The reason for this new formula is not difficult to suggest; Feofan was the leader of the Westernizing, bureaucratic, secularized upper clergy supported by Peter I. As Peter I borrowed the forms if not the content of Western eighteenth-century absolutism, so his archbishop borrowed the forms of political theory provided by the West. For our problem, however, the change from "Orthodox" to "Christian" is meaningful. Certainly, the "Christian Sovereign" is theologically as correct as the Orthodox one; but it did mean a break from the image of the tsar who was Tsar because he was Orthodox, because on him depended the fate of all men's souls; it did mean a greater depersonalization, a greater abstraction of the ruler. All the European rulers were Christian, hence all had equal and identical power. This last conclusion is not explicit, but implicit it certainly was, both in the logic of the argument and in relations with European princes. One can imagine what effect Peter's acceptance of the small German princes as equals would have made on his saintly predecessor, Ivan the Terrible.[44]

It is useful at this point to pause and delimit more precisely the aspects of the ruler-myth with which we have been concerned, and also to remind ourselves of the ob-

42. E. V. Barsov, *Drevne-russkie pamiatniki sviashchennago venchaniia tsarei na tsarstvo, Chteniia*, 1883:1, 113f.; Feofan, a highly educated man, also spoke of the Russian tsars as descendants of Augustus.

43. Cf. Smolitsch, 143.

44. Cf. Prozorovsky, "O znachenii tsarskago titula do priniatiia russkimi gosudariami titula imperatorskago," *I.R.A.O.*, 8, 449–77; P. Pierling, S.J., *La Russie et le Saint-Siège* (Paris, 1890), *1*, 309f.

vious qualifications and *caveats*. For the purpose of exposition, the chronological method served very well to show the changes in the myth of the ruler, through well-defined stages, during the centuries. Yet this linear exposition is, in a sense, a distortion of historical reality. In the evolution of the Russian secular state the expected shift took place from medieval political theory to that of early modern absolutism; in theological terms one can describe it as a shift of emphasis from Christ, the manifest deity, to God the Father, abstract and impersonal. The secular state did not arise with Peter I, however, but developed through the centuries; as one Russian jurist wrote, Peter I put into practice what was theory under Ivan the Terrible.[45] The ideological problems created by the secular state also existed for centuries, and hence the solutions for these problems overlapped. In other words, the Sovereign Emperor did not displace the Most-Gentle Tsar; with the shift of emphasis towards the "emperor," the image of the Orthodox Father Tsar continued to exist, partially contained in that of the emperor, partially living alongside of the latter, or even in opposition to it. Contained in both these images, as well as continuing an independent existence, was the image of the saint-prince with its emphasis on the person of the ruler.[46] The changes which could be rung upon these themes are shown by the various images of Peter I described here: Sovereign Emperor and Antichrist, pious Christian monarch and Earthly God; and, in the course of the eighteenth century, attempts were made to synthesize the images of the ruler. One of the earliest Russian secular poets, a cornerstone in the building of Russian neo-classicism, Kheraskov, in his

45. V. Latkin, *Uchebnik istorii russkago prava perioda imperii* (St. Petersburg, 1909), 249, in Smolitsch, 142.

46. With the *terribile* image of the Tatar khan coming in from the outside, so to say.

epic *Rossiada,* evoked the saintly princes—Vladimir, Ol'ga, Boris, Gleb, Alexander Nevsky, Ivan III (!)—on whom Russia depended for salvation, and, at the same time, portrayed Catherine II as Astrea.[47] The naiveté of Kheraskov's conjunctions can be explained largely by his neo-classicism. For him, as for other Russian poets, the antique images made Russian historical traditions rather meaningless.[48] The difficulty of synthesizing the myth, however, was much greater. While the image of the emperor, such as Peter, could and did contain the various aspects of the ruler-myth, presenting one or another facet to particular groups or individuals, these aspects were intrinsically antithetical. But while the tension between the "saint-prince" and the "orthodox tsar" was mainly theological and hence subdued, while the medieval saintly prince could and did merge into the early Orthodox and Pious Tsar, the antithesis between the latter and the image of the new imperial sovereign was quite explicit. One could be the sovereign emperor without being the pious Russian tsar. In fact, a very large minority of Russians, the schismatic Old Believers, drew the extreme conclusion: beginning with Peter I, to be the emperor meant *not* being the tsar. For masses of Old Believers Peter and his successors remained Antichrists exactly because they were emperors. The more extreme groups refused to pray for the ruler; that is, in effect they refused to recognize the existence of the State as such.[49] When, following a

47. M. M. Kheraskov, *Rossiada* (St. Petersburg, 1895), 160, 170 *et passim;* for allegorical images of Catherine, see Rovinsky, *2,* nos. 229, 438 for Catherine as Minerva; *2,* no. 409 for Catherine as Pallas.

48. See, as one instance among the many possible ones, the famous ode of Derzhavin on the capture of the Ismail fortress: "Opisanie Torzhestva v dome Kniazia Potemkina po sluchaiu vziatiia Izmaila," *Sobranie Sochinenii,* Akademicheskoe izdanie (St. Petersburg, 1868), *1,* 264f.; or his poems on the coronation of Alexander I; *2,* 227f.

49. On the elaborate calculations by which such words as "Senat," "Holstein," and "Nicholas I" signified 666, the apocalyptic number of Antichrist, cf. Andreev, *Raskol,* 344.

temporary liberalization of government policy, the Old Believers, in 1799, agreed to pray for the Emperor Paul I, they insisted on praying for ". . . the Great Sovereign, Tsar Pavel Petrovich of All Russia" but would not include the title of emperor nor the official form of the prayer.[50]

What all this meant was that a split along class lines was taking place with regard to the Russian image of the ruler.[51] While for the Old Believers "emperor" meant Antichrist, for the mass of the Russian peasantry the ruler simply remained the *"Batiushka-Tsar,"* the traditional, pious, Most-Gentle Russian Tsar. A number of reasons can be suggested for this. The split along social lines had existed, of course, for a long time. It was manifested by the cossacks in the sixteenth and seventeenth centuries, in their rejection of even the pious and most-gentle tsars and the growing state, and in their appropriation during the Razin revolt of a personal and private ruler in the person of the Tsar's son. Yet the natural social oppression and resulting antagonism does not explain the problem. That the masses reacted against the Petrine monarchy is not surprising, considering the monstrous new burdens it imposed on them. In the sixteenth century, however, burdens as monstrous imposed by Ivan the Terrible did not produce a comparable ideological reaction, even if one considers the Time of Troubles as part of the same period. The difference seems to be in the fact that by the eighteenth century the myth of the ruler had acquired sufficient complexity, a sufficient number of different aspects, facets, and possible interpretations to perform the function of myth: to allow individuals and groups to express, with ever-growing variety, their personal and collective problems and aspirations within its framework. In the event, the difference between the image of the ruler held by the upper class, created and educated

50. Andreev, *Raskol*, 302.
51. Cf. Smolitsch, 144f.

by Peter's new Empire, and that held by the mass of serf peasantry would be central.

And yet this split does not describe accurately the status of the ruler-myth. Because of historical traditions, over-lappings, interests, and aspirations, the various aspects of the ruler-image were mingled, exchanged, confused. No-where in the eighteenth century does this emerge more clearly than in the case of Peter III. Duke of Holstein, a Protestant by upbringing, heir to the throne of Sweden, Peter was called to Russia by his aunt, Empress Elizabeth, to inherit the imperial throne. Elizabeth died on De-cember 25, 1761. On June 28, 1762, Peter III was forced to abdicate by his wife, Catherine II, and was murdered a few days later by a group of the new empress' lovers. During his brief reign Peter III had had the time, on February 18, 1762, to promulgate the law releasing the gentry from the servitude imposed on them by Peter I and, because of his religious tolerance or indifference, to abolish some of the oppressive measures against the Old Believers.[52]

The palace revolution could succeed only because of the enormous dissatisfaction of the gentry with Peter III, which rendered him helpless against the guards regiments made up of the gentry. When one seeks the ideological reasons for this discontent, they appear rather curious: lack of respect for the Orthodox religion, contempt for things Russian—manifested in language, habits, change of army uniforms to the Prussian model—lack of pride in the Russian state and past, seen clearly in Peter's open worship of and subservience to Frederick the Great of Prussia. Whether these charges were correct or not, what they seem to amount to is that Peter III was acting, in a sense, as an emperor and not as a Russian tsar.[53] Yet the

52. Cf. *Istoriia*, 25, 1241ff.

53. For the ideology of the *putsch*, see for example, the coronation medallion of Catherine II, with the inscription *"Za spasenie Very i*

image of the murdered emperor returned, time and again, to plague the government, the imperial bureaucracy, and the westernized gentry. For in the eyes of the Old Believers, unutterably opposed to emperor and state, Peter III was the Orthodox Tsar, signalizing the return to traditional piety and hence salvation. The extreme sect of the schismatics, the *Skoptsy* (*Castrati*), saw in Peter III both Tsar and Christ, and the reigns of Catherine II and Peter's son Paul I were marked by a steady procession of pretenders, Peters who had escaped death or in fact had been resurrected.[54] Both the gentry and the Old Believers were expressing their own conception of a tsar; the former, however, seeking it in a synthesis of the Orthodox Tsar and the Sovereign Emperor, recoiled before the extreme of absolutism, while the latter sought it in the apocalyptic and mythical Moscovite past of the Most-Gentle Tsars. In other words, both groups sought the same aspect of the myth but according to their own respective needs and desires. The gentry wanted a tsar and called him an emperor; the schismatics took up an emperor and called him a tsar.

While the Old Believers were but a large minority of the Russian population, the Pugachov Rebellion reflected the ideology of the Russian masses in general. The most dramatic expression of social unrest and antagonism, it was also the most dangerous attack that the Russian ruling class and state underwent until the twentieth century. Hence its ideology is the more curious. From the very beginning of his rebellion Pugachov announced himself as Peter III; he had escaped from his gentry assassins and his whorish German wife in order to liberate the common folk and destroy the bureaucratic gentry wall between

---

Otechestva" (For having saved the Faith and the Fatherland), Zhmakin, "Koronatsii," 531.

54. Cf. N. V. Reutsky, *Liudi Bozhii i Skoptsy* (Moscow, 1872), 93f. *et passim*.

tsar and people.[55] He was not indifferent to religion, nor did he plan to change the churches into Protestant ones, but on the contrary the boiars hated him because he wanted to replace the four-pointed cross of the "Nikonians" with the eight-pointed cross of the Old Believers, of true Orthodoxy; and it is significant that most of the cossacks, who were the backbone of the rebellion, were Old Believers.[56] Whatever the social policy of Pugachov was and whatever the mistakes committed by him, formally the rebellion was not directed against the Empire, i.e. against the State and the ruler as such.[57] No matter how many of the Don, Volga, and Ural cossacks knew that they were led by Emelian Pugachov, a Don cossack, and not by Peter III, they kept this knowledge to themselves.[58] The masses were not rebelling against their tsar; if Pugachov is any example, such a conception was unimaginable. They were marching behind their own, Orthodox, popular tsar, to restore him to his rightful place and hence to abolish the oppression and injustice against themselves. And yet Pugachov does not emerge as a peasant tsar. This may be partially explained by the predominant role of the cossacks in the rebellion—men who did not think of themselves as peasants and serfs—but it is not the complete explanation. For Pugachov did not present himself as the pious and Orthodox Tsar, but as the emperor, even if his clerks did not always know how to spell the title.[59] Further, we find that his closest collaborators and commanders become pretenders also; they take on the names as well as

55. For the enormous amount of material on this, see N. Dubrovin, *Pugachov e ego Soobshchiniki* (3 vols. St. Petersburg, 1884); *Pugachevshchina*, ed. S. A. Golubtsov (Tsentrarkhiv, 1929), *1* and *2*.

56. Dubrovin, *1*, 155ff.

57. The chief mistake was lack of a clear policy concerning serfdom.

58. See the interrogations of the captured cossack leaders after the defeat of Pugachov, *Pugachevshchina*, *2*, 187ff.

59. Cf. *Pugachevshchina*, *1*, 25, 29, 35 *et passim*.

the functions of the top dignitaries of the Empire. Pugachov thus had his own Count Chernyshev and Count
Panin to match the ones of Catherine II.[60]

Bizarre though this may have been, it was revealing. If
the gentry, in their image of the emperor, were affected by
the aspect of the tsar, then here we find the masses, an-
tagonistic to gentry and state, affected in their image of
the Russian tsar by the aspect of the emperor. The extreme sects of the Old Believers, by rejecting the aspect
of the ruler contained in the "emperor," were consistent
in their rejection of the new state so closely identified with
the ruler. The masses represented by Pugachov's rebellion
retained the traditional and central myth of the ruler; but
because the Emperor was so closely identified with the
State they were forced to accept ideologically some of the
very elements of the state against which the whole rebellion was directed.

Though by no means exhaustive, the discussion above
allows some conclusions. The emergence of the modern
secular state was accompanied by the development of a
political mythology which has been called here the "Sovereign Emperor"; an image of an absolutist, autocratic
god-emperor, self-contained and self-generated. The older
ruler-myths, however, did not die. They served as the
foundation for the sovereign emperor and they continued
to exist in themselves, revealed to us as pale reflections by
the lightning of great events and crises—pale because the
predominant, official conception was vigorous, and because
the popular sources where one would expect, through the
sheer force of inertia, to find the traditional forms are
largely lacking. Nevertheless, the pattern of the myth was
set. Particular aspects were emphasized by particular
groups who, at the same time, were forced, consciously or
unconsciously, to accept in their image of the ruler other

60. Cf. *Pugachevshchina*, 2, 411, 428ff. *et passim*.

and contradictory facets. The play of this historical dialectic, of the formation of ideas and myths by material
conditions, and the modification of these conditions by
myths and ideas, is already visible in the eighteenth century, which for the purposes of this study ended in 1812.
Both the synthesis of the ruler-myth and the tension
within it that followed were the fruition.

4. *"Holy Russia"* *

> "The Russian people is the God-bearer."
>
> —F. DOSTOEVSKY

HORRIFIED at the European revolutions of 1848, the poet Prince Peter Viazemsky enjoined Russia from following such a dreadful path; Russia was something different and unique. He wrote:

> "Holy Russia! In its very meaning
> Providence foretold her path
> And not for nothing at her Baptism
> Did He endow her with this name." [1]

We lack the evidence to establish the historical validity of the poet's vision. The question then arises, what did Viazemsky mean by "Holy Russia?" That this strange epithet was a common symbol for Russia would be difficult to deny. But if a myth of the ruler, clear and explicit, is discernible virtually from the beginning of Russian his-

* Much of the material and whole passages in this chapter are from my article, "Holy Russia: A Study in the History of an Idea," *A.H.R.*, *63* (April, 1958), 617-37.

1. P. A. Viazemsky, *Polnoe Sobranie Sochinenii* (St. Petersburg, 1880), *4*, 314-15.

tory, things are neither very clear nor explicit when one turns to what is both a corollary and an antithesis of the ruler-myth—a myth of the Land and the People. The commonplace "Holy Russia" is at least a strand of such a myth as we shall endeavor to show; its meaning, however, must be sought in its history.

The article by Alexander V. Soloviev, "Holy Russia (Study of the Development of a Social-Religious Idea)," [2] published in 1927, drew my attention to this history. Soloviev was the first, to my knowledge, to attempt a historical survey of the epithet. In a later study, published in 1954,[3] the Russian scholar explores the question of the possible derivation of "Holy Russia" from early medieval concepts. Soloviev is quite correct when he points out the significance of the epithet. "Holy," after all, evokes the image of the Holy Land, the land where Christ lived and on which he set his foot; Palestine is holy as a sum total of all the holy places within it.[4] Russia is the only other land that has received this epithet with any consistency,[5]

2. Soloviev, "Sviataia Rus' (ocherk razvitiia religiozno-obshchestvennoi idei)," *Sbornik Russkago Arkheologicheskago Obshchestva v Korolevstve S. Kh.S., 1* (Belgrade, 1927), 77–113 (hereafter cited as *Sbornik.*) This work has been recently revised and translated into English: *Holy Russia, The History of a Religious-Social Idea* (The Hague, 1959).

3. Soloviev, "Helles Russland—Heiliges Russland," *Festchrift für Dmytro Čyževskii zum 60. Geburtstag,* Veröffentlichungen der Abteilung für slavische Sprachen und Literatur des Osteuropa-Instituts (Slavisches Seminar) an der Freien Universität Berlin, 6 (Berlin, 1954), pp. 282–89 (hereafter cited as *Festschrift*).

4. The tradition of Terra Sancta derives from the Old Testament; cf. *Zach.* 2:12; *Sap.* 12:3; II *Macc.* 1:7; in the Greek of the Septuagint it appears as 'η γῆ ἡ ἀγια. In Christian times, however, the epithet *Terra Sancta* appears first during the Crusades; see Carl Erdmann, *Die Entstehung des Kreuzzugsgedankens* (Stuttgart, 1935), 279f. The epithet and the idea behind it existed, of course, though in a different form, in classical antiquity; for 'ιεραι 'Αθηναι see, for example, Fustel de Coulanges, *The Ancient City,* trans. Willard Small (4th ed. New York, 1882), 187 and *passim.*

5. The *Sacrum Imperium Romanum* was a legally derived term and in the Middle Ages was used in apposition to the *Sancta Ecclesia.* The

and it is certainly curious, as Soloviev points out, that the problem had not been studied earlier.[6] The intent of his study, however, is revealed by the question he asks after pointing out the uniqueness of the epithet: "Is it deserved?" He then gives a brief survey of Russian history in order to judge whether the Russian claim to holiness is justified. Because of this outlook, Soloviev, while investigating the problem of the history of "Holy Russia," becomes part of that history himself. He sees Russian thought through the ages as peculiarly god-centered, but the historical problem is limited by the fact that Soloviev finds the earliest dated use of the epithet in the writings of Prince Andrew Kurbsky in the seventies of the sixteenth century. He then argues that Kurbsky undoubtedly did not create the term but found it in common usage, so that one may expect to find earlier documentary proof.[7] In his later article Soloviev concludes that Kurbsky is the earliest dated source we possess. He does, however, suggest sources

whole problem of national epithets is a complicated one and deserving of study; implications of sanctity or holiness do appear occasionally in the national states of Western Europe. For the literature on the "holy realm of France" and its connection with the *Terra Sancta* of the Crusades see E. H. Kantorowicz, *"Pro Patria Mori* in Medieval Political Thought," *A.H.R.,* 56 (1951), 479–84. The same connotation is carried by the "Blessed Lady Spain"; see Gaines Post, "Blessed Lady Spain——Vincentius Hispanus and Spanish National Imperialism in the 13th Century," *Speculum,* 29 (1954), 198–210. The closest parallel with "Holy Russia" is "Virginal" or "Holy Ireland"; see, for example, the poem by Giolla Modubhda, ca. 1200, in the *Todd Lecture Series* (Dublin, 1892), 408–37; see also the eighteenth-century poem *The Fair Hills of Holy Ireland,* trans. Sir Samuel Ferguson in *An Anthology of Irish Verse,* ed. Padraic Colum (New York, 1948) 182. For all of the material on Ireland I am indebted to Professor John Kelleher of Harvard University.

6. *Sbornik,* 77, n. 1. As far as I have been able to determine Soloviev is right when he claims that no study prior to his own had appeared on this subject. The traditional acceptance of the epithet was apparently so deep that it occurred to no one to examine it. The example of this kind of acceptance which I have before me, a social and political study of modern Russia by Georges Friedmann, *Dalla Santa Russia All' U.R.S.S.* (Rome, 1949), is one of many.

7. *Sbornik,* 91, n. 2.

that show earlier use of the epithet, namely Russian folk-
songs written down in the eighteenth century and later
but going back in oral tradition, according to Soloviev,
to the fourteenth century.[8]

This contention that in the fourteenth century the folk-
songs used the epithet "holy," cannot be substantiated.
The question then remains: are there any manifestations
of a myth of Russia, prior to the sixteenth century, which
would shed light on our epithet? The earliest document
which bears on our problem, which manifests a self-aware-
ness, whether one calls it tribal, cultural, or national, is
the twelfth-century *Slovo o Polku Igoreve* (The Lay of
Igor); the poet bemoaned the betrayal, for selfish reasons,
of *Rus'*, the Russian land, in the struggles against the
nomads of the South Russian steppes; he appealed to the
princes of the Riurikid dynasty to forget their squabbles
and differences and to unite in the defense of *Rus'*, the
patria, the common fatherland of them all.[9]

The next step in this process of self-identification appeared in another epic, the *Slovo o pogibeli russkoi zemli*
(Lay of the downfall of the Russian land). This too, like
the Igor' tale, was written to describe a catastrophe, in this
case the Mongol attack on Russia. *Rus'* was not just the
fatherland of those who were born and lived in it; in the
eyes of the writer it was the *svetlaia zemlia,* or the *svet-
lorusskaia zemlia*—the Illumined Land, or the Illumined
Russian land.[10] The meaning of the epithet can best be
explained by reference to the one great element of unity

8. Festschrift, 283–85; A. V. Kartashev, "Sud'by 'Sviatoi Rusi'," *Pravoslavnaia Mysl'*, Trudy Prov. Bogos. Inst. v Parizhe, *1* (Paris, 1928), 136–37.

9. *Slovo o Polku Igoreve,* ed. V. P. Adrianova-Perets (ANSSSR, 1950),
17f.; for literature on the *Slovo,* see commentaries to this edition; R. O.
Jakobson, "Izuchenie 'Slova o polku goreve v S.Sh.A.," *T.O.D.R.L., 14*
(1958), 102–21; *T.O.D.R.L., 8* (1951), 1ff.

10. "Slovo o Pogibeli russkoi zemli i o smerti Velikogo Kniazia Iaro-
slava," Serebriansky, appendix, 109; cf. M. N. Tikhomirov, "Gde i kogda

in the politically chaotic and fragmented Russian area, namely by the Christian religion. "Illumined," in this case, meant illumined by the light of true faith, by the light of Christianity.[11]

To interpret this appellation, however, as an expression of a popular idea or myth is difficult. Scarce as the sources for the medieval period are, the epithet appears too rarely to be considered a popular or prevalent one. What one sees here, in other words, rather than an expression of a popular ideology, is an attempt to create a rallying cry, a means of self-identification during times of political crises; one, moreover, which was borrowed from the princely myth, for the term "svetlyi" in the Igor tale appears as an epithet for the prince, not for Russia.[12] Struggling against the pagan nomads from Asia, the Russians' identification with Christianity was a logical one.[13]

All this is not to deny the correctness of Soloviev's arguments that the origin of "Holy Russia" is to be found, both ideologically and etymologically, in the epithets "bright," "enlightened," "illumined."[14] But the line of

---

bylo napisano 'Slovo o pogibeli russkoi zemli'," *T.O.D.R.L.*, *8* (1951), 235–44; cf. Soloviev, "Le dit de la ruine de la terre russe," *Byzantion*, 22 (1952), 113f.

11. *Festschrift*, 282.

12. *Slovo*, 11; cf. *Festschrift*, 282.

13. Cf. speech of Prince Mstislav, ch. 1, n. 45; the epic *Zadonshchina*, celebrating Dimitry Donskoi's victory in 1380 over the Tatars, V. P. Adrianova-Perets, "Zadonshchina," *T.O.D.R.L.*, *5* (1947), 198f., for other examples of this kind of identification. There is little doubt that war, foreign invasion, brought out the need for identity, exalted if at all possible. What was lacking as yet was the rationalization and utilization that accompany myth. To die for the *patria, Rus'*, was to gain salvation, yet *Rus'* was hardly defined except in terms of the prince and Christ. On the development of the idea of *patria* and its relation to Christianity in the medieval West, see Erdmann, *Entstehung*, Halvdan Koht, "The Dawn of Nationalism in Europe," *A.H.R.*, *52* (1947), 265–280; Kantorowicz, *The King's Two Bodies*, 236f.

14. *Festschrift*, 282f.

transmission was not a direct one. The fruition of the imagery of "enlightened" or "illumined" Russia was expressed in the sun imagery employed when referring to the Russian Grand Princes. Beginning with Vladimir, the Beautiful Sun (*Vladimir Krasnoe Solnyshko*), and ending with the letter of the monk Philotheos to Vasily III, the Russian rulers seemed to have provided the illumination which rendered Russia "bright." Hence, if on the one hand the early epics did suggest an image of Russia, of the Russian land as a whole, this tradition remained, on the other hand, at best submerged, vitiated by the vitality and power of the princely myth. One might say that there was, in medieval Russia, a myth of the ruler, but not of the land, of the country and people as a whole.[15]

If that was the case, what of "Holy Russia"? When could the epithet first be used? What conditions were necessary for men to think of Russia in these terms? What could the epithet signify? The meaning of the term must be sought in the analogy with the Holy Land; Palestine was holy because Christ had lived there, because it was the physical setting for the possibility of man's salvation. Thus Russia could be holy, even in Christian times, if it had a

---

15. If anything, the myth of the ruler was created at the expense of the myth of the "land." The twelfth-century *Slovo o polku Igoreve* speaks of the *zemliia russkaia*, the Russian land; in the fifteenth century, one only reads of the prince, who symbolizes state, country, and faith. Historians have noted that a feature of Russian political history was the fact that opposition groups failed rather miserably because they never seemed to have had an ideological foundation or theory to base their actions on. The problem, as we can see, was an old one by the time the boiar opposition of the sixteenth century tried to formulate its views. On the opposition in the sixteenth century, see V. Leontovitsch, *Die Rechtsumwälzung unter Ivan dem Schreklichen und die Ideologie der Russischen Selbstherrschaft* (Stuttgart, 1947), 44–51; Ševčenko, 173–74. On the boiar opposition of the Time of Troubles, see Platonov, *Ocherki*, 300f., 449ff. On the opposition by the Church, cf. Val'denberg, *Drevnerusskie ucheniia*, 395f. On the aristocratic attempts of the eighteenth century (1740), cf. Kliuchevsky, *Kurs, 4*, 268f.

unique and exalted role in the economy of salvation, if in it, and in it alone, Christ still walked, in spirit if not in person. Such times came in the middle of the fifteenth century, for after the Council of Florence and the attempt at the Union of Churches in 1441 Moscovite Russia saw herself as the only orthodox land in the world, that is to say, as the only source of salvation for mankind.[16] Salvation thus coincided with a political boundary; it could only be attained in Russia. The future of the whole world depended upon the faith of the new Russian tsardom.

If we accept, then, the possibility, or rather the applicability, of the epithet "Holy Russia" from the middle of the fifteenth century on, the question of its first appearance becomes highly interesting. For over a century after it was, theoretically, usable, the epithet did not appear in any of the numerous and extremist writings dedicated to the exaltation and virtual deification of the Russian ruler. It first appeared in the writings of Prince Kurbsky. After his emigration he wrote his letters to Ivan and his *History of the Prince of Moscow*.[17] In his answer to Ivan's second epistle, he accuses the tsar of having "dishonored yourself and all the holyrussian land." [18] Eight more times

16. In connection with these events, and particularly with the fall of Constantinople in 1453, there was another expression of national self-identity, of the idea of Russia rather than of the prince. Translating the popular prophecies on the fall of the Reigning City, the Russians substituted, in the "Revelation of Methodius of Patara," the "Russian people" for the "red [haired] people" who, according to Methodius, were eventually to reconquer Constantinople from the infidels and rule it in eternity. The substitution could work because of the play on the word *rous* for red, as meaning *rhos*, Russian. Cf. V. Istrin, *Otkroveniia Mefodia Patarskago i apokrificheskie videniia Daniila v vizantiiskoi i slaviano-russkoi literature*, in *Chteniia*, 1897:2, 240; B. Unbegaun, "Les relations vieux-russes de la prise de Constantinople," *Revue des Études Slaves*, 9 (1929), 13–38.

17. In *R.I.B., 31*.

18. "Na preskvernoe i vechnoe tvoe postydienie i vsea sviatorusskie zemli," *R.I.B., 31,* 134.

in his *History* the prince uses the epithet, five times in
the form of "holyrussian land," [19] once as holyrussian
tsardom," [20] and twice as "holyrussian empire." [21] This is
the only known use of the epithet in the sixteenth century.
Soloviev refers to its use in the letter of Philotheos to
Grand Prince Vasily III but correctly does not place much
credence in it, for the term "All Holy and Great Russia"
is found only in a redaction of the seventeenth century.[22]

The problem then remains: assuming even that the
epithet was in common usage, reflected in the folksongs
and epics, why was there only one reflection of it in the
political literature of the sixteenth century? Kurbsky, after
all, belonged ideologically to a group of boiar opposition
to autocracy that dated from the beginning of the sixteenth century, with the circle around Maxim the Greek.[23]

The answer may be found, at least partially, in the use
Kurbsky made of the epithet. In each case it is used in a
sentence describing the evil deeds of the autocratic tsar:

"Oh, Satan! . . . why have you planted such a godless
seed in the heart of a Christian tsar, from which such a
fire swept over all the Holyrussian land that no words
are needed to witness it from me? . . . Oh evil ones, filled
with various vices and slyness, destroyers of your fatherland, or better said of the whole Holyrussian tsardom!
. . .[24] Such evil, vicious . . . ones that they have torn the

19. *Sviatorusskie zemli.*
20. *Sviatorusskoe tsarstvo.*
21. *Imperiia sviatorusskaia.* This formula probably reflects Kurbsky's
Polish and general Western associations. *Imperiia* would normally refer
to the Western, Habsburg empire; the Roman-Byzantine empire was called
tsarstvo. As one can see, in all usages by Kurbsky, *sviataia* and *russkaia*
are combined into one word, that is, used as an epithet.
22. *Festschrift,* 285, n. 7; "Khristianskomu tsariu i vladeltse vsekh,
brazdoderzhateliu zhe vseia sviatyia i velikiia rosiia," Malinin, Appendix,
p. 50.
23. On this, and also for bibliography, see Budovnits, esp. chaps. 3–5.
24. This was addressed to the tsar's councilors.

belly of their mother, that is of the Holyrussian land, who has born them and raised them."

Warning Ivan, rhetorically, of the example of Herod, Kurbsky tells the tsar that "your majesty's abundance of evil will devastate not only friends but all the Holyrussian land," and he writes of Theodore Basmanov, the tsar's "beloved" and "the destroyer . . . of the Holyrussian land." Ivan killed a great noble whose father, Stepan, "served many years, until he was eighty, served well and honestly the Holyrussian empire." [25] Again, the tsar killed "Nikita, surnamed Kazarinov, with his only son Theodore who was in the bloom of his youth, who [that is, Nikita] had served many years and faithfully the Holyrussian empire." [26] In fact, the tsar had ordered his murderers to wipe out men who were dying in the defense of "Holyrussian" land against the pagans.[27]

In every case the epithet is used to create an antithesis to the tsar, the antithesis of a "Holy Russia." Ivan's actions, dreadful as they were, became the more horrible when directed against his country, which is not just his property but is the Holy Land. Perhaps Prince Kurbsky began to construct that myth of the nation that he found necessary to oppose the myth of the ruler. The "Holy Russian" land, the tsardom or empire, existed apart from the exalted and newly created Tsar. Certainly, in this sense, the epithet would express a political theory consistent with the views of Kurbsky and his ideological predecessors: Russia was a land, exalted by its orthodoxy and purity, entrusted to a princely clan which in common held Russia and in common ruled over it.[28] Thus, for Kurbsky, Ivan became a monster of iniquity after having rejected his

25. *R.I.B., 31,* 216, 262, 266, 271, 305.

26. *R.I.B., 31,* 307. In another variant, the word "region" (*oblast'*) is written in on the margin.

27. *R.I.B., 31,* 306. The pagans in this case are the Tatars.

28. See Kliuchevsky, *Duma,* 241f.

councilors and boiars and acted autocratically, having imagined himself to be "immortal and divine."[29]

Nevertheless, Kurbsky's uniqueness remains a problem. Certainly the argument from silence is a dangerous one, but the epithet appears to have passed unnoticed.[30] Though it was used in a letter to Ivan, the Tsar did not pick it up; it did not appear in the political writings at his court. Yet one must agree with A. V. Soloviev that it is most unlikely that Kurbsky invented the term; more probably the rebellious prince used an epithet in common usage. So much more striking, then, is the silence of official tsarist ideology. It seems to confirm my suggestion that from the very beginning the epithet "Holy Russia" was an anti-tsarist, anti-state slogan.

One more consideration remains as far as Kurbsky is concerned. His letters are dated quite precisely, but the earliest manuscript of his writings that has survived is from the early seventeenth century.[31] There appears to be, therefore, no conclusive evidence for the use of the epithet during the sixteenth century. This is not to say that one must reject the sixteenth-century origin of "Holy Russia," but Kurbsky's uniqueness may have the very simple explanation that "Holy Russia" is a seventeenth-century interpolation. The likelihood that a seventeenth-century scribe casually added "Holy Russia," or substituted it for

29. *R.I.B.*, *31*, 1–2, 281.

30. See, for example, the main "royalist" writers: the monk Philotheos, in Malinin, Appendix; Abbot Iosif Sanin of Volokolamsk, *Prosvetitel'*, in *Pravoslavnyi Sobesednik* (Kazan', 1856, 1857), and also in *Chteniia* (1847); Archbishop Vassian of Rostov in *P.S.R.L.*, *6*. See also, for example, *Zhitie i khozhdenie Daniila russkia zemli igumena*, ed. Mikhail A. Venevitinov, in *Pravoslavnyi Palestinskii Sbornik* (St. Petersburg, 1883–85), nos. 3 and 9; the earliest manuscript is from 1475. In this travelogue and pilgrimage Palestine is frequently referred to as the Holy Land, but the epithet is never applied to the "russian land" for which the abbot prays on his pilgrimage.

31. *R.I.B.*, *31*, v–vii; *Poslaniia Ivana Groznogo*, 529f.

the original name or epithet, must be judged by the history of the symbol in the seventeenth century. What may be called the period of silence extends from the middle of the fifteenth century all through the sixteenth, that is, through the period of the evolution and culmination of Byzantine imperial ideology, of the deification of the state, first in the person of the grand prince and then of the tsar.

The history of the title "Holy Russia" in the seventeenth century is a very different one. It began early in the century, when on June 14, 1619, the metropolitan Filaret Romanov, father of the recently elected tsar, Michael Romanov, returned to Moscow from his long years of captivity in Poland. The joy experienced by the young Tsar and the country was expressed in a song beginning:

> The Moscovite Tsardom rejoiced
> And all the Holyrussian land.[32]

The song then describes the reception of Filaret and his companions by Tsar Michael and the mass that was celebrated, ending with the metropolitan's blessing of his imperial son:

> God grant health to the Orthodox Tsar
> Grand Prince Mikhail Fedorovich
> May he hold the Moscovite tsardom
> And all the Holyrussian land.[33]

This is the first really dated use of the epithet, for, within two months of its creation, the song was recorded

---

32. Pavel K. Simoni, "Velikorusskie pesni zapisannye v 1619–20 gg. dlia Richarda Dzheimsa," *Sbornik Otdeleniia Russkago Iazyka i Slovesnosti,* Akademiia Nauk, *82* (1907), 7.

> Zradovolosia Tsarstvo Moskovskoie
> i vsia zemlia Sviato-russkaia.

33. Carl Stief, *Studies in the Russian Historical Song* (Copenhagen, 1953), 54.

by the Englishman, Richard James, chaplain to the embassy sent out in 1618 by James I.[34] The exact date, of course, is not the issue. What is significant is that the epithet appears to have been in common usage, that it was used in a popular song, and that it emerged in a period of new developments in Russian ideology. The new Tsar and the new dynasty symbolized a new national consciousness. Michael was elected by an Assembly of the Land (*Zemskii Sobor*) after years of civil war and foreign invasions during the Time of Troubles. The threat to national existence and to orthodoxy (for this was how the Russians saw Polish intervention) came at a time, however, when the traditional central authority was virtually absent. Salvation came from the Russian people—towns, monasteries, and lower gentry; there was a conception of a popular, national will expressed in the great assembly. It is against this background that the use of the epithet in a song should be considered.

In the song, the predication "Holy Russia," while not antithetical, is nevertheless separated from the state, from the Moscovite tsardom. The epithet symbolizes a new and a different dimension in the concept of Russia. Despite the historical origin of this dimension in the fifteenth century, in contrast with the historical Moscovite tsardom it symbolizes the nonhistorical, transcendental Russia. The identifying feature of this other Russia is the orthodox Russian people. No one in the seventeenth century seems to have analyzed the epithet, nor even to have been conscious of its use and implications, but the available evidence supports this interpretation. This evidence consists of epics of the Don cossacks, dating from the middle of the seventeenth century.[35] In the so-called *"Poetical" Tale of the Siege of*

34. Stief, 13f.

35. *Festschrift*, 286; *Voinskie povesti drevnei Rusi*, ed. Adrianova-Perets (Moscow, 1949).

Azov,[36] the cossacks are called upon to surrender by a Turkish general of the besieging army: "You have injured . . . the Turkish Lord and Tsar. Truthfully are you still called in Russia the holyrussian heroes; how can you now, you thieves, flee from his dread hand?" When the situation of the beleaguered cossacks becomes desperate, they appeal prayerfully to their patron, John the Baptist: "We shall never be in Holy Russia again! Our sinful death comes in the deserts for your miracle-working icons, for the Christian faith, for the tsar's name and for all the Moscovite state." [37] In the *Lament of the Captives* of the Zaporozh'e cossacks, the enslaved cossacks sing: "Deliver, God, the poor captive/ To the holy-russian bank/ To the happy land/ Among Christian folk." [38]

The use of the epithet in the Azov tale suggests that "Holy Russia" embraced all the values for which the cossacks died: the holy icons, the faith, the tsar, and the state. This becomes clear when one recalls the unique position of the "Great Don Army" (*Velikoe Voisko Donskoe*), as the cossack association called itself. In effect, it was an independent political entity, dealing as a sovereign power with the Turks, Tatars, Poland, and Moscow; and yet, as individuals, as orthodox Russians, the members recognized the sovereignty of the tsar. That is to say, as orthodox, the cossacks *were* Russians, even though by origin many of them were Tatars, Poles, or Lithuanians, and as orthodox Russians they could only acknowledge one ruler—the Orthodox Tsar. Nevertheless, the Moscovite tsardom be-

---

36. *"Skazochnaia" povest' o vziatii Azova,* in *Voinskie povesti drevnei Rusi,* 265f.

37. *"Skazochnaia,"* 62–63, 76.

38. V. Antonovich and M. Dragomanov, *Istoricheskie pesni malorusskago naroda* (Kiev, 1877), *1,* 95, in *Festschrift,* 286, n. 13. Another variant of the song, quoted by Soloviev, illustrates the equation between Russian Christianity and holiness: "Vyzvol', Hospody, nevol'nika / Na iasny zory / Na ruskii bereh / Mezh mir khreshchenyi."

gan across the frontier, and the Don cossacks were always anxious to preserve the right to enter Russia. What is interesting, however, is that Moscow also saw its boundaries as those of the "political" Moscovite state and ordered the cossacks not to allow freemen to enter "Russia and the upper [river] towns." [39] The Moscow government as well as the cossacks acknowledged implicitly the distinction between, or the nonidentity of, the Moscovite state and "Holy Russia."

But in this acknowledgment there was a difference, for the government—that is, the tsar, the bureaucracy, the Church, and the ideologists of Moscovite power—never used the epithet "Holy Russia." This, I believe, is essential. Official political thought did not seem to be aware, or refused to become aware, of this other dimension, the popular dimension of Russia. The focus of all sanctity was in the Orthodox and Most-Gentle Tsar, and the unique function of Russia, manifested in the formula "Moscow, the Third Rome," was from the beginning, in the mid-fifteenth century, dependent on the ruler. Salvation existed only within the political boundaries of Russia, determined by the power and rule of the tsar. The more or less official national pride and consciousness, insofar as it did not speak of the tsar, was symbolized by the "reigning city of Moscow," the "impregnable," the "beautiful," the "New Rome." [40]

"Holy Russia," then, was a popular epithet expressing a popular ideology. It was used by the Don cossacks, outlaws legally but not morally or ideologically. It was a territorial concept insofar as it embraced the land of salvation, with its icons, saints, and the Christian Russian people.

39. *Donskie Dela, 3,* in *R.I.B., 26,* 543. On this whole problem, see S. Tkhorzhevsky, "Donskoe voisko v pervoi polovine semnadtsatogo veka," *Russkoe Proshloe, 3* (1923), 9–28.

40. *Skazanie Avraama Palitsyna,* Arkheograficheskaia Kommissiia (St. Petersburg, 1909), 297–98.

The way in which the epithet was used in popular folk-songs and epics did not prescribe the political form of Russian society; that is to say, Russia could be "Holy Russia" whether there was a tsar or not.

At this point we must deal with the problem of folk-songs and epics; the epithet is found in the song composed for Filaret's entry into Moscow. In addition there are four folk tales preserved in seventeenth-century manuscripts.[41] In one of them, the epic of Michael Potok, are found the epithets "holyrussian hero" and "holyrussian land."[42] It is possible, therefore, that the many songs using the term "Holy Russia" employed it as early as the seventeenth century.[43] In most of them the epithet is used with standard associations. It would be superfluous to quote all the instances of use, running into the hundreds, but it is worthwhile noting that in the great song cycle associated with the history of Ivan the Terrible, whose image has remained so vivid among the Russian people, the epithet, used many times, is not associated with the terrible tsar or with the state; on the contrary, "Holy Russia" is found in bawdy and satirical songs that make fun of the tsar and of his marriage with Maria Temriukovna.[44] Here the antithesis of tsar and "Holy Russia" seems explicit.

All this is not to say that the antithesis was logically necessary. Ideally, a Holy Russia ruled by a holy tsar should create no tension nor present an ideological problem. In the songs on Filaret's return the tsar and the Holy-

41. A. P. Evgen'eva, "O nekotorykh poeticheskikh osobennostiakh russkago ustnago eposa XVII–XIX vv., *T.O.D.R.L.,* 6 (1948), 177–78.

42. *T.O.D.R.L.,* 6, 178, n. 3 and 6. See also Vladimir Ia. Propp, *Russkii Geroicheskii Epos* (Leningrad, 1955), 105f.

43. The Kirsha Danilov Collection. For details on this collection see *Festschrift,* 286–87.

44. See Vsevolod F. Miller, *Istoricheskie pesni russkago naroda, XVI–XVII vv., Sbornik Otd. Russ. Iaz. i Slov.,* Akademiia Nauk, 93 (1915), 41f.

russian land are not antithetical. Yet the distinction between "Holy Russia" and the Moscovite tsardom was
drawn, and it is doubtful that it was purely for the sake
of rhythm. To resolve this problem it is necessary to return
to the evidence for the meaning and the limits of the
epithet. Russia was "Holy Russia" because it was the land
of salvation, expressed in its icons, saints, people, and
ruler. But the historical origin of the term indicates its
concrete limits: "Holy Russia" was what remained, during the Time of Troubles, after Tsar and State and
Church hierarchy were gone; it was the concentrated essence of Russia, visible when the form of Russia was destroyed. Hence, both on the transcendental and concrete
levels "Holy Russia" was an absolute, immutable, because
the land of salvation could not change except catastroph-
ically, nor could the Russian essence change without losing
itself. Hence, also, an inherent antagonism would exist between "Holy Russia" and the Moscovite tsardom, for the
latter could and did change. Between these two the pious
and Most-Gentle Tsar could act as the middle term, preserving the conditions for salvation and ruling the state.
But the line he had to maintain was a very fine one, as
shown by the cossacks in their ambivalence towards Tsar
and State.

Considering the evidence for the seventeenth century
and the dates of the subsequent song collections which appeared in print, the epithet became a commonplace among
the masses, the peasants, from the early seventeenth century
on.[45] What we have here is the emergence of a popular
myth. It is not hard to guess why the tsar and officialdom
disregarded or pretended to disregard "Holy Russia." On

45. For the evidence that the epithet survived to the present, cf.
Propp, 508f.; A. D. Grigoriev, *Arkhangel'skie byliny i istoricheskie pesni*,
St. Petersburg, 1904–1910; *Byliny Severa*, ed. A. M. Astakhova, *1* (Moscow,
1938), 253f.

the transcendental level the epithet symbolized something which, though it included the tsar, was larger than he. On the concrete level the epithet represented something even more dangerous; it symbolized a conception of immutability of function and essence which precluded all change and would require opposition to any social and political changes. In this sense it manifested that perpetual and universal mass inertia which it was the task of the state mechanism to conquer. Through an historical dialectic, the myth of "Holy Russia," which derived out of a tradition of a holy ruler providing salvation for an orthodox society, became a possible standard against which the ruler and the state could be judged. The myth of the ruler, as we have said, was so powerful in medieval Russia, that it suppressed any real myth of the people; with the crisis of the early seventeenth century, when a myth of the people developed, it drew on the same sources as the ruler-myth and became as absolute as its older counterpart. The saint-ruler, unique and absolute, was now confronted by "Holy Russia," equally unique and absolute.

That this tension between the myths, though presented above in an extreme formulation, was inherent is shown by the extreme positions taken during the Petrine crisis. When the emperor in effect rejected the image of the saintly and pious ruler, his extreme counterparts, the Old Believers, rejected the emperor and the state. But they still remained "Holy Russia"; "Holy Russia" was in the past to which one should return, and it also continued in their communities which fled the Russian state. In fact, "Holy Russia" existed in the tsardom of Antichrist-Peter, for all those who believed in "Holy Russia," who held to the old ways, and hence recognized the coming of Antichrist, were of it. Granted that the Old-Believer sects which insisted on the Antichrist idea were extremist groups, isolated fanatics; to the non-schismatic orthodox,

Peter was not quite the Antichrist, and "Holy Russia" was not restricted to the northern communities of the various sects. Nevertheless, the Old Believers drew their ideas from the common source, and only pushed them to their logical and consistent conclusions. Both the orthodox and the schismatics saw "Holy Russia" contained in a system of values which were their own—icons, saints, faith, customs; to all of these the Petrine secular state, beginning with the shaving of beards and ending with the census of "Souls," would be antithetical.[46] It would seem legitimate, therefore, to assume that the Old Believers, in their violent opposition, were expressing and utilizing the beliefs of the masses, the myth of "Holy Russia." [47]

In his survey of the history of the epithet, A. V. Soloviev correctly points out that neither "Holy" nor "Illumined" Russia were thought of in the eighteenth century, that age of borrowed neo-classicism.[48] What he meant was that for the educated upper classes who wrote, the term and the problems it raised would have been meaningless. But if for the westernized gentry "Holy Russia" did not exist, and the peasant masses did not write enough to provide us with conclusive evidence, an interesting problem ensues which bears on our question. The original Russian name for Russia was *Rus'*, and this word was used in official documents, chronicles, and literary works. It is difficult to de-

---

46. The census which, curiously enough, was first taken in Russia by the Tatars, was seen by the Old Believers as an attempt to get everyone marked with the seal of Antichrist (Semevsky, *Slovo*, 108f.; "Istoriia Pechatnaia," *Chteniia* [1863:1], 57f.). The problem was compounded by the fact that the technical term employed to denote an individual was "*dusha*," soul, so that the count was of souls as well as of bodies.

47. The Pugachov rebellion supports this interpretation. Trying, in a sense, to take over the state, the Pugachov movement was not anti-state as such, and did not employ the "Holy Russia" myth, prevalent though it was at the time, for the myth's connotation and usage were anti-state.

48. *Festschrift*, 287. This is necessarily an argument from silence.

termine at what point in time the second and still used name, *Rossiia,* came in.[49] In any case it was used in the titulature of the tsar by 1654.[50] Perhaps it came into use through the Poles, who used it and had occupied Russia during the Time of Troubles.[51] Certainly by the eighteenth century it replaced *Rus'* in secular literature and in all official documents except in the case of some archaic formulas. *Rus'* remained the popular, the common appellation for Russia, and the distinctions between the two names in all their grammatical forms continued through Russian history. From the viewpoint of our problem, the tension between the two myths, the significance of the difference between the names can be stated quite briefly. It was impossible, apparently, to say *Sviataia* (holy) *Rossiia:* one could only speak of *Sviataia Rus'.* And it was equally impossible, apparently, to speak of *Russkaia Imperiia* (Russian Empire); one could speak only of *Rossiiskaia Imperiia,* where the adjectival "Russian" was formed from *Rossiia* and not *Rus'.* The difference was explicit in other forms as well: the word for a Russian which finally prevailed was *Russkii,* derived from *Rus'.* In the eighteenth century,

49. Cf. M. N. Tikhomirov, "Maloizvestnye Pamiatniki," *T.O.D.R.L., 16* (1960), 452–53; A. V. Soloviev, "Weiss-Schwarz-und Rotreussen . . . ," *Jahr. für Geschichte Osteuropas,* 7 (1959), 1–33. For literature and origin, see his *Le Nom Byzantin de la Russie* (The Hague, 1957).

50. *A.I., 4,* no. 83, p. 219, charter of July 16, 1654; *A.A.E., 4,* no. 72, p. 109, document of August 5, 1654; cf. A. V. Soloviev, "Der Begriff 'Russland' im Mittelalter," *Studien zur Älteren Geschichte Osteuropas* (Wiener Archiv für Geschichte des Slawentums und Osteuropa), 2 (1956), 167–68, and n. 98.

51. "Only Poland called us "Rossiia," according to the Latin script, and we have taken it over into our cyrillic writing. . . ." V. Dal', *Tolkovyi Slovar' Zhivogo Velikorusskogo Iazyka* (St. Petersburg-Moscow, 1882), *4,* 114, under "Rusak." The transition was not a sudden one, from *Rus'* to *Rossiia;* through the reign of Michael and the first half of that of Alexis, the name for Russia in the tsar's official title was *Rusia,* obviously a compromise solution. For titulature with *Rusia,* see acts of Michael and Alexis, *A.I., 3, 4; A.A.E., 3, 4.*

however, the poets and writers used their ingenuity to create *Ross,* or *Rossiianin,* derived from *Rossiia.*[52] The antithesis was sharpened by the fact that *Russkii,* a Russian, was expressed among the people by synonyms— *krestiane-khristiane* (peasants-Christians) or *pravoslavnye* (orthodox).[53]

In other words, to be of *Rus'* was to be an Orthodox, a Christian, to indicate one's status in eternity; to be of *Rossiia,* was to be of the political state. What we seem to have here are two different Russias, each expressing a different myth: the common and popular *"Rus',"* material carrier of "Holy Russia," and *"Rossiia,"* the political state, ruled by the *Imperator Vserossiiskii.* This, however, involves an interesting consequence. If the Russian Tsar (*Russkii Tsar'*) could act as a middle term between people and state, this function was reflected in the dual nature of his title. The Russian Emperor (*Vserossiiskii Imperator*) was no longer in the middle; as his title indicated, he was completely of the state, identified with it.[54]

Once again, therefore, we perceive the antithetical relation between the myths we are concerned with, and once again it is necessary to emphasize the dialectic nature of this antagonism. The myths served different functions, but drew upon the same common sources for their justification. Hence the myth of the ruler and the myth of the people were not antithetical in substance but in their confrontation. A peasant, who was within and of "Holy Russia," in-

52. Beginning with Lomonosov, himself of peasant origin.

53. Cf. above, the Don cossacks songs, n. 38.

54. One can suggest a further tangle of distinctions here: the popular term for fatherland was *"rodina"* (birthplace), feminine in gender; the upper-class word was translated from *patria*—"otechestvo" (fatherland), neuter in gender. In this sense the tsar could only be married to the *rodina,* Rus', while the emperor was identified with the neuter state, *Rossiia,* which was the *otechestvo.* Cf. above, chapter 3, n, 26.

sofar as he accepted the State, could and did accept its mythology of the secular absolutist emperor.[55] He could do so by accepting, in effect, the existence of two Russias. If, however, the myths were to be confronted with each other, if only one Russia could exist, the alternatives were obvious: the myths would either have to merge into one, a Holy Russia with a holy tsar, or one would predominate to the exclusion of the other. The possibilities for interweaving and intermingling the various strands of the mythical whole cloth were numerous. In the popular legends and songs, Peter as Antichrist confronted Peter as the Christlike miraculous infant, the angry, mercilessly just, and terrifying tsar appeared also as the essence of piety, with thaumaturgic gifts; the populist *Rus'* of Pugachov became the *Rossiia* of a "Peter III."

All these tensions, vague though the sparse evidence may be for them, existed on the other side, within the mythmaking of the state and the upper class associated with it. In a recent study Hans Rogger described the development of a concept of Russian national character in the second half of the eighteenth century.[56] Under the impact of Western cultures, Rogger points out, Russian gentry, themselves westernized, sought for a national identity, and one which should not make them blush.[57] Our concern is not with the impassioned statements of Fonvizin, Novikov, N. A. L'vov, or P. A. Plavil'shchikov,

55. Cf. Kirsha Danilov, *Drevniia Rossiiskiia Stikhotvoreniia* (2nd ed., Moscow, 1818), 293; Kireevsky, *Pesni, 8*, 1ff.

56. Hans Rogger, "The Russian National Character: Some Eighteenth-Century Views," *H.S.S., 4*, 17–34; also see his "The 'Nationalism' of Ivan Nikitič Boltin," *For Roman Jakobson*, eds. M. Halle, H. G. Lunt, H. McLean, C. H. Van Schooneveld (The Hague, 1956), 423–30. For the general problem, see Rogger's recent book, *National Consciousness in Eighteenth-Century Russia* (Cambridge, 1960).

57. Even Catherine II herself was engaged in this occupation, Rogger, *H.S.S., 4*, 18.

trying to prove that the Russians were as intelligent, talented, gifted, skillful, and virtuous as the Germans, French, and English; in fact, according to these gentlemen, the Russians were more so.[58] Praiseworthy as these qualities may be, one can argue that they do not help us identify a Russian; when the journalist Plavil'shchikov wrote that "What the Russian cannot grasp will forever be unknown to men," [59] we have learned nothing, the chauvinist cliché being so universal and so monstrous. Yet the title of Plavil'shchikov's standard exercise in nationalism is quite revealing: "Something on the Innate Quality of Russian Souls." The writer used the word "soul" to describe character. His argument was that he used "soul" while depicting character, because the former was not a loan-word; [60] yet a number of Russian words existed which were far more synonymous with "character" than was "soul." [61] For Plavil'shchikov all the great qualities of a Russian—intellectual, moral, and even physical —were contained in his soul, in a theological image.[62] But what kind of a soul was the Russian one? The poet N. A. L'vov gives us at least a partial answer:

> "The gigantic spirit of our ancestors
> To men of foreign lands appears
> As a madness supernatural!
> And yet how should it not be so
> For in foreign lands all is measured
> On a balance, words, on a yardstick, steps.
>
> .   .   .   .
>
> But for our own Orthodox,
> Fired is anything in his hands.

58. On the views of these writers, cf. *Rogger*, 19ff.

59. "Nechto o vrozhdenom svoistve dush russkikh," *Zritel'* (St. Petersburg, 1792), no. 3, 173, in Rogger, *H.S.S., 4*, 32, n. 42.

60. Rogger, *H.S.S., 4*, 31.

61. Cf. Dal's dictionary under *"Kharacter"* for synonyms, e.g., *"nrav."*

62. On the mechanical and artisan qualities of the Russian soul, cf. Rogger, *H.S.S., 4*, 32.

> Like a thunderbolt is his speech,
> From his words sparks are everywhere,
> In his steps whirls the dust about." [63]

The Russian soul is an Orthodox one; in fact no other characterization of a Russian is necessary, and the synonym "Russian" and "Orthodox" rings a familiar note for us. Describing a Russian, L'vov necessarily draws on the myth of the people, for there was nothing in the ruler-myth any longer which could help him answer his question.

Yet a new element enters the story here, and one which becomes central. The writers quoted above serve to illustrate the confusion and mingling of the myths; gentry, representatives and products of the Empire, *Rossiia,* they drew on the myth of the people. But their words raise more problems than they answer. Why the sudden search for national identity? and why the search for the Russian soul, for the qualities of a Russian, i.e. for the image of an individual, when the only mythical individual was the ruler, and "Holy Russia" was a collective, concretely and transcendentally? To try to answer these questions within the scope of this study would be impertinent. Yet some kind of an answer must be suggested in order to introduce properly the new element in our story, the *tertium quid* in the equation Tsar and People—what we shall call here the "intelligentsia."

Rogger's explanation, that the gentry's search for national identity was a reaction to the challenge of western cultural identity, is certainly correct; but, for our purpose, it does not go far enough. The challenge of the West had, after all, existed for a long time.[64] And the Russian reaction, one of utter rejection of Western habits, customs,

---

63. "Neizdannye stikhi N. A. L'vova," *Literaturnoe Nasledstvo, 9/10* (1933), 275.

64. One can begin it with the importation of artists by Ivan III at the end of the fifteenth century.

modes, and thought, was well enough established to have
become, in the eighteenth century, the subject of numerous
satires.[65] But when the Russians rejected the offers to grant
the Russian ruler the title of king, or when they rejected
attempts to change their modes of life, this was consistent
with their myths.[66] The Russian ruler as king would be a
betrayal of the ruler-myth, just as changes in habits and
customs would distort their outward behavior which was
an expression of their inward fulcrum—orthodoxy, the
mark of their salvation and of Russia's holiness. Whatever
tensions existed between the two myths, they were both
within the same enclosed universe, and would provide the
same reaction to anything outside their world.

With the secular absolutist state, the image of the ruler,
as we have seen, preserved the traditional aspects of the
ruler-myth. Yet the basic antagonism between it and the
myth of the people became more and more explicit, for
the image of the emperor contained many aspects which
could not be identified as Russian; in superficialities at
least, the empire and emperor borrowed widely from the
outside, the West. For the upper class, the gentry, which
followed the new ruler-image and which, in fact, was
created and molded by the new ruler and state, a question
would necessarily arise: with their duties and habits, they
were not of "Holy Russia"; what, then, were they? Implicitly at least, the answer was that they were of the State,
of the ruler. That they had an awareness, however, of the
ideological gulf growing between the State and the people
the aristocratic Guards regiments revealed in the overthrow of Peter III.

Whatever their awareness, the problem does not appear

65. Cf. Fonvizin's great satire, "*Brigadir*," *Polnoe Sobranie Sochinenii*
(St. Petersburg-Moscow, 1888), 61–102.
66. On the offer of the royal title and Russian reaction, cf. Prozorovsky,
"O znachenii," *I.R.A.O., 8*, no. 6, 449–77.

to have been acute during the first half of the eighteenth century. Necessarily so, for one can argue that a precise date can be given on which the problem of gentry self-identification could become acute. On February 18, 1762, the unfortunate Peter III released the gentry as a class from obligatory state service. In other words, on that date a whole class was created, the only educated class and one which was no longer, inherently, part of the State. But because of its very education, Western in character, imposed by the state, neither was it of the people. Two entities existed in Russian history reflected by their myths: Tsar and People, for the myth of the ruler was strong enough to overwhelm the earlier attempts on the part of the aristocratic bureaucracy to create an ideology of its own. Now a third entity appeared which was neither of the Tsar nor of the People—an entity, however, only in a symbolic sense. Though the decree of Peter III "liberated" the gentry as a class, the government, the State, was still made up of the gentry. The choice for the gentry, to serve or not to serve, to identify with the State or not, had become an individual one; in the search for identity, therefore, the need arose for an individual image as well as for a collective one, for an image of a Russian as well as for an image of Russia. The central issue here was the possibility of choosing. The peasant masses, as we have seen, in their ideological rationalizations, accepted or rejected the State and its myth; their choice, however, did not affect their identity. For the gentry the impact of the problem was immeasurably greater and their ability to choose far more real. Caught, so to say, in a society constricted by the two great myths, the gentry had no identity at all; the solution lay in either creating a myth of their own or of identifying with the existing ones. And in confronting the two myths the choice was the more painful, for there was on the one side the appeal of the State in all of its power, glory, and familiar culture, and on the other the guilt over the fact that "Holy Russia" was the myth of enslaved masses, in servitude to the very class that was liberated and thus free to search for identity.

What one can anticipate, therefore, is an intensity and amount of concern, of emotional and intellectual vigor, which meant a new state in the history of our myths, indicated, however feebly, in the second half of the eighteenth century; for, as far as the gentry were concerned, the myths could provide both personal and collective identity and a rationale for their actions. But if we can expect that this new and numerically small group, due to the great emotional pressure, played a disproportionately great role in the history of our myths, we can expect even more. For this class, driven to find identity, also had a monopoly on education, culture, and thus on intellectual expression; it was, in other words, the intelligentsia. Through the centuries, the myth of the ruler and the myth of the people were expressed by individuals who were neither the ruler nor the collective people; they were, however, within the universe bound by the myths. Beginning with the late eighteenth century those who wrote about the myths (or about anything, for that matter), were no longer within; they were outside, trying desperately to understand what was within and become part of it. This search for understanding gave a new dimension to the problem. In the modern and final period the history of the myth of the ruler and the myth of the people was also the history of the myth of the intelligentsia.

This excursus on the intelligentsia may serve to justify the methodology used in dealing with the problem of the myths in the nineteenth and twentieth centuries. Even with the paucity of medieval material, a statistical method would be incorrect. Exactly because the modern period involves the intelligentsia, which wrote down just about everything it thought about, to prove the patterns and configurations of ideas through a comprehensive collation of all the material would be meaningless. The problem is not to demonstrate a majority or minority opinion. Because for the intelligentsia the myths were involved in the search for individual identity, they acquired the colorings of all the individual inclinations and differentiations. And, at the other extreme, there were many who, because of particular interests and problems, were not at all concerned with these myths. The purpose, rather, is to illustrate the possible uses of the myths, the meanings that could be assigned to them, the tendencies with which they were applied.

5. The New Orthodoxy

IT is difficult enough to periodize history, even without imposing "mythological" standards. Yet, in the case of the Russian nineteenth century, the solution is temptingly easy. Popular myths have been evoked, or have been made explicit, by great national crises, and 1812 could match, as a time of crisis, any of its predecessors. The literary reaction to 1812 has been characterized, correctly, as patriotic Romanticism,[1] and the poems of Derzhavin and Zhukovsky on the Napoleonic wars are full of noble sentiments on Russian heroism in battle and the glory of a soldier's death.[2] When one speaks of patriotism, however, it may become necessary to define the *patria* which is the object of the sentiment.

The Napoleonic invasion was, of course, a serious dan-

1. *Festschrift,* 287.
2. It is interesting to note that the poets who actually fought as soldiers in the war of 1812, such as Batiushkov and Prince Viazemsky, wrote very little poetry on the subject. Warlike romanticism was obviously easier in St. Petersburg than in Moscow in 1812.

ger to the Russian state. The danger was the greater, however, because of the French policy, at the beginning of the
war at least, to promise the serfs emancipation. The threat
to Russia consisted not only in the possibility of military
defeat, but also in the possibility that the overwhelming
majority of Russians would not regard the invasion as a
danger to themselves.[3] Hence, the ideological problem was
to associate the population with the government in a unity
called Russia; the psychological problem was to make this
"Russia" convincing, and, perhaps more important, to
convince oneself, as member of the governing class, that the
unity did exist and that one was also a part of it.

The search for unity found, at the start, an easy object
in the most obvious and prevalent symbol of Russia—the
ruler. Russian memoirs of the Napoleonic wars are full of
the discovery, or rather the rediscovery, that the Russian
Emperor was also the pious and orthodox Tsar, and even
the saintly prince.[4] S. N. Glinka described the reception of
the Tsar in Moscow (July 1812) by the population; as one,
the masses of Moscovites greeted Alexander I: "Father!
Our Father! Let us look at you! . . . Our Father! Our
Angel! . . . Long Live the Tsar, our Sovereign [*tsar-
gosudar*]! Lead us where Thou [in the familiar second

3. One illustration of this fear is in the memoirs of the famous parti-
san, General Denis Davydov; when he captured a Russian peasant who
had taken the French promises seriously and killed all the gentry he
found, Davydov claimed that "this prize was more valuable than 200
Frenchmen." V. V. Kallash, *Dvenadsatyi God* (Moscow, 1912), 120.

4. This rediscovery could take on some fantastic forms. Among them
one should list the medals designed in honor of the war and victory
by count Feodor Tolstoy. One of them shows the emperor as a legendary
Russian hero, and is inscribed "The Rodomysl of the 19th century." The
Emperor is wearing Russian medieval armor, as are all the figures of
Russians on the other medallions, designed in the most ridiculously classical mode. This appears to be the extent of Russification on Tolstoy's part;
*Medalliony v Pamiat' voennykh sobytii 1812, 1813, i 1815 godov, izobre-
tennye grafom F. Tolstym*, Arkheograficheskaia Kommissiia (St. Peters-
burg, 1838).

person singular] will! . . . Our Angel! May the Lord
God guard you!" [5] The courtier Valuev, commenting on
this reception, said to the emperor: "Your Majesty, seeing
you and the people looking at you, one would say that the
common father of the great family of the Russian people
is eating his bread and salt among his joyous intimate
family," but for Glinka himself this was too colorless an
explanation:

"In the heart of the Russian tsardom, within the walls
of Moscow . . . Emperor Alexander was convinced that
Russia will stand in Russia; he saw that . . . the Russian
spirit was fired by the two-centuries old life of the great
times of the citizen Minin and prince Pozharsky . . .
Alexander was embellished not by the diadem but by the
love of the people, gazing at him with the eyes of the soul
and the heart . . . On the altar of pure love, selfless love
. . . the people gladly lay down possessions and life. And
the tribute brought that day, speaking in the words of
Zhukovsky, was: 'Not to the power, not to the crown, but
to the man a tribute!' " [6]

Glinka's views were quite typical, and they become even
more clear when we find that he was complimented, in
1808, for placing on the cover of his journal, *Russkii Vestnik,* the portraits of Dimitry Donskoi and Tsar Alexis.[7]
The acclamations which Glinka reported, however accurately, contained everything he was trying to convey:
the Russian tsardom, with the beloved, Angel-like Tsar
surrounded by his adoring orthodox people, firm in their
faith as they were two hundred years earlier, when faith and
tsar were threatened. The cover of *Russkii Vestnik* com-
pletes the imagery: Dimitry Donskoi, sainted for his de-

5. "Iz Zapisok S. N. Glinki," Kallash, 82–3.

6. Kallash, 83, 82.

7. Kallash, 72. One of the comments came 34 years later. M. P. Pogodin,
the Slavophile historian, wrote Glinka that the journal and its cover, in
1808 "inspired in me the first feeling of love for the fatherland."

fense of Russia, alongside Tsar Alexis, the Most-Gentle, most pious Tsar, evoked an image of the Russian Tsar which could and did inspire the people to rise to his and Russia's defense.

The problem is, however, more complicated. It was the gentry, the ruling class, not the people, who rediscovered the pious Russian tsar. The need for popular support was a very real, not to say desperate one, and the image of the tsar which was evoked was chosen because it was, or was assumed to be, popular.[8] The gentry were expressing both their belief and their hope when they felt that, with this new image of the ruler, the war had become a national one.[9] If, however, the ruler was the popular tsar, to whose call the people had responded so heroically and so completely, what was the tsar ruling, what were the Russian people? Glinka again suggested an answer. In 1806, when a call for a militia was issued, Glinka, traveling in the country, came across a large group of peasants who were tying each other up in order to convey the weaker ones to the *"militsiia."* Our patriot rushed into the crowd and cleared up the misunderstanding which was due to the use of a foreign word: "You are frightened by the word *militsiia.* This means—the army of the land [*voisko zemskoe*]. And this army is gathering on its own land, for its own land, for its fields, for the graves of its fathers, for

8. The accuracy of this image is quite probable. The war of 1812 certainly possessed, in the popular imagination, apocalyptic overtones. The popular reaction to the "Fatherland War," *Otechestvennaia Voina,* however, was a curious one. To a great number of Russian peasants Napoleon was Antichrist, and the war in which they were led by their tsar was a holy one; but there is some evidence that the Antichrist legend was promulgated by the government, cf. Glinka in Kallash, 63. At the same time sects appeared which worshipped Napoleon as Christ, come for the second time; the cult continued past the middle of the century; cf. Andreev, *Raskol,* 291–92.

9. Cf. Prince P. A. Viazemsky, "Vospominanie o 1812 gode," Kallash, 229.

everything with which God has endowed our Russian
land, which he ordains us to keep and to hold in it. I am
such a Christian as you. Here is my cross." [10] Count Feodor
Rostopchin, the notorious Moscow commander-in-chief,
felt that in dealing with the common folk one must know
the four sayings which, he was sure, expressed their essential character: "Great is the Russian God. Serve the tsar
with faith and truth. One cannot die twice. What is fated,
is fated." [11]

That answers even more ludicrous were provided is well
illustrated by the famous proclamations in a supposedly
popular style, issued by this same Rostopchin for popular
consumption in Moscow. Yet in one of them, written
probably in the worst taste of all, Rostopchin hit upon a
valid image: "Remain, brothers, obedient Christian soldiers of the Mother of God, do not listen to empty words!
Respect your commanders and estate owners [pomeshch-
ikov]; they are your guardians and helpers . . . Let us
destroy the remaining enemy forces, let us bury them in
Holy Russia . . . He [the Tsar] relies upon Almighty
God, on the God of the Russian Land . . . He alone is the
anointed of God . . . He is the Father, we are His children, while the evil Frenchman is the unbaptized [nekresh-
chenyi] enemy." [12] The point, of course, is not to register
the very first use of the epithet "Holy Russia" by the governing class. Glinka, writing his memoirs many years later,
assigned the epithet to 1808; [13] The poet K. N. Batiushkov
used it in 1812, before Moscow was captured by the

10. Kallash, 64–5.
11. "Iz zapisok grafa F. V. Rostopchina," Kallash, 8: *Velik russkii Bog.
Sluzhit' tsariu veroi i pravdoi. Dvum smertiam ne byvat'. Chemu byt' togo
ne minovat'.*
12. *Rostopchinskie Afishi 1812 goda,* ed. A. S. Suvorin (St. Petersburg,
1889), 50–51.
13. Kallash, 74.

French.[14] Suffice it to say that the epithet appeared in con-
junction with the "Fatherland War" of 1812.

The meaning of the epithet in Rostopchin's proclamation is quite clear: "Holy Russia" is the Christian, Orthodox Land, the land of piety and of God. The proclamation
drew the logical consequence of the content of "Holy Russia": While Russia was a Christian land, she was holy because she was the only Christian land, the only land where
salvation was possible. Hence it was proper to speak of the
"Russian God" (*Russkii Bog*), an epithet as unique as
"Holy Russia," [15] and which entered the history of the
myth at that time. The "Russian God" did not mean a
territorial limitation of divinity, but neither did it stand
for the Russian equivalent of "Gott mit uns." God was
universal and infinite, the Father of all men, but as Russia
was the only holy land, He must stand in a unique relationship to it. Or, rather, in order for Russia to have become
Holy, God must have manifested himself in a unique way
to the Russians, displayed an aspect of himself which explained and justified Russian holiness. To put it another
way, if the uniqueness of Russia required the transcendental adjective of "Holy," then the uniqueness of God,
at least as far as Russia was concerned, required the ma-
terialistic adjective "Russian." The logic of the argument,
as with all myths, was perfect and circular.

While the meaning of "Holy Russia," written in so casually by Rostopchin, corresponded to the popular myth
and even elaborated on it, the setting of the epithet was
unusual. For Rostopchin, "Holy Russia" was not antithet-

14. *Sochineniia K. N. Batiushkova* (5th ed., St. Petersburg, 1887) 201.

15. Rostopchin's claim that the "Russian God" was a commonplace
among the people (cf. n. 11) cannot be substantiated on the basis of the
available sources. There is no reason, however, to think that the count
had invented the term himself. Considering the logic of the epithet, the
likelihood of its common usage is great.

ical to the State or the emperor; on the contrary, "Holy Russia" was the Russian people, led and guided by God through the tsar. The quality of Russian Christianity was expressed in the tsar, who was the antithesis to the non-Christian Napoleon. In other words, "Holy Russia" and the holy tsar formed a harmonious unity in which the tsar predominated, and which the tsar's image defined. The myth of the people was appropriated for the ruler-myth by Rostopchin, in the same way as Pugachov tried to appropriate the myth of the Sovereign Emperor for his popular purposes. That this appropriation could be dangerous, considering the role of the peasants during the war and their status after it, the government knew; none of the imperial proclamations, calling for loyalty and sacrifice, contained anything resembling a popular conception or language.[16] Yet "Holy Russia" could be conjoined, not with a "foreign" westernized emperor, but with the Russian Tsar, pious, orthodox and saintly in person as well as in office, who would restore the ideal balance between tsar and people.

When victory was achieved in 1814, the Senate met in solemn session together with the State Council and the Holy Synod, in order to find a proper expression of their

16. The discomfort and embarrassment of at least some members of the ruling class was revealed by Alexander I himself. The emperor refused to approve the draft of the great victory proclamation of 1815. The proclamation listed the achievements of the various classes of Russian society, and the rewards given them by the emperor. The last class, the peasants, were informed that God will render them their due, while they are to continue to obey their owners, for the eventual benefit of both. Alexander personally struck out this edifying sentence. Cf. *Zapiski Mneniia i Perepiska Admirala A. S. Shishkova*, eds., N. Kiselev, Iu. Samarin, *1* (Berlin, 1870), 303f. Interesting to note, the admiral-literateur Shishkov, who had drafted this proclamation, had written all of Alexander's wartime manifestoes and decrees. The admiral explained Alexander's reluctance to approve the draft by the emperor's unfortunate education at the hands of the revolutionary Swiss, La Harpe (309, n. 1). For the text of the imperial proclamations, cf. *Shishkov, 1*, Appendix.

love and admiration for the emperor. Unanimously the governing institutions of Russia decided that their feelings, representative of the Russian people, could be best expressed by giving the emperor a new and personal title— "The Blessed" (*Blagoslovennyi*). For, as the dignitaries pleaded in their petition, which was carried to the emperor by three envoys picked for their first name, Alexander:

"What shall we render to You, Who has ensured the safety of our Fatherland . . . What praises can be equal to You Who has punished the arrogant foe . . . who had desired to subdue all tsardoms and peoples under his iron sceptre! Exalting You as victor, we also bless Your mercy . . . Who among the rulers of the earth is equal to You! . . . The Universe, awed by Your greatness . . . has awarded You all possible titles. You, however, the worthy elect of the All-highest, assigning all Your great deeds only to His benevolent Will . . . with Your modesty silence our mouths. Obeying You, Sovereign, we will not offend by loud praises Your gentleness . . ." [17]

One hears familiar echoes from the *vitae* of St. Alexander Nevsky and St. Dimitry Donskoi resounding in the St. Petersburg of 1814. And, for the nineteenth century, *Aleksandr Blagoslovennyi* was an equivalent for what, in earlier centuries, would have been St. Alexander.

The effect was obvious: for the Blessed Tsar, as for the saintly princes, the myth of the people, of "Holy Russia," should not be as dangerous as it was for the Sovereign Emperor. In effect, "Holy Russia" was an adjunct of the tsar; the tsar was not the "Blessed" because he ruled over Russians, but Russia could be "Holy" ruled by such a tsar. Consequently "Holy Russia" could, and did, become

17. Cf. Shishkov, 469f.; *P.S.Z.*, No. 25,629; *Sbornik Istoricheskikh Materialov izvlechennykh is Arkhiva Perv. Otd. Sobst. E.I.V.Kantseliarii* (St. Petersburg, 1876), 120f. The envoys were prince Alexander B. Kurakin, Alexander P. Tormasov and count Alexander N. Saltykov; cf. *Sbornik*, 123 and n. 1.

an innocuous commonplace among the upper class, an epithet which casually embraced it too, due to the overarching image of the emperor-tsar.[18] But the submergence of the myth of the people in that of the ruler did not fully solve the problem of "Holy Russia." Many of the gentry-intelligentsia who had accepted the idea of a Peoples' War, of a National unity, in 1812, were aware that the popular myth, the myth of "Holy Russia" was the myth of slaves who had remained slaves and that the question of what they themselves were remained for the gentry. The most dramatic formulation of the problem comes from the pen of P. G. Kakhovsky. A participant in the Decembrist revolt of 1825, Kakhovsky wrote to the new emperor, Nicholas I, while imprisoned in the *Petropavlovskaia* fortress, awaiting the death sentence: "It is a bitter thing for a Russian not to have a nation, and to terminate everything in the Sovereign alone." [19]

Was this bitterness justified, was there nothing for a Russian to focus on except the ruler? In the fairy-tale opening of *Ruslan i Liudmila,* Pushkin describes a magic place where a cat on a golden chain tells stories and sings songs, where the wood-spirit and the river mermaid live, where "on unknown paths/Are tracks of never-seen beasts," where all the Russian folk-tales are true, "There's the Russian

18. How casual a commonplace it became can be illustrated by a single example. General Count Benkendorff, a German educated in Bayreuth and at the famous Jesuit *pension* of Abbé Nicole in St. Petersburg, wrote to his old friend, Count (later Prince) M. S. Vorontsov, brought up and educated in England and who, like Benkendorff, thought, spoke, and wrote in French. The subject of the letter was the good treatment extended to Benkendorff's command which was quartered in the provinces, by the local population. Benkendorff commented: "C'est incalculable ce qu'on peut faire de la bonne volonté des gentilshommes, de la richesse et de la prospérité croissante de notre Sainte Russie." *Arkhiv Kniazia Vorontsova,* ed. P. Bartenev (Moscow, 1889), *35,* 186.

19. *Iz Pisem i Pokazanii Dekabristov,* ed. A. K. Borozdin (St. Petersburg, 1906), 30.

spirit . . . it smells of Russia!"[20] What was this Russia for Pushkin, what kind of a solution to Kakhovsky's question did it offer?

The epithet "Holy Russia" occurs quite frequently in Pushkin's writings. In *Boris Godunov* Pushkin describes the approach of the False Dimitry, at the head of his army, to the Russian frontier. One of his followers, the young Prince Kurbsky, son of the exiled enemy of Ivan the Terrible, gallops up to the border and exclaims: "Here, here it is, here's the Russian border! Oh Holy Russia, my fatherland, I'm yours!"[21] It is more than likely that Pushkin, in his historical research for his great drama, read the writings of the elder Kurbsky and gave his words to the son. The meaning of the epithet, in that case, is quite clear. "Holy Russia" was the great and immutable ideal, through which one could identify oneself as a Russian, and by which one could judge even tsars, who were within "Holy Russia" and only a part of it. In terms of this ideal the elder Kurbsky judged Ivan IV to be a tyrant, and his son judged the same of Boris Godunov. One could speculate further, for there is an interesting parallel between the Kurbskys, members of the great boiar opposition of the sixteenth century, and Pushkin, a member of the liberal aristocratic opposition of the early nineteenth; and Pushkin's insistence upon his great lineage is, sometimes, overdone. In this sense, "Holy Russia" was an answer to Kakhovsky, a patriotic rather than a popular one; Pushkin was offering the *otechestvo, patria* as something greater than the ruler, and he undoubtedly remembered that in the days of the most recent tyranny, during the reign of Paul I, the emperor had struck the word *otechestvo* from the language and had ordered, as synonymous, *gosudarstvo,* "state."[22]

20. *"Tam russkii dukh. . . . tam Rusiu pakhnet!"*

21. Scene xiv; *"Vot, vot ona! Vot russkaia granitsa! Sviataia Rus', otechestvo, ia tvoi!"*

22. Cf. Khakhovsky's complaint about this, in Borozdin, *Iz Pisem',* 14.

If in *Boris* Pushkin gave his own particular interpretation of "Holy Russia," what was his reaction to the epithet in its popular, mythical sense? In the eighth chapter of *Evgeny Onegin,* the so-called "Travels," Onegin returns home: "Onegin rides: for he shall see Holy Russia, her fields,/ her deserts, cities and her seas." [23] The context of the novel, the description of life in Russia and Onegin's activities, makes the use of the epithet ironic. But if some doubt remains about Pushkin's meaning in *Onegin,* little of it is left when reading his "First Epistle to the Censor": "Tell me, are you not ashamed that in Holy Russia/Because of you no books are to be seen?" [24] And still less when one reads the letter to his younger brother, Lev. Trying to get his *congé* and refused twice, Pushkin wrote from Odessa where he had been exiled: "There is one thing left—to write directly to him [the tsar]—such and such, in the Winter Palace, that is opposite the Peter-and-Paul fortress; or perhaps one should quietly take one's hat and cane and go off to see Constantinople. Holy Russia is becoming intolerable for me. *Ubi bene ibi patria.* And for me, it is *bene* there where I don't care, my brothers." [25] Pushkin, in his own age, rejected "Holy Russia," because it was appropriated by the ruler. "Holy Russia" is the Russia of the censor, the Russia of the emperor, crude and unjust.[26]

23.   "*Onegin edet: on uvidit.*
                 Sviatuiu Rus', eia polia
                 Pustyni, grady i moria."

24. "*Skazhi, ne stydno li, chto na Sviatoi Rusi/Blagodaria tebia, ne vidno knig dosele?*"

25. "*A mne bene tam, gde rastet trin-trava, bratsy.*" Letter to L. S. Pushkin, January (after the 12th), 1824. Considering the number of Pushkin editions that are available, a specific reference to any one would only be confusing.

26. Cf. Pushkin's letters to Viazemsky, 6 February 1823, L. S. Pushkin November (20?) 1824, M. P. Pogodin, July 1, 1828. In all, the epithet was used consistently and with bitterness. That Pushkin was not alone in

The poet's ambivalence towards the epithet was a rejection of the logic of the myth, and hence of its utilization. While he accepted "Holy Russia" as the popular symbol for a popular ideal, he rejected its claim to reality. Instead of justifying reality by the myth, Pushkin used the epithet to question the Russia and tsar of reality. Implicit in his use of "Holy Russia" were two alternatives: the rejection of the popular myth, corrupted as it was by the association with the myth of the ruler, or its acceptance as an ideal, a standard by which to judge reality; and, if reality is found lacking, he must condemn it.

If Pushkin did not accept the myth of "Holy Russia" as pressed into the service of the State since 1812, then what of his image of the ruler? Most powerfully and dramatically it is shown in his *Bronze Horseman.*[27] The Introduction is a paean of praise to Peter I and his City, which he created out of nothing, against the forces of man and nature, by his will alone. Part I describes the great flood of 1824, when the Neva overflowed its banks and swept through the city. Men were helpless before the fury of nature; Emperor Alexander I, sick at heart, sent his aides out to do whatever they could but he knew that "Tsars cannot overcome God's elements." The victim-hero of the poem, the young poet Evgeny, found himself, at the height of the flood, astride one of the marble lions on the Senate square. Obsessed with fear for the life of his fiancée who lived on one of the islands of Peter's city, he suddenly saw the one unshaken and unshakeable object in the chaos, the bronze statue of Peter on horseback by Falconet:

---

his views can be seen from one of the earliest uses of the epithet, by Batiushkov, in 1812; cf. Batiushkov, 200–01.

27. For recent literature in English, cf. C. M. Bowra, "Pushkin," *Oxford Slavonic Papers, 1* (1950), 1–15; W. Lednicki, *Pushkin's Bronze Horseman,* U. of Calif. Publ. Slavic Studies, *1* (Berkeley, 1955). My own interpretation draws heavily on Professor Lednicki's work.

> There, on high,
> With Neva still beneath him churning,
> Unshaken, on Evgeny turning
> His Back, and with an arm flung wide,
> Behold the Image sit, and ride
> Upon his brazen horse astride! [28]

In Part II, the flood having receded, Evgeny, finding that his beloved was dead, goes mad. In his wanderings about the city he returns to the square and sees the horseman:

> Appalling there
> He sat, begirt with mist and air.
> Proud charger, whither art thou ridden,
> Where leapest thou? and where, on whom,
> Wilt thou plant thy hoof?—Ah, lord of doom
> And potentate, 'twas thus, appearing
> Above the void, and in the hold
> A curb of iron, Thou sat'st of Old
> O'er Russia, on her haunches rearing.

The poor madman shakes his fist at the one he considers responsible for his own unhappiness, and is punished:

> For now he seemed to see
> The awful Emperor, quietly,
> With momentary anger burning,
> His visage to Evgeny turning!
> And rushing through the empty square,
> He hears behind him as it were
> Thunders that rattle in a chorus,
> A gallop ponderous, sonorous,
> That shakes the pavement. At full height,
> Illumined by the pale moonlight,
> With arm outflung, behind him riding
> See, the bronze horseman comes, bestriding
> The charger, clanging in his flight.
> All night the madman flees; no matter

28. I've used the translation by Oliver Elton, *Verse from Pushkin and Others* (London, 1935), 159ff.

> Where he may wander at his will,
> Hard on his track with heavy clatter
> There the bronze horseman gallops still.

Pushkin tells us of the individual, a poet, crushed, driven mad, and killed by the overwhelming, elemental power that is the ruler. But his image of the ruler is again ambivalent. Alexander I, as emperor, submits before the divine power of nature, yet Peter had mastered it, and Pushkin's love and loyalty are for the expression of that mastery, the new imperial city, St. Petersburg, which replaces the old symbol of the Russian tsardom, Moscow.[29] The elemental quality of Peter's will is monstrous, yet it seems that his Creation is worth the flood and the tragedies which ensue. For poor Evgeny, for the individual, there is no choice, no solution. In other words, the individual cannot find his personal solution in the ruler, whose interests are antithetical, yet the Sovereign Emperor is justified if he has a purpose higher than himself: the good of his country, of Russia. Because this was Peter's purpose in creating St. Petersburg, the bronze emperor was justified in pursuing one who was too small to see the great goal.

Here is the key to Pushkin's ambiguity. He rejected the old ruler-myths revived in 1812, and the popular myth which was also being used to justify present reality.

His acceptance of the Sovereign Emperor, however, was not total, and frequently in his writings he referred to Peter I as a revolutionary; his own aristocratic prejudices made him look with great disfavor on the consequences of the Petrine revolution.[30] Yet, despite this, he accepted Peter's revolution and the concept of Russia which derived from it. Rejecting the myths of the "Blessed Tsar" and

29. On Pushkin's views of St. Petersburg, cf. Lednicki, 43f.

30. For references on Pushkin's views of Peter I, cf. *Dnevnik A. S. Pushkina,* Trudy Gos. Rumian. Museia, *1* (Moscow-Petrograd, 1923), 506f.

"Holy Russia," Pushkin accepted the idea of the State, i.e. of Russia as a state led by the emperor towards a future ideal. The myth of the ruler and the myth of the people were replaced, in effect, by the myth of revolution: revolution not in the tradition of "Holy Russia," not in the popular tradition of Bolotnikov, Razin, or Pugachov, but revolution through and with the State. It was this conception which infused the Russian revolutionary intelligentsia until 1917, when it saw that the popular idea of revolution was much closer to Pugachev than to Peter I. Pushkin's own ideas justified his patriotism, his defense of the Russian state.[31] The poet's personal solution is expressed in the following passage from one of his last poems, "Monument":

Through all great Russia's spaces shall my name be spoken,
And every living tongue of man my name shall tell;
Proud breed of Slav, and Finn, and Tungus still unbroken,
And Kalmuck whom the steppe knows well.

And I shall for long years be loved by all the nation
Because for noble passions with my lyre I call,
Because in pitiless days I prayed for liberation,
Asked clemency for those who fall.[32]

For his personal salvation, Pushkin needed neither ruler nor people. But not many could escape the myths of their society through personal apotheosis. In the poet's works we find all the aspects and uses of the myths, reflected and commented upon: the revived image of the Holy Tsar superimposed on "Holy Russia"; "Holy Russia" as a national ideal, apart and opposed to the ruler; the Sovereign Emperor, supreme and absolute; and, in a new twist, the Sovereign Emperor associated with the na-

31. See his patriotic and chauvinist poems: "To the Calumniators of Russia," "Borodino," "Refutation of M. Berangér" et al.

32. 3rd and 4th verses, translated by C. M. Bowra, A Book of Russian Verse, ed. C. M. Bowra (London, 1943), 22.

tional myth of Russia. Pushkin's contemporaries and his successors pursued all these possibilities.

Many of them were aware of the problem raised by Pushkin: the primacy of reality over myth, or of the myth over reality. In his memoirs, Prince Viazemsky, a close friend of Pushkin, discussed the disgrace of M. M. Speransky under Alexander I and his return to the government under Nicholas I: "What would have happened if Speransky . . . would not have lost the sovereign's trust? What would have happened? It is difficult to answer this question. Perhaps only the Russian God knows the answer . . . One can suppose that perhaps we have thought up the Russian God because so much happens with us outside the laws which rule the rest of creation . . . In the same way that the Russian God had advanced Speransky, He pushed him aside." [33] To explain Russia, Viazemsky has need of the Russian God, even though he makes no use of "Holy Russia"; but the latter is implicit in the idea of the Russian God. This idea, however, could impose a standard of judgment, and in 1828 Viazemsky wrote to his friend, A. I. Turgenev: "Russian patriotism can consist only of hatred for Russia, such as she appears to us . . . Any other love for the fatherland among us I find incomprehensible." [34] The poet worded his dilemma much more strongly, at about the same time, in a poem entitled "The Russian God":

> God of road-ruts, god of snow-storms
> God of winding country roads
> God of bedless travel stations—
> That's him, that's the Russian god.
>
> God of cold and god of hunger
> Beggars each and every way,

33. P. V. Viazemsky, *Staraia Zapisnaia Knizhka*, ed. L. Ginzburg (Leningrad, 1929), 145.
34. *Ibid.*, 337.

God of lands without a profit—
That's him, that's the Russian god.

God of alien newcomers,
Flooding over the threshold here,
God especially of Germans—
That's him, that's the Russian god.

God of all who wear an order.
God of lackeys without boots,
Of the masters who're like lackeys—
That's him, that's the Russian god.

Full of good will for the stupid,
Ruthlessly severe with brains,
God of everything that's awkward,—
That's him, that's the Russian god.[35]

For a short time, Viazemsky rejected the myth.[36] The myth of the Russian God was false because Russia did not live up to it, because it justified everything evil in Russian life and, in fact, exemplified it. Yet the rejection was not an unqualified one, for Viazemsky was attacking not so much the idea of a Russian God, as the distortion of the idea, its use by those who did not understand it.

The doubts which assailed Viazemsky at the confrontation of myth and reality place him in the generation of the Decembrists; of those who questioned the society for whose preservation the myths had been evoked. Yet if these doubts were strong, so was, apparently, the need to accept the myths, to find identification for oneself and one's society, even a negative one, with the distorted Russian God. An illustration of this tension can be found in Alexis Khomiakov, who in the '40s and '50s of the century became a founder and leader of Slavophile thought. In 1832 Khomiakov wrote a poem "Inostranke" ("To the foreigner"), addressed to a society beauty, A. O. Rosset. He describes

35. Viazemsky, 3, 452; for another, very similar version, see 450.
36. See below, chap. 6, for Viazemsky's later views.

the lovely girl from the south of Europe, whom he cannot
love:

> I sing to her a song of native land,—
> She does not listen, does not heed!
> Before her if I utter "Holy Russia!"
> Her heart won't tremble even here.[37]

What was it that her heart should tremble about, or rather,
why did Khomiakov's or any Russian heart tremble at the
sound of "Holy Russia!"? Philosopher and historian as
well as a member of the liberal gentry-intelligentsia,
Khomiakov was well aware of the evil in Russia, both past
and present.[38] If, in the facts of Russian life and history,
Russian holiness was not easily discernible, how was one to
identify it? Khomiakov's answer to this came in his poem
"*Rossii*," ("To Russia") written in 1839. He pleads with
Russia not to heed flatterers who speak of her physical
glory and might. Rome and the Mongols, mightier still,
had vanished, as everything based on arrogance and false
pride must vanish. "But because you are humble, because
with childish simplicity, in the depths of your heart, you
have accepted the Word of the Creator,—He has granted
you your bright fate: To safeguard for the world the treasure of high sacrifices and pure deeds; to safeguard the holy
brotherhood of peoples, the vessel of vivifying love, the
riches of fiery faith, and truth, and justice without
blood." [39]

The logic of the myth had triumphed. For Khomiakov,
"Holy Russia" was a given, a premise from which he started,

---

37. A. S. Khomiakov, *Polnoe Sobranie Sochinenii, 4* (Moscow, 1900), 209.
Quite rightly the fair recipient was very angry at the poem; cf. A. S.
Khomiakov, *Stikhotvoreniia*, ed. & comment by V. A. Frantsev (Prague,
1934), 143–44. Also see Khomiakov for evidence that the poem was probably written before 1832.

38. Cf. his articles in *Pol. Sobr., 3,* 11ff.

39. *Pol. Sobr., 4, 230.*

rather than a conclusion which he reached. To justify it, however, he had to separate "Holy Russia" from the state, from the empire, from everything that he assigned to false pride and arrogance induced by the flatterers. "Holy Russia" was the antithesis of all the earthly glory and power; it was described by humility, childlike simplicity and faith, qualities of the simple Russian people. Thus far, Khomiakov returned to the popular conception of the myth of the people. Yet he was not of the people, so that the argument could not stop at this point. The virtues of the people were demonstrated by the fact that they did not seek earthly glory, that they bled selflessly for other peoples' freedom; in effect, the virtues which manifested "Holy Russia" were virtues which explained the evil of Russian life. Russian conquests and government injustice were possible because the people were Christian, patient, humble, because power and conquest were not the things that mattered to them. The sharp antithesis between "Holy Russia" and the state was restored in Khomiakov's thought, but one can also see in it the beginning of that fantastic inversion which reached its fullest development with Dostoevsky. The proof of "Holy Russia" was contained, in a sense, in the misery of Russian life.

The myths, revitalized by 1812, were powerful enough and widespread enough to have involved, in varying degrees, the poets we have been discussing, members of the gentry-intelligentsia. The solutions they chose become the more understandable if we now examine other, less intellectual conceptions of Tsar and People. The immediate popular response to the ideological propaganda during the Napoleonic wars is difficult to judge because all the observations of popular patriotism came from the gentry, and Alexander I himself made no attempts to live up to the image of the Blessed Tsar, one with his Russian people. Yet there is striking confirmation that the old image, revived, made a strong impression on the masses. The emperor died in 1825 while at Taganrog on the sea of Azov. Within weeks of his death, before his body had reached St. Petersburg, the legend was current that he had not died, that the coffin contained the body of a common soldier and that the Tsar had gone away.[40] The legend persisted and, through the years, became more specific: Alexander I had gone away to wander over the Russian land, to live with and like the common people, suffering their pains. In the 1830s he was identified in the person of a mysterious hermit, Feodor Kuzmich. Feodor lived in various towns of Siberia after having been flogged and exiled for not owning a passport. He died in 1864, and, while it would be impossible to judge how widely the belief was held that he was Alexander I, he was listed as a saint because of popular adoration.[41]

The legend of Feodor Kuzmich exhibited the features of the saint-prince cult. At the same time, however, it displayed significant similarities to the legends which circulated in Russia after the death of Peter III. Certainly the legend was a manifestation of the enormous power of the ruler-myth; the person of the saint-tsar, adapted to nineteenth-century conditions, dominated popular political theory. Yet if the intention of government propaganda in 1812 was to conjoin all the aspects of the ruler with "Holy Russia," the propaganda failed. In the popular tradition, the image of the tsar, saintly in person and office, was appropriated into the myth of the people and hence became antithetical to the State. According to the legends, Alexander I fled the state, fled pomp and ceremony in order to live with his people, in order to destroy the wall be-

---

40. On the history of the legends and for all the literature on the problem, see Lev Liubimov, *Taina Imperatora Aleksandra I* (Paris, 1938). The author himself firmly believes in the "mystery" of Alexander's death.

41. Golubinsky, 343.

tween the ruler and "Holy Russia." [42] The danger for the
government, implicit in this appropriation, was manifested
very clearly during the long reign of Alexander's successor, Nicholas I (1825–1855). Thousands of peasants literally risked (and lost) their lives, in order to appeal directly
to the emperor against their oppressors, despite the law
that forbade the serf to complain against his master. Hundreds of peasant uprisings took place during the thirty
years of Nicholas I, for which the justification was the
utter conviction of the peasants that their tsar had decreed
their liberation, and that his order was being disobeyed
and suppressed by the gentry and the bureaucracy, that is,
by the State.[43] The Russian peasants had excellent reasons
for rebellion, without any mythological justifications; they
did not rebel because of the myth of the ruler, but the
image of the Blessed Tsar played a dual role. It manifested
a contradiction between the image of the benevolent state
and the reality of slavery, and it gave the peasants such
strong support that they, in their rebellions, withstood for
years incredibly brutal punishments without giving up
their cause.[44]

That the attempt to join together the secular state manifested in the Sovereign Emperor, and "Holy Russia"
should have failed among the peasants is not surprising.
Their idea of the State was far too clear and non-mythical,
while the image of the Blessed Tsar was familiar to them

42. In this connection, it is interesting to note that the early rumors
about Alexander's death were to the effect that he was kidnapped or
exiled by his enemies, the aristocracy, or that he fled in order to escape
assassination. Cf. Liubimov, 123f.

43. On peasant unrest, cf. V. Semevsky, *Krestianskii vopros v Rossii*
(St. Petersburg, 1888); E. Kots, "Volneniia krepostnykh v Nikolaevskuiu
epokhu," *Russkoe Proshloe*, 2 (1923), 74–88; N. Varadinov, *Istoriia Ministerstva Vnutrennykh del* (St. Petersburg, 1862), *5*, 123ff.; *4*, 58ff.

44. On the image of the tsar as protector of the common people, cf.
e.g., songs on the death of Peter, collected by Kireevsky during the reign
of Nicholas I, P. Kireevsky, *Pesni, 8,* 278ff.

through a long tradition. The incongruity and also the danger of such a synthesis was noted by Pushkin in 1834. Both he and Grand Duke Michael Pavlovich were furious about a description of the emperor's visit to Moscow, published in the officially patriotic *"Severnaia Pchela"*:

"After the parade, the Emperor went [*izvolil otpravit'sia*] to the Granovitaia Palace. Going up on the Red Steps [*Krasnoe Kryl'tso*] He turned to the square and bowed low to the people. Oh! what indescribable enthusiasm was reflected in the total, thunderous acclamation of the whole great crowd when the Lord of the Russian Land, great-grandson of the Great Peter, bowed his sacred head before the inhabitants of Moscow."

The writer was sorry that no enemy of Russia was present at the sight for: "He would then see of what the utterly unconquerable power of holy Russia consists." [45] The anger of Michael Pavlovich is comprehensible; as Pushkin pointed out, this business of the emperor bowing low would be read by all the tradesmen, and, Pushkin implied, give them wrong ideas. The image of the ruler bowing to his people, in close communion with them, belonged to the old days of a Tsar Alexis. It had no place in the ceremonial of the Emperor. Yet the article in the newspaper serves to illustrate the most extraordinary attempts made to synthesize the myths and to live up to the synthesis.

It is a truism to state that the reign of Nicholas I was the culmination of despotism. The nature of this despotism, however, was quite unique. Its ideological underpinnings were provided by the famous minister of education under Nicholas I, S. S. Uvarov. Russia, according to his formula, was contained in three ideas: Autocracy (*Samoderzhavie*), Orthodoxy (*Pravoslavie*), and Nationality

45. Pushkin, *Dnevnik*, 65 and 507. The editor of the diary cannot understand why the Grand Duke should have been angry over the low bow of the emperor.

(*Narodnost'*).[46] The meaning and the interrelations of these concepts in theory are difficult to determine. Yet even Uvarov's vague description gives us the relative weight of each idea:

"Genuinely and deeply devoted to the church of his fathers, the Russian looked at it, from time immemorial, as a guarantee of public and familial happiness. Without love for the faith of one's fathers, a people as well as an individual, must perish. The Russian, devoted to the fatherland, will as little consent to the loss of any single dogma of our *Orthodoxy*, as he would consent to the theft of a single pearl from the crown of Monomakhos. Autocracy is the main condition of Russia's political existence. The Russian colossus bases itself on it as on the keystone of its own greatness . . . Together with these two national principles there is a third, no less important, no less powerful: *Nationality*. The problem of nationality does not possess the same unity as the preceding ones; but all of them flow from a single source and are tied together on every page of the Russian tsardom. Concerning nationality, the whole difficulty was contained in agreeing ancient and modern views; but nationality does not force us to go backward or forward; it does not demand *immutability* of ideas . . . It would be wrong to oppose the natural flow of events in time; it is sufficient if we preserve unsullied the sanctuary of our popular conceptions." [47]

It is quite clear that Uvarov knew the ideas of German romanticism far better than he knew Russian myths, for

46. The difficulty of translating *"narodnost'"* accurately has faced every historian of this period. N. Riazanovsky gives as its closest meaning *Volkstumlichkeit*. In English he, too, translates it by "nationality"; cf. his *Russia and the West in the Teaching of the Slavophiles* (Cambridge, Mass., 1952), 9, n. 7. On the whole question of *narodnost'*, see N. Riazanovsky, *Nicholas I and Official Nationality in Russia 1825–1855* (Berkeley and Los Angeles, 1959).

47. S. S. Uvarov, "Desiatiletie Ministerstva Narodnago Prosveshcheniia 1833–1843 gg.," in *Epokha Nikolaia I*, ed. M. O. Gershenzon (Moscow, 1911), 110. On the origin of the formula, cf. N. Barsukov, *Zhizn' i trudy M. P. Pogodina, 4* (St. Petersburg, 1888–1910), 82–85.

otherwise he would not have separated orthodoxy and nationality for the Russians. Nevertheless his formula was a synthesis of the Russian myths, in which orthodoxy could serve as a third term, as a bridge from the Sovereign Emperor to the people by way of the pious, Orthodox Tsar.[48] But in the synthesis, the keystone was Autocracy. The paradox was that, while Autocracy was no better defined than the other terms of the new Trinity, it defined itself through each government action and therefore was the only standard available, the measure of all things.[49] In effect then, the synthesis broke down from the very beginning, for the myth of the people was absorbed in the myth of the ruler. But both the difficulty of analyzing the reign of Nicholas I and our fascination with it are due to the fact that the ruler-myth was expressed not in words as much as in actions. More than anyone else, apparently, Nicholas I believed in the image of the "Blessed Tsar."

A. I. Herzen, from his exile, gave an accurate description of the emperor:

"Nicholas wanted to be a tsar rather than an emperor, but failing to understand the Slavic spirit, he failed to reach his goal and limited himself to the persecution of any yearning for freedom, of any idea of progress . . . He wanted to create a military Byzantium out of his empire; hence his nationalism and orthodoxy, cold and icy like the climate of St. Petersburg . . . In his system there was no motor, and even nothing national; without becoming a Russian, he ceased to be a European. During his long

48. For the role of this official Orthodoxy, serving purely a state function, oblivious to the myth of the Orthodox people, see, for example, the sermons of the Metropolitan Filaret of Moscow, *Slova i Rechi, 3* (Moscow, 1845), 3ff., 165f., 305f., 509ff.

49. An illustration of this is in the memoirs of the military historian A. I. Mikhailovsky-Danilevsky. The revolt of December 1825 against the succession of Nicholas I was seen by him as also an attack against "Holy Russia." The issue is not in Mikhailovsky's hypocrisy but rather in the fact that autocracy, the emperor, was the expression and standard of "Holy Russia"; "Zapiski," *Russkaia Starina, 68* (1890), 508f.

reign he affected in turn nearly all institutions, introducing everywhere the element of paralysis, of death." [50]

Herzen gave an accurate picture both of Russia and of the emperor's intentions, but the question remains, in what way Nicholas I saw himself as tsar rather than emperor? His most famous or infamous institution was the corps of gendarmes, created in 1826 under the control of the "Third Section of the Personal Chancery of His Imperial Majesty." [51] The purpose of this organization was indicated in an apocryphal story: the emperor, asked for a statement of general policy by the chief of the new organization, Benkendorff, handed his general a handkerchief and said: "Here are all your instructions. The more tears you will wipe away with this handkerchief, the more you will reflect my purpose." [52] The fact that the whole episode is a legend is irrelevant. The Corps of Gendarmes was created as part of the Personal Chancery, in order to wipe away tears or to cause them, because Nicholas saw the fulfillment of the Tsar image in personal government. The gendarmes intruded into every aspect of Russian life, personal and institutional, exactly because Nicholas I saw them as the extension of his personal will; and his will as Tsar, as person, intruding into private lives, contradicting his own laws, could only be beneficial.[53] Examples of horror and of pettiness inherent in Nicholas I's system would not make the argument more convincing. The principle according to which Nicholas I formulated his system is sufficiently clear. When the Emperor decided cases that were being tried simultaneously in the law courts, when

50. A. I. Herzen, *Polnoe Sobranie Sochinenii i Pisem*, ed. M. Lemke, *8* (Petrograd, 1919), 54.

51. Cf. M. Lemke, *Nikolaevskie Zhandarmy i literatura 1826–1855* (St. Petersburg, 1909), 14f.

52. *Zhandarmy*, 17.

53. On this conception, and examples of what chaos followed, cf. Presniakov, *Russkoe Proshloe, 2.*

he punished without trial, when he ordered divorces and reconciliations, payments of dowries and debts of honor, when he ordered some men to be fired from their jobs, and ordered others to take jobs, the principle was the same.[54] The imperial system, the State with the Emperor at the head, went on functioning (though rather badly). Superimposed above it, however, was the Blessed Tsar, whose personal qualities and judgment were the real guarantee of justice and happiness. Though the great codification of Russian law was done under Nicholas I, on his orders, the emperor found it impossible to admit that his human impulses, exactly because they were his, and therefore just, could be limited by his own laws.[55]

While the State performed its essentially negative function of controlling and limiting individual desires and interests, the Tsar had the higher and positive function of guiding and ordering the individual to good deeds. Nicholas' "system," however, was more comprehensive even than this. If the tsar was truly the Blessed Tsar, his duty would be to guide and direct not only men's deeds but their thoughts and desires as well. And if the Russians, as a whole, were "Holy Russia," there would be a unanimity of opinion, a homogeneity of judgment which would make this guidance effective and easy at the same time. Physically and morally Russia should be a harmonious whole. It was this conception which made possible the monstrous intellectual oppression and obscurantism of Nicholas' censorship and educational program. Uvarov's purpose, ordered by the emperor, was to unify all Russian thought, to make all of it good and "well-

54. See the case of Prince P. V. Dolgorukov, who had enough courage to point out that the gentry had, since 1762, the right not to serve in the government, Lemke, *Zhandarmy*, 540–41.

55. This applied not only to laws. Nicholas dealt with the Imperial Budget in the same "human," "personal" way. Presniakov, *Russkoe Proshloe, 2,* 14.

disposed." [56] If there was a "Holy Russia," then those who thought differently, oddly, individually, were outside of it, against it; the Decembrists who attacked the emperor, with their Western ideas, were against "Holy Russia" too.[57]

It is agreed by historians that the system of Nicholas I failed politically (in the Crimean War) and ideologically. This last contention, however, requires some elaboration; success or failure in the realm of ideas is difficult to measure.[58] Practically, the centralized despotism of the emperor resulted in an anarchy, because there arose hundreds of petty despots, and his supralegalism resulted in universal corruption. In the realm of myths, however, the issue is not failure or success. Nicholas was able to maintain the identity of the people, of "Holy Russia," with the State. Unlike his older brother, he used the epithet in an official proclamation. On the occasion of the European revolutions of 1848, he wrote, rather hysterically: "We are ready to meet our enemies, wherever they may appear, and, without sparing ourselves, we will, in an indissoluble union with our Holy Russia defend the honour of the

56. Uvarov, in *Epokha Nikolaia I*, 110; "Tsenzura v tsarstvovanie imperatora Nikolaia I," 6, *Russkaia Starina, 113* (1903), 577ff. One may wonder whether the famous idea of Admiral Shishkov, Uvarov's predecessor as chief of censorship, that the purpose of censorship was to raise the level of Russian literature, did not derive out of a similar conception.

57. Cf. n. 49 for an example of this reasoning by Mikhailovsky-Danilevsky.

58. Perhaps Nicholas I himself would have regarded the testimony of an invalid veteran of his wars as supreme proof of success. Reminiscing about the late emperor, while in an appalling "home for veterans," one of the old soldiers defended the old way and discipline against the liberalization of the early years of Alexander II: "It used to be, when you were handed over (as a recruit) and had your head shaved, that your mother and all the others would weep over you, as if you were dead. Well, you really were dead: You belonged to God and the Tsar! (*Bozh'im da Tsarskim stal!*)"; "Iz vospominanii raznykh lits o Nikolae Pavloviche i ego vremeni," *Russkii Arkhiv* (1895:8), 186–87.

Russian name and the inviolability of our borders." [59]
That the epithet had other, contradictory meanings, for
the intelligentsia and the peasants, Nicholas I and his government knew. The intelligentsia, corrupted and non-
Russian in this sense, was the particular object of dislike
and concern. As for the peasants and the problem of serfdom, Nicholas' concern revealed yet another tension
within his mythmaking.

That serfdom contradicted "Holy Russia" and, in fact,
negated the whole conception of personal government,
was quite clear.[60] Yet Nicholas, discussing a project for a
very minor amelioration of peasant life in his State Council, formulated his position in the following words: "I am,
of course, absolute and autocratic [*samoderzhavnyi i
samovlastnyi*], . . . but I shall never *order* the gentry to
make any agreements." [61] The issue here is not the political
conservatism of Nicholas I which made him feel that even
though serfdom was evil and should be abolished, he will
do nothing about it, nor his political judgment that he
cannot alienate the gentry. None of these considerations
required such a statement from a man such as Nicholas I,
whose faith in his own absolutism and autocracy was total.
These words, however, Nicholas spoke as *emperor,* absolute and autocratic also, but in a different sense. As *emperor,* Nicholas I maintained the laws of his empire which

59. Cf. M. K. Schilder, *Imperator Nikolai Pervyi*, 2 (St. Petersburg, 1903),
629. The epithet appears very rarely indeed in the writings of the imperial family and high officials. One of the exceptions, also in connection with 1848, was in the diary of Grand Duke Konstantin Nikolaevich;
cf. A. S. Nifontov, *Rossiia v 1848 godu* (Moscow, 1949), 202.

60. Out of some 52 million Russians, *circa* 43 million were serfs, private
and state owned, and were not within Russian society; by law, they were
not in any real relation to the ruler. Cf. Presniakov, *Russkoe Proshloe*,
2, 14. For Nicholas' recognition of the moral and political need to abolish serfdom, cf. the memoirs of Baron M. Korf, in *Materialy i Cherty k
Biografii Imperatora Nikolaia I, S.R.I.O., 98* (1896), 101ff.

61. *S.R.I.O., 98* (1896), 110.

was based on the gentry and guaranteed the gentry's rights.

The example is not a striking one, but it serves to illustrate the fact that in his image of the Blessed Tsar, Nicholas included, consciously or unconsciously, the aspects of the Sovereign Emperor. And it was this that gave his conception such monstrous forms. We are reminded here of Herzen's image that the emperor stopped being a European without becoming a Russian, for Nicholas I tried to be a Tsar Alexis by means of his *fligel'-* and *general-adiutanty*. The myth of the Pious Tsar was executed through the secular state which was contained, for Russian emperors generally and for Nicholas particularly, in a military mold. This tension, or dualism, within the image of the ruler Nicholas could not and did not want, perhaps, to resolve. While the ladies of the court were ordered to appear, on formal occasions, in a nineteenth-century version of old Russian dress, in order to express Nationality, the emperor at all times wore his uniform, for which even Uvarov could not have found Russian antecedents. To repeat, there is no question of failure about Nicholas' attempt to live up to the myths of the Most-Gentle Tsar and the Sovereign Emperor. The result was the image of the Blessed Tsar, overwhelming in his power and in his person. But the difficulty of maintaining a balance between the two aspects and the danger of emphasizing the person of the ruler were reflected, ironically, in the case of Nicholas I, who had tried so hard to be the Blessed Tsar. In a century when every Russian ruler received a spiritual epithet—Alexander I the Blessed, Alexander II the Emancipator, Alexander III the Peacegiver (*Mirotvorets*)—Nicholas I was seen as the Colonel.[62]

For the intelligentsia, that *tertium quid* so hated by Nicholas I, the power and scope of the official conception, despite its internal tensions, only intensified the problem

62. Cf. Kakhovsky, in Borozdin, *Iz Pisem'*, 25.

pointed out by Pushkin. The myth of the people was over-whelmed and absorbed by the ruler-myth. Without it, the individual, lacking identity, stood helpless before the Bronze Emperor. But accepting "Holy Russia" meant either accepting its corruption and identification with the state mechanism, or accepting its original popular mean-ing, expressed vaguely by the masses who were utterly foreign to oneself. In the reign of Nicholas I the problem for the gentry-intelligentsia, as individuals and as Rus-sians, was to create a balance between ruler and people, to answer Kakhovsky's implicit plea.

The intensity of the problem, the feeling of crisis, can be illustrated by an event of the intellectual history of the time. In 1836 Peter Chaadaev published his famous "Philosophical Letters." [63] His thesis was simple and strik-ing: Russia has had no history, no culture or civilization; her people have contributed nothing to humanity and have absorbed virtually nothing of value from the civilized world; neither nationality nor religion are meaningful, applied to Russia. The work created a furor in all groups of the intelligentsia, and even the most Western-minded mem-bers of the gentry attacked Chaadaev for his views. The benevolent emperor declared the writer officially insane, with all the consequences which followed from this diag-nosis. Yet Chaadaev did not attack the ruler-myth.[64] What he brushed away were the other two members of the of-ficial trinity (religion and nationality), or, in other words myths of the people. The first answer Chaadaev received, one that was not published for many years, was from the editor of the journal in which he printed his letter, Pro-

63. P. Chaadaev, *Sochineniia i pis'ma,* ed. M. Gershenzon, *1* (Moscow, 1913), 74–142. On the publication and subsequent events, see M. Lemke, *Zhandarmy,* 402ff.

64. Even in his "Philosophical letter" Chaadaev gave all credit for whatever good was in Russia to Peter the Great, and this he emphasized still more in his later "Apology of a Madman."

fessor N. I. Nadezhdin.[65] There is little doubt that Nadezhdin was trying to get out of the extremely uncomfortable situation he got himself into by publishing the letter, yet the logic of his argument is revealing. In effect he agreed with Chaadaev, except for one significant difference. True, the Russian people had no history or civilization; what did exist was the Russian State, the creation of the Russian rulers. Everything that Russia achieved, everything that Russia was, was due to the ruler. This was cause for Russian pride and for Russian joy, and this was the supreme guarantee for the Russian future.[66]

Symbolically, this debate which never took place can serve as the starting point for a new stage in the development of our myths. In effect, Chaadaev had swept the ground clear for the intelligentsia. By denying the very existence of Russia as a recognizable entity, he forced the need for an answer. An image of the people, of Russia, had to be recreated, or, if necessary, created. But Nadezhdin, pushing the ruler-myth to its logical and absurd conclusion, illustrated the danger: the overwhelming image of the Tsar.

65. Cf. Lemke, *Zhandarmy*, 411ff.
66. Lemke, *Zhandarmy*, Appendix, 592–604.

6. *The Russian God*

"Holy Russia demands holy deeds."

—V. SOLOVIEV

THE gentry-intelligentsia rejected Chaadaev's conception, even though it offered a solution. For, if there was no such thing really as Russia, and if Western culture was the measure of all things, then the problem of self-identity could be solved rather positively by the only class which possessed Western culture. But if it was not possible for a generation imbued with the ideas of German patriotic Romanticism to abandon the idea of nationality, it was, to repeat, equally difficult to adopt the popular solution contained in "Holy Russia." The nature of this difficulty is best illustrated by one striking exception.

Sentenced to hard labor in Siberia for his participation in the Decembrist revolt, Prince A. I. Odoevsky continued to write poetry. In 1827, in answer to a poem of Pushkin's which offered sympathy and hope, Odoevsky proudly replied that "Behind the bars of our prison/In our hearts we laugh at tsars." [1] The cause is not forgotten or lost "And our

1. A. I. Odoevsky, *Polnoe Sobranie Strikhotvorenii i Pisem,* eds. I. A. Kubasov and D. D. Blagoi (Moscow-Leningrad, 1934), 116.

Orthodox people/Shall gather to our holy banner." The epithet "orthodox" the poet associated with a revolutionary people, who will rise against the tsars. He was more explicit in a historical poem on the Time of Troubles; in it, Liberty complained to the Russians:

> Oh Russians! I have been dear to you:
> I could breathe in the fatherland of the Slavs,
> And for me stood then Holy Russia
> . . . The Mongol fell; but slavish habits
> The people took as ancient ways.
> At princes' feet, forgetting its own glory.[2]

In the same historical cycle, in a poem on the siege of Smolensk, the people, on hearing the news that tsar Vasily Shuisky was overthrown, exclaim: "Vasily is uncrowned, but our tsar is Russia!" [3] More and more clearly Odoevsky developed the tsar-people antithesis, the inherent historical antagonism between the two, the betrayal of "Holy Russia" by the rulers and by the people who suffered the rulers.[4] The fullest expression of this view is in his "Verses on our transfer from Chita to Petrovskii Zavod." Lacking any rhyme, the poem is in the nature of a solemn hymn:

> What tents are visible
> Among the burning fires,—
> Gay fellows are going behind bars
> For Holy Russia.
> For Holy Russia prison and punishments—
> Joy and glory.
> Gaily will we die alive
> For Holy Russia.

Each verse, describing the journey, ends with the refrain of the last four lines. The last verse no longer deals with the trip:

2. "Deva. 1610 g. K. Vasiliiu Shuiskomu," *Pol. Sobr.*, 133.

3. "Osada Smolenska," *Pol. Sobr.*, 136.

4. See, for example, the long historical poem on the Kievan period, "Vasil'ko," *Pol. Sobr.*, 153 and *passim*.

Sleep, sullen slaves.
You've forgotten how to sing.
Awake! Free songs
Deafen you.
We glorify our Russia, in prison we sing
Holy freedom.
Gaily will we die alive
In the tomb for Holy Russia.[5]

In chains, in Siberia, deprived of all rights and of his gentry status, Odoevsky was a revolutionary who had broken openly with the Tsar and, through punishment, was one of the people. His path could not be followed by the gentry, dependent for its very existence on the imperial state, and more alienated from the peasants than the emperor for whom the "Blessed Tsar" provided a bridge. Odoevsky himself, hoping for an amnesty, wrote poems in which the Tsar and "Holy Russia" appeared in necessary and harmonious unity, and while one can debate the sincerity of his sentiments, it is clear that he saw such sentiments as proper, as a gage for re-entering the world.[6]

While Odoevsky's mythologizing was exceptional, his logic was more acceptable. If Russia was holy, then it must have specific and unique qualities, and these qualities must be recognizable in its history; but more than this, if "Holy Russia" was the essence of Russia, then at some time, in the past if not in the present, this essence must have been explicit, not just an adjunct of the Russian ruler. Hence Odoevsky sought "Holy Russia" in the Russian historical past, in legendary times or times of crises, and this procedure was followed by those who tried to establish the validity of the myth of the people, as well as by those who tried to deny it.

The attempt to define and clarify the concept of "Russia" took place within the context of what is called the

5. *Pol. Sobr.*, 190–91.
6. Cf. "Otsu," "Na proezd naslednika prestola v Sibir'" 1 and 2, *Pol. Sobr.*, 208–09, 213–221.

Slavophile-Westernizer controversy. The justification for discussing the thinkers of both camps here is not the desire to present the intellectual history of the mid-nineteenth century; nor the assumption that these men represented large homogeneous groups.[7] Rather, it is that these men, particularly the Slavophiles, in dealing with the problem of "Russia," its dimensions and meanings, necessarily encountered various aspects of the myths and reflected them, according to their own views, in various combinations; thus far, they can be considered representative of Russian thought. The Slavophiles, tradition-minded as they were, saw traditional Russian myths loom far greater on their horizon than did their opponents; the Westernizers, in their rejection of the Russian past, could afford to discard much of the mythological baggage from it.[8]

The search for national ideals, i.e. for self-identity, in the past, was certainly not unique to Russia; the technique of this search the Russians had, in fact, acquired from German Romanticism.[9] But for the Russians the scope of the search was limited by the popular myth. Trying to discover what Russia was, they found that it already had an epithet, and one which made some of them, like Khomiakov, tremble. The question remained, why was Russia holy? One of the first Slavophiles, Ivan Kireevsky, tried to answer this question: "If the Russian land has sometimes been called 'Holy Russia,' it was only with the thought of the holy relics, monasteries and temples of God which existed in her; not because her status was . . . like that of

7. For Khomiakov's joke on the small number of Slavophiles, cf. A. F. Tiutcheva, *Pri Dvore Dvukh Imperatorov*, eds. S. V. Bakhrushin and E. V. Ger'e, 2 (Moscow, 1929), 104.

8. For the best account in English on the Slavophiles and the whole controversy, see N. Riazanovsky, *Russia and the West;* also his studies, "Pogodin and Shevyrev in Russian Intellectual History," *H.S.S., 4* (1957), 149–167; "Khomiakov on *Sobornost'*," *Continuity and Change in Russian and Soviet Thought,* ed. E. J. Simmons (Harvard, 1955), 183–197.

9. Riazanovsky, *Russia and the West,* 12f.

the 'Holy Roman Empire'." [10] The answer was not very satisfactory; obviously many countries had relics, monasteries, and churches as fine as those in Russia. Kireevsky grew more explicit: "the uniqueness of Russia has been contained in the fulness and purity of the expression which Christian teaching received in her." [11] Kireevsky was trying to solve a very difficult problem. "Holy Russia" could not be located in the physical superficial aspects of Russia, for by definition it was a transcendental quality; yet this holy essence had to be manifested in order for it to be recognized, in order that it could be proven.

The danger of Kireevsky's approach was obvious to Khomiakov, who reviewed the work. Russian history, Khomiakov argued, could not serve as proof that Russia was uniquely and supremely Christian, and his examples were obvious and convincing. [12] Khomiakov's argument was unassailable, and yet a few pages later in his review of Kireevsky, discussing the introduction of Christianity into Russia, he wrote:

"A new land, unfettered as yet in the forms of an established political society, unspoiled by conquest, perhaps because of its basic customs and the milder [national] character ready to receive the supreme spiritual principle, she [Russia] became immeasurably higher [spiritually] than Byzantium from the moment she was illumined by the light of true faith. She understood just how holy and immutable was the law of truth and justice, how indissoluble the idea of mercy and the conception of Christian society, how precious the blood of man to God and hence to human justice. She became not only higher than Byzantium but higher than all the countries of Europe." [13]

10. Ivan V. Kireevsky, "O Kharaktere prosveshcheniia Evropy i o ego otnoshenii k prosveshcheniiu Rossii," *Polnoe Sobranie Sochinenii,* ed. M. Gershenzon, *1* (Moscow, 1911), 205.
11. *Polnoe Sobranie Sochinenii, 1,* 219.
12. Khomiakov, *1,* 213f.
13. Khomiakov, *1,* 219–20.

The contradiction is not surprising, even in a philosopher like Khomiakov. It serves to illustrate a new and specifically "intelligentsia" stage in the history of the myths: a need to justify and demonstrate rationally the validity of the myth. The logical sequence was necessarily circular in all attempts, since the only proof for a myth is the myth itself: The major premise was established and unshakeable. The problem was not whether Russia was holy, but how to demonstrate her holiness, and what conclusions to draw from it. The importance of the Slavophile philosophers is in the rationalized expansion of the myth of the people which they achieved.

While Kireevsky was cautious about the use of the epithet "Holy Russia," Khomiakov's most casual references to Russia were in that form.[14] The real proof of "Holy Russia" was that it made a Russian's heart tremble, and the poet-philosopher could not challenge his own premise. Yet the contradiction remained between what the transcendental Russia was, and what the Russia of historical reality had done in her past. Both Kireevsky and Khomiakov were agreed that the essence of Russia, the basis and justification of her holiness, was her Christianity. "Our old Russia was created by Christianity itself. St. Nestor felt this, as well as St. Ilarion who had prophetically foreseen the task of the Russian land; there was this same awareness in the first of our known pilgrims to Jerusalem, where, before the tomb of the Saviour, he united in one prayer all of Holy Russia and her princes," wrote Khomiakov.[15] Then how to explain her non-Christain past? Khomiakov's solution had

14. Khomiakov, *1*, 85; *3*, 166, 167.

15. Khomiakov, *1*, 231. It is interesting to note that Khomiakov makes of Nestor the Chronicler a saint; also that the abbot Daniel who made the pilgrimage to Palestine in the twelfth century, did not use the epithet "Holy Russia" when praying for the Russian land; cf. chapter 4, n. 30. For Khomiakov, *Rus'* and *Sviataia Rus'*, "Russia" and "Holy Russia" were synonymous.

far-reaching consequences in Russian intellectual history. In effect, he argued that the intelligentsia had existed from the ninth century. The *druzhina,* the warriors of the Russian Varangian princes, served the prince; removed from the people, the warriors and administrators, no matter what their national origin, developed the vices of individualism. They did not possess the national, collective awareness of Christianity and hence their actions did not reflect the particular spirituality of the Russian faith.[16] Even though they were the ruling class with all their advantages in education and sophistication, as a result of their alienation they were morally far below the Russian peasant masses.[17]

The solution was an ingenious one. Khomiakov separated "Holy Russia" from the gentry, the ruling class, which represented the state and was active in history. "Holy Russia" was the Russian people, the mass of the peasants, imbued with true Christianity and living according to its precepts. The logic of his argument remained circular, of course. The Russian people were "Holy Russia," and "Holy Russia" was whatever the Russian people were. But for Khomiakov and others of the intelligentsia, the Russian masses were something distinct from themselves, something apart and very little known. Hence it became possible to begin to create the Russian character, to describe a being who was of "Holy Russia," for no real test of such a description was possible. Discussing the differences between Eastern and Western Christianity, Ivan Kireevsky described a Russian Christian:

"His meal is eaten with prayers. Each action he begins and ends with a prayer. With a prayer he enters a house and with one he leaves it. The least peasant, entering the palace of the Grand Prince . . . does not bow to the master

16. Khomiakov, *1*, 222f.
17. Khomiakov, *1*, 243; cf., also, Kireevsky, 2, 247.

before he bows in front of the holy image which always stood in the place of honour in every building, large or small. Thus the Russian associated every action of his, whether important or not, with the highest conception of his mind and with the deepest concentration of his heart." [18]

Quite obviously Kireevsky's description of a Russian did not apply to the gentry-intelligentsia of his time, but it did not have to, for it described a Russian, a member of "Holy Russia." One could seriously doubt whether it even described a Russian peasant, at any time or place, but in this doubt was the crux of the whole conception. One could be sceptical about Kireevsky's description, and the many opponents of the Slavophiles voiced their scepticism most vociferously, but one could not prove or disprove any statement about such a *persona incognita* as the Russian peasant. And Kireevsky himself did not offer his description as proof of Russian holiness, which did not require proof; given that Russia was holy, all evidence on the Russian was significant, for it all, by definition, described holiness.

Khomiakov's solution, however, did more than provide a rational structure for possible mythmaking about the Russian individual, or the Russian soul. Though he separated "Holy Russia" from the state, he could not see it as inherently antithetical to the state. This would require the acceptance of a permanent disharmony, of permanent antagonism, which could not be reconciled with Khomiakov's optimistically Christian eschatology. "Holy Russia" was not discernible in Russian history, nor did Khomiakov accept the official conception that the epithet described Russian reality of his day. Only one direction remained: "For Russia, only one task is possible: To become a society founded on the highest moral principles." [19] The trans-

18. Kireevsky, *1*, 211.
19. Khomiakov, *3*, 335.

lation of Kireevsky's premise from the past to the future was accomplished by Khomiakov through a kind of Hegelian dialectic. Russia, whose essence was "Holy Russia" should be and was in the process of becoming, completely and fully, "Holy Russia." The significance of this conception was not in its muddled Hegelianism, but in the fact that it provided a solution for those who were not of "Holy Russia," the gentry-intelligentsia. They, and the state which was of them, could become "Holy Russia" by re-discovering the values of the people who made up "Holy Russia," by accepting the customs and habits of the Russian people as their own, by becoming truly Russian.[20] The fanatic observance of religious rituals and customs by the Moscow Slavophiles, Khomiakov's Russian "native" dress which, according to Moscow wits, made the peasants think he was a Persian—these were steps on the way to becoming Russian.

As philosophers and historians, the Slavophiles were not consciously mythologizing. Rather, they attempted to construct rational justifications and historical explanations for the Russian myth of the People. No matter how inconsistent their arguments, and how unhistorical their speculations,[21] they were bound to some extent by their method.[22] The

20. For, as Khomiakov wrote: "Our life is still firm and whole. It has been preserved, as an absolute gage, by that much-suffering Russia which has not, as yet, received into itself our meager semi-education. This life we can restore within ourselves; one has only to love it with a sincere love." *1*, 91.

21. Examples even more radical than Kireevsky's can be found in the works of Konstantin Aksakov: "The history of the Russian people is the only history in the world of a Christian people . . . not only in its profession of faith, but also in its life, or at least in the aspirations of its life." *Polnoe Sobranie Sochinenii, 1* (Moscow, 1861–1880), 19; if this statement exhibits some caution still, the following does not: "Russian history reads like the lives of the Saints." *1*, 625.

22. In a letter to the historian M. Pogodin, Kireevsky could inquire sarcastically as to the meaning of the epithet "Russian God," *Russkii Bog*, used by Pogodin in his eulogy of Karamzin. (Kireevsky, 2, 240; Barsukov, *Pogodin, 7*, 195f.; *Moskvitianin* [1845], no. 9, 5f.). Logically and theologi-

poets had an easier time of it. To express his own yearning
and the mystery of Russia, Tiutchev wrote his famous qua-
train: "Not by brain can Russia be understood, Not by a
common yardstick can she be measured; She has a unique
dimension—One can only *believe* in her." [23] Yet the Slavophile thinkers were responding to the yearning in Tiutchev and others to fathom Russia's meaning and to discover
one's own place within the mystery. Most powerfully was
this dual desire expressed by Gogol' in *Dead Souls*:

"In you, all is open, desolate, flat; your lowly towns lie
scattered like dots, like specks invisible among your plains;
there is nothing to allure or captivate the eye. But what
mysterious inexplicable force draws one to you? Why does
the mournful song that floats all over your length and
breadth from sea to sea echo unceasingly in the ear? What
is in it, in that song? What is it that calls and sobs and
clutches at my heart? . . . Russia! what do you want of
me? What unthinkable bond hides between us? Why do
you look at me so and why is everything there is within
you turning its eyes on me, full of expectation? . . . And
still, full of perplexity I stand motionless while an awful
cloud heavy with coming rains looms above my head, and
thought is dumb before your immensity. What does this
limitless space prophesy? Is it not here, in you that there
is to be born infinite thought, when you yourself are
without end? . . . And I am engulfed menacingly by the
mighty space which reflects with fearful force deep within
me; a supernatural power has enlightened my eyes: Oh,
what a radiant, marvellous, unknown to earth distance!
Russia!" [24]

---

cally there could be no answer to Kireevsky's query. The "Russian God"
was as meaningless or as meaningful as "Holy Russia" in which Kireevsky
himself believed so firmly.

23.   *"Umom Rossiu ne poniat'*
                      Arshinom obshchim ne izmerit'
                      U nei osobennaia stat'—
                      V Rossiu mozhno tol'ko verit'.

F. I. Tiutchev, *Polnoe Sobranie Sochinenii,* ed. P. V. Bykov (St. Petersburg,
1913), 202.

24. Nikolai V. Gogol', *Polnoe Sobranie Sochinenii, 6* (Moscow-Leningrad,
1951), 220–21.

Gogol' is overwhelmed by the immensity, the grandeur
of Russia, the Russia of the people, "Holy Russia," though
the epithet is not used. What is revealed to him, however,
is not the meaning of the mystery, but only the mystery
itself. Gogol's awareness was the awareness of those on the
"outside" of Russia, and his words convey the awe, the
terror before the full dimensions of the myth, for that was
what he evoked. But they also convey the yearning to pene-
trate the mystery and to be one with it, to forge the bond
between the individual and the myth, much more powerfully than Khomiakov's trembling at the sound of "Holy
Russia." It is through this urgency, the nakedness of the
psychological need, that Gogol' reflects his age; not the
age of 1812 and the liberal Decembrists, but the height of
the "Nicholas system," the growing awareness of the serfdom issue and the political isolation of Russia.

The response to Gogol's yearning came in the context
of this last factor. The European revolutions of 1848 were
seen by Viazemsky as a threat to the one stable society that
remained, as a new 1812. And the poet who had scoffed at
the Russian God now wrote:

> Holy Russia! In its very meaning
> Providence foretold her path
> And not for nothing at her Baptism
> Did He endow her with this name . . .
> Oh, safeguard then your pledge
> Keep to the same self-chosen path
> Before all men and before God
> Oh Holy Russia, Holy be! [25]

Under the pressure of extreme danger, as he saw it, the
poet did not philosophize or hesitate. He accepted the existing myth, whose proof was its own existence through all
time.

While Viazemsky's response was the most explicit, it was
not the only one. In 1850, the reserved and aristocratic

25. Viazemsky, *Sochineniia*, *4*, 314–15.

Tiutchev wrote a poem attacking the Imperial Vice-Chancellor, Count Nesselrode, for the latter's alleged betrayal of Russian political interests in the Balkans:

> No, little dwarf, unheard of coward,
> No matter how you wiggle now or fear,
> With your half-empty soul
> You can't tempt Holy Russia.
>
> Destroying all her holy hopes,
> Destroying her beliefs,
> Her task and purpose
> Could she deny for you?
>
> Whoever wants, can disbelieve in Holy Russia,
> As long as she herself believes in it,
> God victory will not defer
> To please the cowardice of men.[26]

The prize of victory, as Tiutchev saw it, was to be the "crown and sceptre of Byzantium." And, while Viazemsky and Tiutchev were regarded as political reactionaries, the liberal Slavophile, Khomiakov, burst out at Russia, at the beginning of the Crimean War:

> You have been called to holy battle
> You're the beloved of our Lord
> You has He given strength so awful
> That you may crush the evil will
> Of blind, and mad and wild force
>
> .   .   .   .
>
> But hearken; to be God's weapon
> For earthly creatures is a heavy load
> His slaves He judges harshly
> And over you, alas, how many,
> How many dreadful sins repose.
>
> In courts you're black with blackest falsehood
> And marked with slavery's awful stamp

26. Tiutchev, *Sochineniia*, 193.

With rotting lies, with godless flattery,
With sloth both deadening and shameful
With endless filth you're full.[27]

Despite all the sins, however, Russia was God's elect. She
is to do penance, "With humbly kneeling soul, With head
reposing in the dust" but then go on to battle with God's
sword in hand. And shortly afterwards, in a poem addressed
to "Repentant Russia," Khomiakov saw her before the
whole world "In a new and holy radiance," bringing sacred
freedom to peoples, "Awesome, beautiful—God's Angel
With sparkling countenance of flame." [28]

It is evident that these poems express the sentiments of
conservatives (a liberal Slavophile would still be consider-
ably to the right of center) and a foreign war or danger
would always bring out elements of chauvinism contained
in most people. Within the Russian context, one must
also remember that the poets and writers, no matter how
conscious and interested, could express virtually no opinions on internal problems, in mythological or other form.
Hence, to find such patriotic poems at such times is not
surprising. Their importance for us is in the fact that the
poets seem to resort almost instinctively to formulas and
images based on the myth of the people. Whatever the individual doubts and misgivings may have been, whatever
individual yearnings for and conceptions of "Holy Russia"
existed, seeking the Russian essence, something that would
awaken an emotional response in any Russian, the poets
turned to the myth. This is the more interesting as we remember that all three poets, particularly Khomiakov, tried
to separate the myth of the people, "Holy Russia," or even
"Russia" as such from the State; yet in the poems this distinction is lost, for the "Holy Russia" which wins wars,
gains Constantinople, and resists revolutions, is the Rus-

27. Khomiakov, _4_, 255–6.
28. Khomiakov, _4_, 257.

sian State. In order to justify the actions or existence of
the Russian State, the poets evoked what they believed to
be a much higher, transcendental entity, "Holy Russia";
but by involving "Holy Russia" in politics, they themselves
brought it down to mix with the idea of the Russian State.
This kind of mythological dialectic could result, for an
uninitiated reader, in a virtual *non sequitur.* The poet
V. G. Benediktov, consoling Russia on her defeats in 1855,
described at length all the rational reforms that Russia
would introduce, all the natural wealth of the country,
Russian loyalty to the tsar who will accomplish all good
things, and ended his poem with the claim that the enemies
of Russia would realize: "what means Both Russian God
and Russian man." [29] Benediktov's dialectic was implicit
only, and the evocation of the Russian God and man appears to be quite sudden and unfounded. Similarly, the poet
N. M. Iazykov, in a violent, Slavophile poem attacking his
ideological enemies, drew, in his defense, on the image of
"Holy Russia" and the "Great Russian God," the foundations of his beliefs and of national life, and then, in another
poem addressed in gratitude to his doctor, recommended
the latter to the "great Russian God." [30] Despite Benediktov's claim that even the enemies of Russia would understand the meaning of the epithets, it remained sufficiently
vague to allow the contradictions and the non-sequential
petty uses noted above.

While Russia's enemies did not respond to the challenge,
a striking attempt was made to answer the question what
"Holy Russia" and the "Russian God" were. The occasion
for it was Viazemsky's poem on "Holy Russia"; in response
to it, the poet V. A. Zhukovsky wrote his old friend a letter

29. V. G. Benediktov, *Sochineniia,* ed. I. P. Polonsky, *1* (St. Petersburg-
Moscow, 1902), 313.

30. N. M. Iazykov, *Polnoe Sobranie Stikhotvorenii,* ed. M. K. Azadovsky
(Moscow-Leningrad, 1934), "K ne nashim," p. 625; "Poslanie k F. I. Inozem-
tsevu," p. 599.

in July of 1848, which he later published in the *Russkii Invalid* [31] and it is worth quoting at length:

"HOLY RUSSIA—what deep meaning this word acquires now, when we see how everything around us crumbles, only because the common denominator has already crumbled, without which there is nothing to unite all these tiny, differing fractions, which cannot make up any whole. The *Holy* is lost; the strong cement, which had held so firmly together the stones of the ancient building built according to plan, has gradually vanished, eaten away by the acid activities of the human mind . . . Meanwhile our star, *Holy Russia,* shines on high, shines undisturbed, and may God preserve it from an eclipse . . . *Holy Russia*—this word is coeval with Christian Russia. It was given to her, as your verses say, at its baptism, and it will never lose its profound meaning even though it has become one of *lieux communs*. Let me say, in passing, that I value most highly these so-called commonplaces; they are in life and language as the air which invisibly surrounds and without which one cannot live or breathe. That which has become a commonplace, is accepted by all, is undeniable for everyone; it has lost its novelty because of its own antiquity, for which very reason it is a universal and necessary truth. It suddenly acquires the character of a revelation, marvellously expressing the supreme truth, only when it is opposed by something which denies this truth. So is it in this case: *Holy Russia*—how frequently and for how long has this word been repeated, how accustomed we are to it, how many of us use it even in an ironical sense—yet uttered now . . . does it not astonish us with its freshness and its validity? Does it not express, in one sound, with a new conviction for us, everything that became through the centuries our faith, love and hope? Is not there marked more clearly in it our particular *union* with God, as a result of which we have received from our forefathers his wondrous name, the *Rus God (Russkoi Bog,* ne *Rossiiskii Bog* . . .) not the *Russian God,* the way Oserov ends his "Dimitry Donskoi" [32] The Russian

31. No. 207, 1848.

32. Zhukovsky distinguished here between Rus' and Rossiia, an old and meaningful distinction.

God, Holy Russia—such names for God and fatherland
no other European people has. . . . In the expression
Holy Russia—there is reflected a whole unique history;
this name Russia has from its Baptism, but its deepest
meaning is acquired from the appanage period, when over
many small princes there was one chief one, the Grand
Prince, when under one grand principality there were
many small ones dependent upon it, and when all this was
combined into a whole, not into a *Russia* but into a *Rus'*,
that is, not into a state but into a family, where all had
one motherland, one faith, one language, . . . this is why
. . . when there was no *Russia* . . . for all there was the
one living, indivisible, *Holy Rus'*. A particular strength
was given to this word by the sad times of Mamai: Then
it became for us a unifying, patriotic battle cry; our church
consoled us with it, our princes pronounced it when they
offered to the Horde their heads for the fatherland, it
rang on the field of Kulikovo; it must have received a
marvellous meaning on the lips of the great Ivan III, who
had destroyed the Tatar yoke and who suddenly appeared
as the autocratic ruler of *All Russia*. From that time Russia was a state, the particular property of the Tsar, while
Holy Russia remained a tradition, a joint treasure of
Tsar and People. *There* is our might, our far-flung borders . . . ; *here* is . . . our popular inner life, our faith
. . . everything that is ours and *Russian* . . . *Russia* be-
longs to the complex of European states; *Holy Russia* is
the separate hereditary property of the Russian people,
guaranteed it by God. All the holiness of this Russia and
the wonderful character of the Russian people . . . were
expressed particularly at the moment, when the Moscow
boiars went to the monstrous Ivan IV begging him to exe-
cute them if he so desires, but not to abandon the Russian throne . . . The other expression of our people,
Russian God, has a similar, profound historical meaning
. . . The expression *Russian God* conveys not just our
faith in God, but also a particular popular tradition
about God. He is from ancient times the champion of Russia, visible to our ancestors at all times both good and
bad, glorious and miserable . . . *Russian God* is in the
same relation to our faith in God, as *Holy Russia* is in re-

lation to Russia . . . This conception of the Russian God
. . . is derived by the Russian people out of the revelation
contained in its own history. It is a conception of a tangible God, of a proven God; recognized universally without any propagandizing . . . It would be ridiculous to
say: English, French, or German God; but at the sound
Russian God the soul is transported. It is the God of our
popular life in whom, so to say, there is personified for
us our faith in the God of our soul. It is the image of the
heavenly savior, visibly reflected in the earthly history of
our people." [33]

The political conservatism of Zhukovsky, court poet and
tutor of the heir to the throne, is beyond any question; it
is not surprising that he ended the letter by hinging the
Russia of holiness and godliness on the autocracy of the
Russian ruler. "The foundations of Russia are: the Church
and Autocracy," he argued finally.[34] Thus, in effect, he
virtually denied the "Holy Russia" which he declaimed on
so vividly and lyrically.[35] Nevertheless, his was the most
explicit and complete answer to the question—what were
"Holy Russia" and "Russian God"? His logic, given the
limitations imposed by the myth, was representative. The
main limitation is rather obvious: to put it most simply, the
intelligentsia knew that "Holy Russia" was the popular epithet for Russia, but they did not know that it was created
in time, that there had been no "Holy Russia" before the
seventeenth century. For those who discovered the myth
of the people, the meaning of the epithet, by definition, indicated that it was beyond time. Russia was made holy not
by men, within time, but by God, within eternity. Historically, "Holy Russia" must have existed from the same moment as Russia itself existed. Yet it would be impossible to
speak of a "Holy Russia" before Christianity. Hence both

33. V. A. Zhukovsky, *Sochineniia*, 6 (St. Petersburg, 1878), 164–167.
34. Zhukovsky, *Sochineniia*, 6, 171.
35. These are the adjectives chosen by A. V. Soloviev, *Sbornik*, 100, n. 1.

"Holy Russia" and Russia begin at the moment of baptism, in the tenth century, or rather, from the moment of baptism the vague geographic area which was to become the Russian state, was "Holy Russia." Zhukovsky tried to maintain the separation between "Holy Russia" and the State; the former was the transcendental essence of the Russian people, including the intelligentsia, while the latter was the superficial political form of Russian society. As "Holy Russia" preceded the State in time, however (which was certainly correct theologically) the Russian ruler, present already at the moment of baptism and in fact instrumental in Russia's Christianization, partook of both.

Despite individual nuances, the pattern of Zhukovsky's logic is the same as that of Khomiakov, Kireevsky, and others, and just as circular: The meaning of "Holy Russia" was contained in everything Russia was, and whatever Russia was, defined "Holy Russia," while the proof for this interpretation was offered by the existence of belief in the myth. His disquisition on the "Russian God," though, was more original, perhaps because he had so few models to follow. The logic of the epithet emerges quite clearly. While "Holy Russia" could become manifest only in time, at the moment of Russia's baptism, it expressed the Divine plan which must have existed through all eternity. In other words, "Holy Russia" was the historical manifestation of God's unique purpose. The utility of such a God was obvious. It allowed one to eliminate the contradiction between Russian holiness and Russian history. As Khomiakov pointed out, God judged His own people particularly severely. All the events of Russian history, all the misfortunes of people and state, such as the Tatar conquest, were designed by God to strengthen "Holy Russia," to prepare it for the final triumph. Zhukovsky developed further the idea suggested by Khomiakov, that Russian holiness was manifest, perhaps most strongly, in the miseries of

Russian history. The poet Maikov expressed this conception
more explicitly than Zhukovsky:

> "Be patient! . . . And you had suffered
> Oh Holy Russia, everything
> That God had sent you: all the burdens
> Oppression, exiles and deaths.
>
> A heavy hammer has been forging you
> Into a people, through the ages—
> But you believe that God, through love
> Has punished—and this makes you firm." [36]

While Zhukovsky was right in interpreting "Russian God"
as a corollary of "Holy Russia" and as a uniquely Russian
epithet, he was wrong in feeling, apparently, that such an
idea would be incomprehensible to any non-Russian.
Though certainly sneered at in its Russian manifestation,
the myth would be quite understandable to a Jew of the
Old Testament, with his God of Israel, to Joan of Arc
whose France was the kingdom of King Jesus,[37] and to any
citizen of God's Country.

The idea of a tribal God was not unique to Russia, though
the vigor of the Russian myth was probably matched only
by the American one. The image of the "Russian God,"
however, was quite singular. "Russian God," according to
the poet, was apparently the Russian way of doing things,
the hypostasis of Russian national life; this would be,
of course, a rather pagan conception to apply to the Christian God.[38] But the "Russian God" was also the essence of

36. A. N. Maikov, *Polnoe Sobranie Sochinenii*, ed. P. V. Bykov *1* (St.
Petersburg, 1914), "Uprazdnennyi Monastyr'," 156.

37. Cf. Kantorowicz, *"Pro patria,"* 484 and n. 29.

38. It seems to be quite close to the Roman idea of the Genius of the
Roman people. See, for example, the rather typical formulation by an
optimistic Russian during World War I, in Konstantin Paustovsky's auto-
biography: "Great is the God of the Russian land . . . great is the genius
of the Russian people." "Povest' o Zhizni," *Sobranie Sochinenii, 3* (Moscow, 1957), 352.

Russian faith and, Zhukovsky emphasized, visible to the Russians at all times, "visibly reflected" in their life and history. Zhukovsky did not really explain what kind of god the "Russian God" was, and in what relation he stood to the supreme and universal God of mankind. But an answer was suggested by Tiutchev in one of his most famous poems:

> These poor hamlets, humbly faring,
> Nature sunk in desolation,
> Land of mine, such sorrows bearing,
> Land of all the Russian nation!
>
> Nothing knowing, nothing seeing,
> How can haughty foreign faces
> Mark what mystery has being
> In thy lowly, naked places?
>
> There was one, my land, who knew thee:
> With a cross upon him pressing,
> Like a servant passing through thee,
> Heaven's King once gave his blessing.[39]

The translation is a brilliant one, but it weakens the import of the last lines by rendering the blessing as a single act in time. Literally, the last verse would read: "Burdened by the cross, the Tsar of Heaven, in the guise of a slave has walked all over you, native land, blessing you." [40] According to Tiutchev, the "Russian God" was not a euphemism, nor a pagan *Genius Rossiae*, but Christ Himself who visited, in person, every corner of Russia, blessing it.

Tiutchev's image raised an interesting problem. The poet himself, hearing that Emperor Nicholas I was dead, remarked: "It is as if one has been told that God is dead." [41]

39. Tiutchev, *Sochineniia*, 126; the translation is by Bowra, *A Second Book of Russian Verse*, ed. Bowra, 34.

40.   *Udruchennyi noshei krestnoi*
                      Vsiu tebia zemlia rodnaia,
                      V rabskom vide Tsar Nebesnyi
                      Iskhodil, blagoslavliaia.

41. Tiutcheva, *Pri Dvore*, 185.

What was the relation between the ruler, who was the earthly god and "Holy Russia," which described the epiphanic Christ? Zhukovsky presented a curious symbol of this relationship when he described the action of the boiars in pleading with Ivan the Terrible as the epitome of "Holy Russia." By offering their lives if necessary just so the Tsar would remain on his throne, they revealed those qualities of the Russian people which symbolized "Holy Russia." The question then is, what was the role of the ruler in "Holy Russia" and what were the "wonderful qualities" of the Russian people?

Although, as we have seen, in their emotional outbursts the Slavophiles tended to bring together all the emotion-laden symbols and myths, in their rationalizations they continued to attempt the separation of the image of the people from that of the ruler and the State.[42] A solution for this problem was indicated by Khomiakov in his dichotomy of an individualistic, alienated ruling class on the one hand and a mysterious, collectively moral and good peasant mass on the other. But that the problem was difficult of solution, that the image of the Tsar was an overpowering one, is indicated by Tiutchev's reaction to Nicholas' death. It is revealed by the statement of the great anarchist, Michael Bakunin: "The Tsar is the ideal of the Russian people, he is a kind of Russian Christ"; [43] and by the reactions of the

42. Maikov is witness to these attempts and to the Slavophile reputation on this issue. Though he felt more sympathy with them than with their opponents, he wrote, he abandoned their camp, as to remain in it would have meant "denying history and with it, the whole of the Russian Empire." Maikov, *Sochineniia, 1,* xxiv.

43. Michael Bakunin, Narodnoe delo: *Romanov, Pugachev ili Pestel'* (Moscow, 1917), 42. Another enemy of Nicholas I, though on a different scale of career, general A. P. Ermolov, the hero of the Caucaus, wrote to Prince Vorontsov in 1851 about the enthusiastic reception of the emperor in Moscow: "Under present conditions, this kind of thing does not take place among other peoples, and not for nothing is our country called *Holy Russia." Arkhiv Vorontsova, 36,* 401.

revolutionary Chernyshevsky and the émigré Herzen to the emancipation of the serfs in 1861—both men saw it as the personal achievement of the emperor against all odds.[44]

The search for the innate qualities of the mysterious peasant Russia, "Holy Russia" resulted in the idealization of the *obshchina,* the agricultural community.[45] Konstantin Aksakov described its meaning: From the beginning of history, the Russians lived, free and peace-loving, in autonomous village communities. The moral symbol of the community was its name, *mir,* a word which in Russian also means world and peace.[46] The community was founded on tolerance and mutual respect and, since the Christianization of Russia, on brotherly love.[47] In order to solve, however, the problem of living in an evil world, the Slav communities called in a government. Unlike all the European states, "The Russian state was formed not by conquest, but by a *voluntary invitation of authority* . . . In Russia the people understood the need for state power on earth, and authority appeared as a welcome guest, by the will and conviction of the people . . . Hence, as the foundation of the Western State: *force, slavery and hostility.* As the foundation of the Russian State: *free will, liberty and peace.*" [48] The Russians maintained the *mir* as the focus of national life while they called upon state power to defend it. But "they did not want to become a state themselves; on the contrary,

44. Cf. G. Chulkov, *Imperatory* (Moscow-Leningrad, 1928), 299f.

45. For a good summary of the evolution of the *obshchina* idea among the Russian intelligentsia, see James H. Billington, *Mikhailovsky and Russian Populism* (Oxford, 1958), 64ff.; also cf. Henri Granjard, "Du Romantisme Politique: Slavophiles et Populistes," *Revue des Etudes Slaves, 24* (1957), 73–80; Riazanovsky, *Russia and the West,* 149ff.

46. The interpretations of this etymological symbolism were legion, of course.

47. "The *Obshchina* is a union of men who have renounced their egotism, their own personality, and expresses their common agreement; it expresses an act of love, an act of Christianity, which is reflected, more or less vaguely, in all of its actions." K. Aksakov, *Sochineniia, 1,* 291–92.

48. K. Aksakov, *Sochineniia, 1,* 8 and *passim.*

they wished to continue their community life. Hence they called upon the outside for a state, as a foreign construction." [49]

The conclusions Aksakov drew from this historical scheme were consistent: "The Russian people is not a political people, that is, it does not aspire to political power, does not want political rights, does not contain in itself even the germ of the love of power." [50] This quality of the Russian people was, in fact, a direct manifestation of "Holy Russia," for, as Aksakov noted, "The State, in principle, is evil." [51] Indifferent to the state, the Russians distrusted its works and its structure, including law. Living in communities based on Christian love, the Russian peasant could not accept the formal, inhumane legal conceptions of the West; instead he sought and obtained human justice, Christian forgiveness, awareness of guilt, and spiritual penance.[52]

The concept of the *obshchina,* distinct from the state and, actually, antithetical to it, preserving the *true* qualities of the Russian people, of "Holy Russia," gained the enthusiastic adherence of the majority of the intelligentsia, no matter from behind which ideological barricade they had been sniping.[53] Herzen in his revolutionary stage felt that because of this historical foundation of the Russian character, once rid of the state, the Russian was the freest of all men.[54] Despite all the misery and oppression in Russian history, the Christian *mir* enabled the Russian peasant to remain truly Christian, part of "Holy Russia." What then did it mean to be a Russian peasant, truly Christian? The

49. Aksakov, *1*, 55–56.

50. L. Brodsky, *Rannie slavianofily* (Moscow, 1910), 69.

51. K. Aksakov, *Sochineniia, 1*, 56, note. This sentence was written in on the top of the page in the manuscript.

52. Cf. Kireevsky, *1*, 206f.; Khomiakov, *1*, 139f.; *3*, 73ff., 321ff.

53. Billington, 85.

54. Herzen, *Sochineniia, 8*, 25–26; cf. Bibliographical commentary, 563f.; E. Lampert, *Studies in Rebellion* (London, 1957), 242f.; Martin E. Malia, "Herzen and the Peasant Commune," *Continuity and Change,* 197–217.

answer was given in one of the most popular poems of nineteenth-century Russia, Nekrasov's *Vlas* (1854). Vlas was an old, grey-haired peasant, wandering through Russia, wearing iron fetters as self-punishment, collecting alms in order to build a church. Once he had been a cruel, beastly man; he had beaten his wife to death, oppressed his neighbors, robbed the poor. But during a sickness he had repented and promised God his penance:

> Then gave away Vlas all his property
> Left himself naked and bare
> To collect for the erection
> Of God's temple he prepared.
> Since that time he has been wandering
> Now it's nigh to thirty years
> Only feeds himself by begging,
> Firmly to his oath he holds.
> All his soul's great power
> Into God's work has gone:
> As if wild greed had never
> From his birth been known to it.
> Full of sorrow inconsolable
> Tall and straight and dark of face
> Walks he with unhurried pace
> Through the villages and towns.
> Walks he with a book and icon,
> Talking softly to himself,
> And his heavy iron fetters
> Gently ring as he walks on.
> Walks he in the ice of winter
> Walks he in the summer's heat,
> Calling on the Christian Russians
> Each to give what he can give.
> And they give, they give, the people.
> So from their working-alms,
> Grow God's temples everywhere
> On the face of native land.[55]

55. N. A. Nekrasov, *Polnoe Sobranie Sochinenii i pisem*, eds. V. E. Evgenev-Maksimov, A. M. Egolin, K. I. Chukovsky, *1* (Moscow, 1948), 103–05. For Nekrasov's view of "Holy Russia" as the common people, whom one serves even against the regulations of the state, see 526–7.

Nekrasov gave, in embryonic form, an image which was to proliferate profusely throughout Russian thought, the image of the Russian soul. It was an extreme and wild soul, capable of beastliness but also capable of denying itself through love of man and God. No matter what evil it performed, it recognized it as evil and found its greatest fulfillment in union with God.[56] Nekrasov picked up the strand of Russian mythmaking begun by N. A. L'vov and Plavil'shchikov in the eighteenth century, but he placed it in the logical context. Just as the tribal conception of the deity was made a corollary of "Holy Russia" and was placed within the context of the Russian myth, so the image of the Russian character, which was originally within the sphere of general European nationalistic romanticism, was placed within the aura of the popular myth. The extremes of the Russian soul were due to its intimate relation with the Russian God. When a true Russian, i.e. a peasant, denied God, there was nothing to limit and control his transgressions; when he accepted the Russian God he was saintly. With the myth of the "soul" added to those of the "God" and "Holy Russia," the mythological structure was complete and self-inclosed. Yet this latest myth raised a problem. The Christian Russian soul, intimate with God, saintly in its manifestations, came rather close to infringing upon the ideal image of the saintly ruler. If such was the Russian soul, and if the state was evil in principle, then what of the ruler?

Konstantin Aksakov's brother, Ivan, tried to supply an answer. It was really criminal to try to involve the Russian people in politics, in constitution-making and the like; these are the Russian people, "Holy Russia," who have no name for themselves other than "Christians" (*khristiane*) or "peasants" (*krestiane*).[57] In the eyes of these people: "The Russian Tsar with his innate, hereditary power is not ambitious or power-mad: power, for him, is a penance and a

---

56. Cf. Khomiakov, *1*, 253ff. and *passim*.
57. Ivan S. Aksakov, *Polnoe Sobranie Sochinenii*, 5 (Moscow, 1886), 34.

burden; to be tsar is a true sacrifice [*podvig*]. The Russian
Tsar, in the eyes of the people is not at all the chief bureaucrat . . . In Russian history . . . there had been uprisings against *voevodas,* boiars, gentry, but in popular eyes
the Tsar was never identified with them." [58] And the Russian people expressed their inherent supreme Christian
love and faith in man by entrusting the horrible burden of
power to a Christian man, rather than to institutions and
laws.[59] The argument was ingenious; it was possible to
avoid the antithesis between tsar and people by excluding
the state. The Tsar who willingly bore the burden of
power, through his self-sacrifice, through his quality of
Christian love, was within "Holy Russia." He and the people confronted each other in harmony while the necessary
evil of the state remained outside. If the tsar bore his power
as a sacrifice, however, the question remained as to what
his function was, and what kind of a man he was in order
to offer himself thus.

The most powerful and radical answer was given by
Gogol' who had, earlier, felt most deeply and poignantly
the mystery of Russia. In his *Selections from correspondence with friends* Gogol' wrote:

Our poets foresaw the supreme meaning of the monarch;
they understood that he must, inevitably and finally, become all *Love,* and in this way it will become clear to all
why the sovereign is the image of God, which fact is
now understood instinctively by all our land . . . Loving
everything in his state down to the last man of every class
and calling, transforming everything in it as if into a part
of his own body, sorrowing for all, weeping, praying night
and day for his suffering people, the Sovereign will ac-

58. I. Aksakov, *5,* 34. Cf. the discussions on this issue among the
Petrashevsky circle, recorded in the testimony after the arrest of the
group, *Delo Petrashevtsev,* Pam. Obshch. Mysli, 2 (Moscow-Leningrad,
1941), 221, 236.

59. I. Aksakov, *5,* 120.

quire the allmighty voice of love which alone can reach
sickly humanity . . . There only will the people be cured,
where the monarch will grasp his own highest function
—to be the image of him, on earth, who is love itself.[60]

Gogol's ideas were rejected virtually unanimously by the
Russian intelligentsia. The poet, ill and more than slightly
mad, had gone too far. He had pushed the myths of the
people and of the ruler to their ultimate synthesis and
conclusion, and the gentry, for all its needs and desires,
could not accept Nicholas I as *Love,* as the manifest Christ.
The whole book appears to be a sort of a concave mirror
which focused the rationalizations of the Slavophiles to
their logical final consequences, and reflected them back
at their authors. Discussing community justice, Gogol' ad-
vised an estate-owner, *pomeshchik,* to judge twice: once,
according to reason to decide on the guilty party, and a
second time according to divine, Christian justice, when
both parties should be condemned and punished, for both
were guilty before Christ for quarreling and not forgiving
each other.[61]

Though rejected by nearly everyone, Gogol's solution,
nevertheless, appears logical. Even Bakunin had felt that
the tsar was Christ in the eyes of the Russian people. And,
given a people imbued with Christ, a "Holy Russia," who
but the God of love, the manifest Christ should lead them?
The *Correspondence* cost Gogol' the friendship of Belinsky. In a furious letter the critic pinpointed with great accuracy the pattern of Russian mythological thinking so
fully and madly displayed by Gogol': "According to you,
the Russian people is the most religious people in the
world; that is a lie! The basis of religiosity is pietism, awe,
the fear of God. A Russian utters the name of God while

60. "O Lirizme nashikh poetov," *Vybrannye mesta is perepiski s druziami,*
in *Pol. Sobr. Soch., 8,* 255–56.
61. "Sel'skii sud i rasprava," *8,* 342.

scratching his————." [62] The reason for Belinsky's insistence on Russian popular irreligiosity becomes clear: "I should like to remark on one thing: when a European, particularly a Catholic, is overcome by the spirit of religiosity, he becomes a denouncer of unjust authority, like the Hebrew prophets . . . With us, it is the reverse: the minute a man, even a decent one, is possessed by a sickness, which is known among doctor-psychiatrists as the *religiosa mania,* he tries to make up to the earthly God even more than to the heavenly one; and in this he goes so far that even if the earthly God wants to reward him for his slavish devotion, he cannot do it for fear of compromising himself in the eyes of society." [63]

Gogol's significance lay exactly within the framework of Belinsky's idea. The poet posed more sharply than anyone else the problem whether it was possible, within Russian Christian myths, to separate the Holy Tsar and "Holy Russia," and answered it more vividly than others. Belinsky's distrust of religiosity was evoked, legitimately by the synthesis of the two myths, where the image of the tsar overshadowed rather completely that of the people, and this emphasis was continued by such writers as M. Katkov and Iu. Samarin, and the second generation of the Slavophiles in general.[64] For these political conservatives the state was not excluded from the union of tsar and people, but for the majority that could not perceive the holiness of the Russian Empire there still remained the image of the Christlike tsar leading his Christlike people to the realm of love. And such an image could persist the more easily in the reign of Alexander II (1855–81), the Emancipator-Tsar who had liberated the serfs, instituted reforms in all areas of Russian life, provided justice in the new and honest

62. Letter to Gogol', July 3, 1847; Vissarion Belinsky, *Pis'ma,* ed. E. A. Liatsky, *3* (St. Petersburg, 1914), 233.

63. Belinsky, *Pis'ma, 3,* 234.

64. Cf. G. Liwoff, *Michel Katkoff et son Epoque* (Paris, 1897); Iu. Samarin and F. Dmitrev, *Revoliutsionnyi Konservatism* (Berlin, 1875).

courts. Despite all his good deeds, Alexander II was assassinated by revolutionaries on March 1, 1881. Most of the intelligentsia and, perhaps, most of the people, were shocked and outraged by this deed, and the expression of their shock took on specific forms. Ivan Aksakov wrote in his eulogy of the dead emperor:

Autocrat, He was humble in spirit . . . His soul did not know arrogance or pride. He did not seek for earthly fame but fame sought Him and the historian with amazement balances the account of great deeds which took place in the period from 1855 to 1881. But God raised the humble one to a height above any earthly height: The Tsar of the greatest state on earth, by Whose hand there was ready to go into battle for the defence of His throne . . . a whole ocean of people, was worthy to die truly martyred. His image stands before us now in the radiant glory of a Passion-sufferer. The people, praying for the soul of Alexander II, count him among the intercessors for the Russian land.[65]

The hagiographers who wrote the *vitae* of Saints Boris and Gleb, of St. Andrew Bogoliubsky, of Dimitry Donskoi, would have recognized their own ideas and even words, while the future Metropolitan, Pitirim, was a young man already at this time. The poet Afanasy Fet left his lyrical intimate muse to describe Christ's crucifixion after his betrayal by Judas; out of His overwhelming love, however, Christ forgives even Judas:

> In front of evil's silent victim
> Seeing the sinless flowing blood
> The sun was dark, the coffins opened,
> But much more strongly there shone Love.

> It shines now with a new-found justice,
> And having blessed its shining dawn
> His crown of thorns and cross of sorrow
> He handed to the tsar on earth.[66]

65. I. Aksakov, 5, 21–22.

66. A. A. Fet, "I Marta 1881 goda," *Polnoe Sobranie Stikhotvorenii*, eds. N. N. Strakhov, B. V. Nikol'skii, *1* (St. Petersburg, 1912), 397.

The popular reaction was in the same vein. Verses made up by Old Believers describe the death of the emperor as a second Crucifixion. "You have laid down your life/Because you have done good! You have done good to your enemies/ And this is why Your blood was shed! Our father, the earthly God." [67]

By his death Alexander II seemed to have ensured the supremacy of the ruler-myth. Sovereign Emperor in his power, Orthodox Tsar in his defense of the peasants, he was now also the saint-prince. This last aspect was particularly striking. In his cantata in honor of the coronation of Alexander III, Maikov had the new emperor plead: "In me, oh Lord, In me is there strength enough for the Heavy cross You give me? I am unworthy of Your love . . . Like a faithful slave I give myself to You, And I am ready for any sorrow, For dear to me is not worldly honour, but the crown of Christ." [68] All the strands of the ruler-myth were gathered into one overwhelming image of the Christlike God on earth.

And yet Gogol's image failed and Belinsky's fear was unfounded. In his letter to Viazemsky, Zhukovsky had referred to the satirical use made of the epithets which symbolized Russian myths. Irony and satire, of course, could not be applied to the ruler-myth, in published material at least, but they persisted in regard to the myth of the people.[69] In 1871 the poet Count Alexis Tolstoy wrote a

67. "Kak Vsplakalas' Rossia o svoem Belom Tsare," *Russkaia Starina,* *68* (1890), 689–90. Cf. the feeling of utter loss and bewilderment over the death of the emperor, expressed by servants and "common people" which is described by I. Shmelev, in his reminiscences; "Fear," *Izbrannye Raszkazy* (New York, 1955), 125–134.

68. Maikov, *Sochineniia,* 2, 199.

69. Cf. M. Lermontov, freest from the myths of all the Russian poets, and hence most appealing, for his coining of the ironic epithet "Unwashed Russia," *Neumytaia Rossiia,* in *Polnoe Sobranie Sochineii, 1* (Moscow-Leningrad, 1948), 62; the amusing foreign contribution, on the occasion of the Crimean War, by Gustave Doré, *Histoire pittoresque,*

poem on the Russian epic hero, Potok. After his great ex-
ploits, Potok had gone into a sleep of five hundred years.
Upon awakening (obviously in the reign of Ivan the Terrible) Potok sees the excesses of the Tsar and the people's
adulation. The hero is astonished: "If he is a prince, or
even Tsar, why do they sweep the ground before him with
their beards? . . . Am I really in Russia? God preserve us
from an earthly God, for the Scriptures tell us only to recognize the heavenly one." In disgust, Potok goes back to
sleep and wakes up three hundred years later. He is addressed by a patriot: "Tell me, do you honour the peasant?
But Potok asks in turn 'Which one? ' 'The peasant in general, who is great through his humility!' " is the answer he
gets. Discouraged, the hero muses: "Perhaps . . . I woke
up too early? Only yesterday, lying on their bellies they
adored the Moscovite khan, and to-day they order me to
adore the *muzhik!*" His conclusion, before sinking back in
sleep, is that the Russians seem to have a bad habit of adoring someone at all times.[70] The satire is vicious, coming
from the pen of an acute observer. Tolstoy was saying, in
effect, that the image of the Russian peasant, the *muzhik,*
had replaced that of the tsar. The statement is a little exag-
gerated. Nevertheless, though the image of the Tsar-Christ
was triumphant, gradually, a possible counterbalance appeared to it, the image of the Christlike peasant. The question could be posed, which Christ, if any, was to triumph?

dramatique et caricaturele de la Sainte Russie (Paris, 1854); the dry irony
of perhaps the most civilized of the Russians, Turgenev, who "cannot
help smiling at your appeal for help to the Russian god—I suddenly remembered Berangér's verses: Si je conçois comment l'on s'y comporte/ je
veux, mes enfants, que le diable m'emporte." Thus in a letter from Paris
to his friend P. V. Annenkov, commenting on March 1, 1881: *Krasnyi
Arkhiv, 32* (1929), 196; the famous "collective" satirist Kuz'ma Prutkov,
Polnoe Sobranie Sochinenii (Leningrad, 1933), 97, for a take-off on
Khomiakov; Count Alexis K. Tolstoy, *Polnoe Sobranie Sochinenii,* ed.
I. Iampol'sky (Moscow[?], 1937), 375–6 "Pesnia o Katkove, o Cherkasskom,
o Samarine, o Markeviche i o Arapakh."
    70. A. K. Tolstoy, "Potok-Bogatyr'," 286–292.

7. The Russian Soul

WHEN the revolutionaries who killed Alexander
II had been tried and condemned to death, Leo Tolstoy
wrote to the new Emperor, Alexander III, asking him, as
an act of Christian forgiveness, to pardon the murderers of
his father.[1] And, in Moscow, the young poet and philosopher Vladimir Soloviev, in a public speech, pleaded for the
same: "Only the spiritual force of Christ's truth can conquer the forces of destruction and evil," and "the present
dark moment gives the Russian tsar an unequalled opportunity to show the strength of the Christian basis of
all-forgiveness." [2] That these pleas were rejected by Alexander III was to have been expected; despite Maikov's image, the emperor had no intention of being a saint-prince
and this role did not really suit him. The passing up of a
unique opportunity to perpetuate the myth of the saintly
ruler stood for more than a political decision of Alexander

1. Lev N. Tolstoy, *Polnoe Sobranie Sochinenii*, ed. V. G. Chertkov, *63*
(Moscow, 1935), 44–52.
2. In Chulkov, *Imperatory*, 347.

III, however. Symbolically, it can be taken to indicate the dying of the ruler-myth.

This is a strong statement to make on the basis of what is largely negative evidence. But if the vitality of a myth is measured by further elaboration, by continued myth-making rather than by continued and rigid perpetuation, then the myth of the ruler was dying, for few seemed to be interested in it. This is not to say that the old formulas, epithets, and even feelings, vanished overnight. On the extreme political right, the association of the "Blessed Tsar" with "Holy Russia" continued, and Alexander III himself accepted this image.[3] And the traditional myth of the Russian Tsar must have also continued in a people who sang in a love song: "Perhaps you came down with the dew?/ Perhaps I see you only in a dream?/ I guess my warm prayer/ Has reached the tsar!", and whose proverbs, static remnants of a changing past, reiterate the popular image.[4] These same people marched, on January 9, 1905, with

3. Letter to Konstantin Pobedonostsev, March 12, 1883; *K. P. Pobedonostsev i ego korrespondenty*, intro. M. Pokrovsky, *1:1* (Moscow-Leningrad, 1923), 302. For such sentiments in general, see the numerous letters of Pobedonostsev's correspondents.

4. *Ne s rosoi li ty spustilas'?*
   Ne vo sne li vizhu ia?
   Znat' goriachaia molitva
   Doletela do tsaria!

M. M. Prishvin, "Kashcheeva Tsep'," *Sobr. Soch., 1*, 38. The proverbs, from I. I. Illiustrov, *Zhizn' Russkago Naroda v ego poslovitsakh i pogovorkakh* (3d. ed. Moscow, 1915), are interesting enough to deserve quotation: "The Sovereign is father, the earth is mother" (p. 84, and n. 3); "One sun shines in heaven, and the Russian tsar [shines] on earth" (84, and n. 8); "Everything is under the power of God and the Sovereign" (85, n. 5); "Through God and Tsar is Russia strong" (85, n. 6); "Only God and the Tsar know" (85, n. 18); "Don't think that it is far to the Tsar and high up to God; even though God is up on high, His Eye is below; even though the Tsar is far off, but whatever is on his palm is in God's hand" (85, n. 19); "God's will, the Tsar's power" (86, n. 3); "Close to the tsar is close to death" (86, n. 6)—this proverb dates from at least 1714, i.e. from the reign of Peter the Great, which may explain the sentiment.

icons in hand to see their *Batiushka Tsar'* and obtain justice and help. Yet the image had lost its impact, and the
same priest Gapon who had organized the workers for
their appeal to Nicholas II, exclaimed after they had been
shot down by the troops: "There is no tsar anymore!" [5]
Again symbolically, the change in the ruler-myth is represented by two famous public monuments in St. Petersburg:
Peter I, the Bronze Horseman by Falconet, and Alexander
III's equestrian statue by Trubetskoy. The former:
"Trampling proudly in victory/The fury of the serpent in
a bow,/On the granite gallops the Bronze Horseman—/
With imperially outstretched hand"; the latter: "on the
heavy-footed horse,/Sinking forcefully into the earth its
hoofs/In a half-dream untouched by emotion,/Motionless,
with tight reins sits." [6] And many Russian writers were
struck by the contrast between the image of an emperor and
that of a policeman.[7] From the passion and vigor of the
Bronze Horseman, only sheer power remained, motionless
and sinking into the earth from its own weight.

5. This massacre by the troops was the beginning of the 1905 revolution.
For a description by an eyewitness who tried to prevent the bloodshed,
cf. M. Gorky's letter to his wife, January 9, 1905; M. Gorky, *Sobranie
Sochinenii*, *28* (Moscow, 1949–55), 346–49. For Gapon's proclamation, cf.
348; Gapon was hiding from the police in Gorky's apartment.

6.   *Popiraia, v gordosti pobednoi*
               Iarost' zmeia, szhatogo dugoi,
               Po granitu skachet vsadnik mednyi—
               S tsarstvenno protianutoi rukoi.

     .   .   .   .

               [Tretii], na kone tiazhelostupnom,
               V zemliu vtisnuvshem upor kopyt,
               V polusne, volneniu nedostupnom,
               Nedvizhimo, szhav uzdu, stoit.

Valery Briusov, "Tri Kumira." The poem describes three monuments:
Peter I's, Nicholas I's (in front of St. Isaac's), and that of Alexander III.
(This last had been on the Znamenskaia square, and is now in the back
yard of the Russian museum in Leningrad.) *Izbrannye Stikhotvoreniia*, ed.
I. Briusova (Moscow, 1945), 289.

7. Cf. Dimitry S. Merezhkovsky, "Svinia Matushka," *Polnoe Sobranie
Sochinenii*, *12* (St. Petersburg-Moscow, 1911), 156ff.

The reasons for this transformation were many. They were contained in the changing political and social structure of Russian society: The failure of Alexander II's reforms, the consequent growth of political radicalism, the decline of the gentry and the rise of a lower class radical intelligentsia, the shift from the villages into a growing city proletariat, the enormous dissatisfaction of the peasants over the conditions of their emancipation, and the consequent growing tension between the various classes which the government did little to resolve. Within the context of the myth, the reforms of Alexander II, in particular the emancipation of the peasants, of "Holy Russia," led to the change. By liberating "Holy Russia," Alexander II was living up to the highest conception of the Blessed Tsar. The danger of this conception, however, had already been felt by Alexander I. The "Blessed Tsar," a nineteenth-century translation of the "Most-Gentle and pious Tsar" had strong eschatological overtones. The Orthodox Tsar led his people to beatitude in heaven, in the earlier myth. In the nineteenth century, in effect, the beatitude had been secularized, as in 1812. The Blessed Tsar led his people to victory and salvation on earth. This meant that the tsar could not possibly live up to the image, even if he wanted to, and Alexander II himself apparently approved of the peculiar rhythm of Russian reforms: about four steps forward and three steps back. All that was left was the image of the Sovereign Emperor, particularly harsh and stark because it represented an attempt to go back. The ideologues of this conception tended to be uncomfortable when dealing even with a "Holy Russia" of the Uvarov type, and, as an antithesis to it there was the famous description of Russia by Pobedonostsev, Alexander III's tutor, as an "Icy desert on which there wandered Man." [8] All these factors,

8. "ledianaia pustynia po kotoroi brodit Chelovek," in Grand Duke Alexander Mikhailovich, *Kniga Vospominanii* (Paris, 1933), 189; cf. Pobedonostsev, *Moskovskii Sbornik* (Moscow, 1896); Konstantin Leontiev,

as well as others less tangible which will be discussed below, affected the ruler-myth and signaled its decline.

Many of these same reasons were instrumental in the intensification of the myth of the people. The emancipation of the peasants made them a social reality as well as a mythical one. Hence, the need to know the people, to identify Russia, became even more urgent, while at the same time the possibility of self-identification through the Russian people became a little more real. Ever since the decree of liberation on February 19, 1861, there were only two real entities in Russia, two giants facing each other, argued Ivan Aksakov,[9] but while one was known and understood, what were the people like among whom Christ had walked? Or, rather, what was the significance of Christ having walked throughout the Russian land?

Maikov, a conservative, saw that: "Russia goes on, and as her leader, / The Crucified before her is ever carried, / Who had redeemed us on the cross," [10] but for the guilt-ridden gentry-intelligentsia the image was not specific enough. The greater the inherent qualities of the Russian people, the greater had to be the guilt of those who had owned and exploited them. And if the people displayed evil habits and traits, for these, again, the guilt lay within the gentry, for the evil in the Russian people was a consequence of their history, and not of their nature.

The cult of the people, exhibited most clearly in the

Vostok, Rossia i Slavianstvo, 1 (Moscow, 1885), 280f. However, for a quite fantastic and interesting attempt to preserve the traditional image of the Russian Tsar and even resurrect the myth of the saintly ruler, see the diary of A. N. L'vov, "Kniazia Tserkvi," *Krasnyi Arkhiv, 39* (1930), 147, n. 36. There L'vov describes the attempt, in the court circles around Grand Duchess Aleksandra Iosifovna, wife of Grand Duke Konstantin Nikolaevich, to canonize the emperor Paul I.(!)

9. I. Aksakov, *Sochineniia, 5*, 21, 74, 118.

10. "Na 25-letie Tsarstvovaniia Gosudaria Imperatora Aleksandra Nikolaevicha, 19 Fevralia 1880," *Sochineniia, 2*, 196; Maikov's image anticipated Blok's in *The Twelve.*

Populist (*Narodniki*) movement, displayed this type of circular logic.[11] Volume after volume of Gleb Uspensky's stories revealed the dichotomy: the evil and poverty of Russian peasant life; and the virtues of the Russian people which underlay this surface and which must be so much the greater for having survived in spite of the evil. Having borrowed heavily for their ideology from the French socialists, the populists introduced a non-transcendental explanation of popular virtues by evoking yet another myth, that of the land. Living on the land, working it, dominated and obsessed by it, the Russian peasant had the qualities that nature and virtuous toil give.[12] But the intelligentsia had discovered "Holy Russia" before it had encountered socialist populism, and the myth imposed its own standards on the *narodniki*. Peasant toil in itself did not provide the highest values and virtues, argued Uspensky. It had to be combined with divine truth, and, condemning the intelligentsia, Uspensky contrasted it with the real, popular (*narodnaia*) intelligentsia, the prototype for which were the saints of Russia.[13] In other words, Christ had to have walked on Russian soil for it to offer salvation. But while for Tiutchev it was the slavelike Christ, the radical populists created the image of the revolutionary Christ. "Of Truth the Messiah is born,/The all-powerful God-man/He is incarnate in our thought/He is truth, brotherhood and peace for ever" wrote one of their leaders, Peter Lavrov.[14] The conception of the God-man and of the earthly Messiah was borrowed from the New Christianity of St. Simon and

11. Cf. P. A. Boborykin, *Le culte du peuple dans la Russie contemporaine* (Paris, 1883); Billington, *Mikhailovsky*, and for the literature on the Populist movement, F. Venturi, *Il Populismo Russo* (2 vols. Turin, 1952).

12. Cf. Gleb Uspensky, *Polnoe Sobranie Sochinenii*, "Krestianin i krestianskii trud," "Vlast' zemli," 5 (1908 ed.), 3–194; "Malye rebiata," 7 (1909 ed.), 3–50, *et passim*. On the influence of socialist thought on Mikhailovsky and populist ideology generally, cf. Billington, 42ff.

13. Uspensky, 5, 115–19.

14. *Golos Minuvshago* (1916), no. 7/8, 142.

Proudhon, but in Russia its consequences were more striking than in France.[15] A revolutionary Christ meant a revolutionary people, and it is significant that the political
criminals of Alexander II's reign, from Karakozov to Zhe-
liabov offered themselves as Christian martyrs.[16] The
struggle, for them, was between Christ and the earthly god.

As was the case with the Slavophiles, the Populists were
a comparatively small group in the Russian intelligentsia.
But they made explicit(and in their case also acted out)
the issues which concerned intelligentsia mind and con-
science. The censor and literateur, A. V. Nikitenko, born
a serf himself, wrote in his diary for 1867: "Russian spirit,
. . . Russian nationality (narodnost')—what are these except words, commonplaces in our discussions, and yet, in
reality, great, meaningful essences?" [17] These great, meaningful essences, however, Nikitenko himself did not understand, nor, he claimed, did anyone else in Russia.[18] Yet
the need to understand, to know Russia in the proper way,
was present, for how else was one to escape the problems
which made Nikitenko open his diary for 1875 with the
words: "Everything is a lie, a lie, a lie in my dear fatherland." [19] For the critical and conservative censor there was
no rebuttal to his cry, because "We have the good eastern
orthodox religion. But in the mass of the people reigns

15. Cf. Billington, 126ff.

16. Billington, 132–33; Chulkov, Imperatory, 308. The appeal of the
"God-man" operated on yet another level. The image of Christ was, in
this case, an individualist one, beyond class or groups. For the intelligentsia,
as for some of the more radical sectarians, it solved the problem of
identity by removing it from the realm of the collective, of "Holy Russia."
A group around N. Chaikovsky founded the sect of the "God-men,"
where each individual could achieve the status of which Christ was the
forerunner. On this Joachite adaptation in nineteenth-century Russia, see
M. Frolenko, "Chaikovsky i Ego Bogochelovechestvo," Katorga i Ssylka
(1926), no. 5.

17. A. V. Nikitenko, Zapiski i Dnevnik, 3 (St. Petersburg, 1893), 133.

18. Nikitenko, 3, 133.

19. Nikitenko, 3, 375.

crude superstition; in the upper classes reigns either indifference or atheism."[20] To deny "Holy Russia" was to
block the possibility of escape from the lie, but Nikitenko's
realism was rare.

Far more acceptable to the gentry-intelligentsia was the
solution offered by L. Tolstoy in *Anna Karenina*. Not that
Tolstoy did not, in a sense, struggle against it. Talking
about the Russian volunteers with the Balkan Slavs just
before the Russo–Turkish war of 1878, the liberal and hard-
working *pomeshchik*, Levin, denies that they represented
the feelings of the Russian people. His opponent, Sergei
Ivanovich, angrily remarks that, even if Levin lacked the
feeling of compassion for the oppressed, the Russian people
have always had such sentiment. "Perhaps,—Levin ans-
swered . . .—but I can't see it; I am also of the people
(*Ia sam narod*) and I don't feel this."[21] Because he works
hard with his hands, because he adopts some peasant habits
and food, Levin feels that he is one of the people and has
as much right to speak for them as anyone.[22] Yet he is un-
happy and restless, unable to determine true values and
true principles for his life. Wandering in the woods, he
meets a peasant, and in talking to him hears the latter
describe another peasant: "He lives for the soul, he remembers God. How does he remember God? How does he
live for the soul? nearly shouts Levin. Obviously how, according to truth, according to God. Men are different . . .
For example you, you also will not hurt a man. Yes, yes
goodby—said Lenin, choking with excitement and, turning
around, he took up his cane and walked quickly away."[23]
Tolstoy would be unable to admit that he was excluded

20. Nikitenko, *3*, 375.
21. *Anna Karenina*, *19*, 388.
22. Compare this with Potok, in Alexis Tolstoy's poem, insisting that
he cannot worship the people as he is one of them himself; cf. n. 69,
chapter 6.
23. *Anna Karenina*, *19*, 376.

from the "truth," that he, Tolstoy, could not know, by
virtue of being a gentleman, what the Russian peasant
knew; yet Levin, in spite of his claim to be one of the people, learns the supreme truth and reality from a Russian
peasant. The discovery is not in the words themselves, of
course; Levin had certainly heard them before. Uttered
by the peasant, however, they are imbued with a power
which makes them, suddenly, truly meaningful. Nothing is
really settled for Levin by this conversation, his doubts do
not vanish, and in this Tolstoy differed from the orthodox
populists. Nevertheless, the answer to Levin's confusion,
as to Nikitenko's lie, was contained in the person of the
simple Russian peasant.[24]

Tolstoy incorporated in the episode both strands of populist thought: the belief in the saving power of natural
manual labor, and in the particular revelation embodied
by the Russian peasant. Yet his limited adherence to populism was strongly criticized by Dostoevsky. For the latter,
the fact that Levin did not approve of war against the Turks
was exactly proof that he was not of the people. He was of
"that upper-middle class whose historian Count L. Tolstoy
chiefly is." [25] He was, in fact, of the intelligentsia, and this
group, with the best intentions in the world, could not and
did not know Russia any better than old Verkhovensky
in *The Possessed*.[26] The Russian people, Dostoevsky insisted, had the fullest and most active compassion for the
Slavs who were being massacred by the Turks, and also

24. Levin's experience summarized, in essence, Tolstoy's idea which he
expressed at greater length in the relations between Pierre Bezukhov
and Platon Karataev in *War and Peace*. For Tolstoy's explicit views of
the Russian people and his acceptance of "Holy Russia," cf. his Diary
for February 6, 1906, *55*, 188–89; also *56*, 542, n. 532.

25. *Dnevnik*, III, July–August 1877, 285.

26. Who babbled on about his knowledge of "la sainte Russie"; *Besy*,
7, 101.

had complete understanding of Russia's needs and goals in the so-called Eastern Question.[27] Those who see the Russian people as a drunken mob, stupid and driven, are wrong, for the people are united with their tsar and desire the same things for Russia as he does.[28] This unity makes Russia stronger than any power, and its reward will be the achievement of the Russian dream, the possession of Constantinople.[29]

The Diary of a Writer, in fact, is full of outrageous chauvinism and xenophobia, and all of it on a rather primitive level.[30] But political conservatism and imperialism pure and simple did not satisfy Dostoevsky and his readers. Russia's conquest of Constantinople, her solution of the "Eastern Question" would not be due to her military strength, or even to her tsar.[31] "The Russian people . . . is orthodox, and lives out fully the orthodox idea . . . *Actually* there is no other "idea" in our people except this one, and everything derives from it alone; at least, this is what our people desires . . . I speak of the perpetual thirst for universal . . . brotherly union in Christ, which is inherent in our people." [32] It is impossible, therefore, according to Dostoevsky, to judge Russia as if it were just any political state. The political aims of the Russian state are only a manifestation of the Russian popular soul. Hence the political actions of Russia are deceptive, for Russia's purposes are not political. "According to the Russian idea . . . the state must end by becoming a pure church, and nothing else. And this shall come to

27. *Dnevnik,* III, July–August 1877, 300f.
28. *Dnevnik,* III, March 1877, 90; April 1877, 129.
29. *Dnevnik,* III, March 1877, 97.
30. Cf. *Dnevnik,* II, December 1876, 493f.; III, March 1877, 44ff. *et passim.*
31. Though Dostoevsky passionately proclaimed his loyalty and love for the tsar, the references to the ruler are few and far between; cf. n. 27.
32. *Dnevnik,* III, January 1881, 584–5.

pass, it shall come!" exclaims father Paisy in the *Brothers Karamazov*.[33] This solution, this light will come from the East, from Russia.[34] In spite of all the sneers of foreigners about the assertion that the conquest of Constantinople is not really a conquest, this claim is true. The Russians will shed their blood not to grab territories and peoples, not to increase their own power and wealth, but in order to liberate suffering humanity. "Whoever wants to be highest in the kingdom of God must become everyone's servant. This is how I understand the Russian purpose," wrote Dostoevsky in the *Diary*.[35] In his scheme he solved the old and increasing tension between the Russian state and "Holy Russia." Rather than undercutting the idea of the state through a union of tsar and people, as the Slavophiles did, Dostoevsky expressed a solution more satisfying psychologically. The tsar seemed to retire into the background, and the Russian State became the expression of the Russian people, made manifest in the political crisis of the seventies in the Balkans. The image of the tsar which tended to overwhelm the myth of the people no longer dominated the idea of Russia. Thus Dostoevsky avoided the official ideology of Blessed Tsar and "Holy Russia" which identified "Holy Russia" with the Russian State. For the writer, "Holy Russia" remained separate from the State, but imbued it with its own essence and justified its actions. If 1812 revealed the intrinsic quality of Russian holiness, then the Pan-Slavic crisis and ideology unmasked the political consciousness of "Holy Russia," its readiness to undertake its messianic mission.

What prevented Tolstoy's Levin, however, from sharing the true sentiments of the Russian people—and this despite his goodwill, his decency and his willingness to

33. *Bratia Karamazovy*, 9, 82.
34. *Ibid.*, 86.
35. *Dnevnik*, II, June 1876, 254.

work? Because his values are essentially different, argued
Dostoevsky. "The common man is vile, he cannot stop
himself from committing the foulest of sins [*smradnyi
grekh*], but he still knows that it is a foul sin . . . always
our people believes in truth, recognizes God, weeps in
joyous repentance," wrote Father Zosima in his teachings.[36] More than once in his writings Dostoevsky emphasized this image: "Yes, our people are sinful and crude,
beastly is their image . . . The people sins and fouls itself daily, but in its best moments, in the moments of
Christ, it will never mistake the truth." [37] The upper
classes, the intelligentsia are not like this; they have lost
the conception of truth, because they have lost their
faith.[38] But the difference between the gentry and the
people is greater than this, so that even faith would not
assure for Levin his being one of the people. Discussing
in his *Diary* a Russian soldier, captured by the Kipchaks
in Central Asia, and tortured to death supposedly for
refusing to deny Christianity, Dostoevsky concluded:
"Listen, gentlemen, do you know how I see this obscure,
unknown soldier of the Turkestan batallion? He is, so to
say, the emblem of Russia, of all Russia, all our national
[*narodnoi*] Russia; he is her true image." [39] The meaning
of his image he made clear in another context: "I believe that the chief, the most basic spiritual need of the
Russian people, is the need to suffer, perpetual and unquenchable, everywhere and in everything." [40] The need,

36. *Bratia Karamazovy, 9,* 394–95.

37. *Dnevnik,* III, August 1880, 532–33; cf. for similar images Dnevnik,
III, January 1877, 20; Ivan Karamazov's introduction to his "Legend of the
Grand Inquisitor," *Bratia Karamazovy, 9,* 311; Dostoevsky backed up
this conception with numerous examples from his own experience in
Siberia; cf. *Zapiski iz Mertvogo Doma, 3,* 394ff., *et passim.*

38. Father Zosima in his teachings and precepts, *Bratia Karamazovy,
9,* 395.

39. *Dnevnik,* III, January 1877, 17.

40. *Dnevnik,* I, 1873, 225.

however, is not a pathological one. The suffering was imposed on the people, during centuries of oppression and horror. Through it, in slavery and indignity, they had the ability "to join together in love and in Christ's truth." [41] Levin cannot join them because: "The main school of Christianity that they had were the centuries of uncountable and infinite suffering . . . when they, abandoned by all, oppressed by all, working for all, were left alone with only Christ the Consoler, Whom they received into their soul for ever, and Who, in return, rescued their soul from despair!" [42] It is for this reason that God will save Russia, no matter what her sins. "God will save his own people, for great is Russia in her humility." [43] Again Dostoevsky solved the problem that had plagued Russian thinkers since Pushkin, and which had obsessed Khomiakov: the contradiction between Russian reality and Russian essence. Dostoevsky did not argue that the sins of the Russian people were a good thing. They were the manifestation of Russian suffering, and insofar were excusable. In their suffering, however, the Russian people had Christ alone as a consoler. More than that, in effect Dostoevsky argued that it was only through suffering that they received Christ, that anyone can receive Christ. Hence the suffering of the Russian people was, in fact, proof that they had Christ in them. The circle of mythical logic was now complete, and reality could be absorbed by the myth. The oppression inflicted on the Russian people, their misery, were the very proofs of "Holy Russia." Without excusing the oppressors, oppression both sanctified the Russia who bore it so patiently, and demonstrated that Russia was chosen by God, as all His martyrs were, to suffer for a higher Divine purpose.

41. *Dnevnik*, II, July–August 1876, 332.
42. *Dnevnik*, III, August 1880, 531.
43. Father Zosima in *Bratia Karamazovy*, 9, 395.

All the qualities of the Russian soul, of Father Zosima's plain and simple "Holy Russia," [44] derived from the experience of suffering alone with Christ. The Russian soul was compassionate in its entirety, yearning to suffer and at the same time to alleviate the suffering of others, brothers in Christ.[45] It even led the Russians into committing actions which were wrong socially and politically. Discussing the jury trials in the new reformed courts, Dostoevsky wrote: "We [sc. the people] are frightened by this terrible power over human fate, over the fate of our own brothers, and, until we will grow up to citizenhood, we keep on pardoning . . . We sit as jurymen and . . . think: 'Are we ourselves better than the accused? We are rich, well-off, but if we were in his situation, we, perhaps, would do worse things than he . . .' . . . And this may be a pledge for something in the future so sublimely Christian that the world has seen nothing like it!" [46] Even the sins of the people reflected directly their unique relation with Christ. Dostoevsky criticized Nekrasov's poem, *Vlas,* as artificial and forced in parts, but felt that the essential point, Russian ability to repent, was correct. To support it, he told his readers about two peasants who tried to commit the worst crime they could think of, simply on a bet. Finally, they decided on the supreme outrage—to shoot at the bread of communion which one of them had saved. At the last moment, as one of the peasants lifted his gun, he saw the crucified Christ and fainted.[47] The ultimate crime for the Russian was that of blasphemy, and the peasant who had attempted it crawled on his knees from monastery to

44. *Bratia Karamazovy, 9,* 355.

45. *Dnevnik,* III, July–August 1877, 300f.

46. *Dnevnik,* I, 1873, 197; cf. 257. On Dostoevsky's insistence that the Russian people regarded criminals as "poor ones," "unfortunates," rather than evil, see *Zapiski is Mertvogo Doma, 3,* 409f. *et passim.* This supposedly Russian trait was already emphasized by Gogol', *8,* 321f., 341.

47. *Dnevnik,* I, 1873, 220ff.

monastery, convinced that there could be no forgiveness for him. The breadth and violence of the Russian soul was due to its constant and intimate communion with Christ; the Russian judged everything in terms of this relation and because of this his actions could appear to be extreme and radical by human standards. In fact the Russian must always be utterly radical according to human, "civilized," Western judgment; he is always the absolute revolutionary, because his thought is not within the earthly, temporal framework.[48]

There was little hope for the intelligentsia to become part of these Russian people, to acquire a Russian soul. Dostoevsky offered a *nostrum* in the diary: it is not sufficient to love the people for their suffering, one must love it for itself. "And what does it mean to *love it for itself?* 'Love what I love, worship what I worship' this is what it means." [49] Not much better was Shatov's advice to Stavrogin in the *Possessed:* "Listen, attain God through work; this is the whole point," [50] but these prescriptions were not very specific, nor did they touch upon the central issue of suffering, which was both the essence and the property of the Russian people. In his speech on Pushkin (June 8, 1880), Dostoevsky offered a solution: "Humble yourself, proud man, above all break down your pride." [51] "Holy Russia" was glorified by Christ because of the humility of each individual. In order to become part of "Holy Russia," each individual *intelligent* must humble himself, lose his pride, dissolve himself in the mass of people imbued with compassion, brotherly love and suffering. Personally Dostoevsky could rest content. The years in Siberia were

48. *Dnevnik*, II, June 1876, "My Paradox," 240ff.; cf. Dostoevsky's famous "Pushkin" speech, III, 511: "A Russian wanderer desires . . . universal happiness, in order to relax; he will not settle for less."

49. *Dnevnik*, III, December 1877, 473.

50. *Besy*, 7, 271.

51. *Dnevnik*, III, August 1880, 514.

his passport to "Holy Russia," for he had suffered. But
the solution was more than a personal one. Russian ter-
rorists, and Russian *narodniki* went out to work and to
suffer, and attained at least the second goal. Was this suf-
cient, however, to achieve the goal, to become Russian
and obtain salvation? The answer was ambiguous. In *The
Possessed,* Stavrogin asks Shatov whether the latter believes
in God. "I believe in Russia, I believe in her orthodoxy
— — — I believe in the body of Christ. — — — I believe that
the Second Coming will take place in Russia — — — I believe — — — Shatov babbled madly.—But in God? In God?
—I — — — I will believe in God." [52] Shatov was murdered
by the revolutionaries before he had gained the faith for
which he was searching, but the question remained, could
one achieve faith in such a way? Stavrogin's face on which
"not a muscle moved" after Shatov's reply, suggests Dostoevsky's doubt at least. Theologically, Shatov's answer was
virtually blasphemous. Yet, if God was the Russian God,
if Christ walked in Russia, what better way than Shatov's
could one find?

The ambiguity of Dostoevsky's theology becomes
greater, if anything, when one considers the thesis he set
forth in the January 1877 issue of his *Diary:* "If it wishes
to live long, every great people believes and must believe
that in it, and in it alone, is contained the salvation of the
world; that it only lives in order to stand at the head of
all the peoples, to assimilate them into itself and to lead
them, in a harmonious choir, to the final goal foreordained
for them all." [53] Dostoevsky believed this proposition to be
correct, but there was, obviously, an enormous difference
between a people believing that it is the salvation of the
world because it wants to believe, and one which believes
this about itself because it is true. The writer tried to re-

52. *Besy,* 7, 268.
53. *Dnevnik,* III, 22.

solve this problem in the famous conversation between Shatov and Stavrogin in *The Possessed*. The opening statement is by Shatov: "Do you know who is now on earth the only 'God-bearing' people, who is destined to renew and save the world in the name of a new God, and to whom alone are given the keys of life and the New Word?' "[54] Despite Stavrogin's irony, the answer could only be the Russian people. Furious at the irony, Shatov goes on questioning his former teacher: "Do you remember your expression: 'An atheist cannot be Russian, an atheist ceases to be a Russian,' do you remember?" and reminds Stavrogin of yet another definition: "A non-Orthodox cannot be a Russian."[55] Dostoevsky raised a fundamental point. If the Russian people were the "God-bearer," in a unique communion with Christ of which the external manifestation was the Orthodox religion, then clearly someone who was not Orthodox or, worse, an atheist, could not be a true Russian.[56] But the question was still unanswered, what made a people the God-bearer? Shatov insists on reciting to Stavrogin the latter's thoughts of earlier days:

"The purpose of every popular movement or motion, in every people and at every moment of its being, is, exclusively, the search for God; its own God, only its own . . . God is the synthetic personality of the whole people taken from its beginning till its end. There had never been one common God for all or many peoples, but each people had its own particular one . . . When the Gods are shared in

54. *Besy*, 7, 262.

55. *Besy*, 7, 263–64.

56. In this connection, see the story told by Baron Del'vig, nephew of the poet. Del'vig, of Baltic origin, was talking to General Anrep, also a Balt. The latter reproached him with having abandoned his Baltic knighthood by being Orthodox and hence a Russian. Anrep insisted that he himself, having remained a Baltic German, served the Russian emperor, not Russia. Del'vig, of course, found this argument rather shocking, though familiar. A. I. Del'vig, *Polveka Russkoi Zhizni*, ed. S. Ia. Straikh, 2 (Moscow-Leningrad, 1930), 345–46.

common, then they die and the faith in them, together
with the peoples themselves, also dies. The stronger the
people, the more exclusive its God. There had never been
a people without religion, that is, without the conception
of good and evil and its own, unique, good and evil." [57]

Shatov is justifying the writer's thought from the *Diary*,
and Stavrogin's answer is purposefully obvious: "You
have reduced God to a simple attribute of nationality."

"Reduce God to an attribute of nationality?—exclaimed
Shatov,—on the contrary, I raise the people up to God.
And could it be otherwise? The people is the body of
God. Every people only remains such while it has its own
God and while it rejects all the other gods in the world
uncompromisingly; while it believes that with its God it
will conquer and drive from the world all the other
gods . . .
     "A truly great people can never be reconciled to a sec-
ondary role amongst humanity, or even to a primary role,
but only and exclusively to the first role . . . But truth
is only one, and therefore, only one of the peoples can have
the true God, even though the other peoples have their
own great gods. The only "God-bearer" people is the Russian one, and . . and . . and do you really take me for
such a fool, Stavrogin,—he suddenly screamed madly—
who does not distinguish whether his words at this time
are old, worn-out nonsense, ground over on all the Moscow Slavophile mills, or are a completely new word, the
last word, the only word of renewal and resurrection, and
. . . what do I care about your laughter at such a moment!" [58]

With frightening clarity Dostoevsky reveals the ultimate
circularity of the Russian myth. Russia was "Holy Russia"
because the Russian people were the "God-bearer," because Christ walked among them and lived within them.
But this Christ, this Russian God, was created by the Russian people themselves. The object of myth, they emerge,

57. *Besy*, 7, 265–66.
58. *Besy*, 7, 266–67.

in reality, as its propagator. Shatov struggles against this conclusion; all the gods may be false, created by men, but the Russian God does coincide with the true and real God. Yet the tension remains intolerable. The Russian people *have* to create a Russian God and, at the same time, so to say, God chose the Russian people as His own, became the Russian God. Who was the true God, in Whom was a Russian to believe?

Ivan Karamazov posed the problem in the sharpest way possible: If the harmony of the world requires the forgiveness of all suffering, all horror and brutality, then, says Ivan,

"As an honest man, I must return my ticket as early as possible . . . It isn't that I don't accept God, Alesha, I am only returning to Him, most respectfully, my ticket.
    This is rebellion,—quietly and somberly said Alesha. Rebellion? . . . Tell me honestly . . . if you were erecting the temple of human fate with the final purpose of human happiness . . . and for this it were necessary to torture to death only one little being, . . . a child, and on his unrevenged tears to erect this temple, would you be willing to act as architect?" [59]

Ivan was rejecting God, but was he also rejecting the Russian God? Dostoevsky insisted that the two were identical, and to deny God meant to deny humanity; without God, not only would there be no moral law, but evil would be the logical, proper and necessary thing to do.[60] Yet he demonstrated, with utter conviction, the power of the purely Russian God, the human God, in *The Possessed:* the revolutionary leader, Peter Verkhovensky, demands Stavrogin's consent to start the revolution.

"There will be such a storm as the world has not seen . . . *Rus'* will be darkened, the land will cry for its old gods . . . Well, that's when we let out . . .

59. *Bratia Karamazovy, 9,* 307–08.
60. *Bratia Karamazovy, 9,* 90–91.

Someone!
—Whom?
—Ivan-tsarevich.[61]
—Who-om?
—Ivan-tsarevich; you, you!
Stavrogin thought for a moment.
—A pretender?—he suddenly asked . . .
—We shall say that he is 'hiding' . . . said Verk-
hovensky.—Do you know what that word means, 'He
is hiding'? But he will come, he'll come. We will create
a better legend than the *skoptsy* did. He is, but no one
has seen him.
And do you know, one can even show him to one out
of every hundred thousand. And it will travel over all
the land 'We saw him, We saw him.' They saw Ivan
Filippovich, the God Sabaoth, how he went up to heaven
in a chariot, they 'saw' it with their own eyes.[62]
And you are not Ivan Filippovich; you are beautiful,
proud as God . . . with an aura of suffering, 'hiding'
. . . You will conquer them." [63]

Dostoevsky was describing the chaos and horror of disbelief, of revolution which could only come with disbelief,
yet Peter Verkhovensky was outlining the creation of a
Russian God. A false god, it is true, but one made completely possible by the power of Dostoevsky's writing. The
whole issue was posed with terrifying irony and much
more simply, earlier in *The Possessed:* listening to a group
of officers discussing the existence of God with Verkhovensky, "a grey-haired bourbon of a captain sat," according to
the latter, "sat all the time quietly, didn't say a word, then
suddenly stands up in the middle of the room and says
loudly, you know, as if talking to himself: 'If there is no

61. The traditional hero of Russian fairy tales.
62. Verkhovensky was referring to a sect of the Old Believers whose
leader, Daniil (Dostoevsky made a mistake in his first name) Filippovich
was adored as God and was supposed to have been seen ascending to
heaven in a chariot. Cf. Mel'nikov-Pechersky, *Pol.Sobr.Soch.*, *6*, 312f.
63. *Besy*, 7, 441–42.

God, then what kind of a captain am I?' picked up his cap,
shrugged his shoulders, and went out." [64]

This was the crux of the problem: what kind of a captain, what kind of a Russian would one be without God?
The Russian God was the God of suffering which was both
existence and purpose. To reject suffering was to rebel
against God, and thus become God oneself, "Man-God"
rather than "God-man." [65] But in rebelling against suffering one could create a Russian God, even if he were a
false pretender; and even if he did not coincide with the
true and universal God, he could be more true and more
acceptable humanly. Dostoevsky was convinced that he
knew the Russian popular soul, the true meaning of "Holy
Russia." His understanding of the Russian people was on
about the same level of reality as that of Khomiakov or, for
that matter, of Tolstoy but he did understand and expose
the conceptions and myths of an intelligentsia for whom
God was dead. Two alternatives were possible for them:
to rebel against God by rejecting Russian reality, to become gods themselves, creating a new reality like the one
of Peter Verkhovensky, Ivan Karamazov or the Man from
the Underground; or, to humble themselves, to give up
their human pride and accept the manifest Christ of the
Russian people, one, however, who was a God on earth
rather than in heaven. But, Dostoevsky felt, the psychological motivation of both groups was the same: the need
to transcend an intolerable reality. Hence both these
strands of thought were within the framework of the Russian myth. Those who rejected God did so because they
were seeking Him through their awareness of the horror
of life; as Russians, they could not help seeking Him and,
as Russians, they had a right to question Him. Those who

64. *Besy*, 7, 240.

65. *Chelovekobog*, rather than *Bogochelovek*; cf. Kirillov's argument in
Besy, 7, 124, 251f.

accepted the Russian God of suffering did so because that was the only way Russian suffering could be meaningful; and the greater the suffering, the greater the reward for it. One, however, which would come here, on earth, as the Russian God was here, on earth. To sum up, Dostoevsky's writings reflected the secularization of the Russian myth and of its eschatology. Russia was to lead the world to salvation not in the arms of the Heavenly Father, but in the arms of the Russian God, who was as much a God on earth as was the emperor.

To those for whom God was not dead, the danger of Dostoevsky's ideas was obvious. The philosopher and poet Vladimir Soloviev warned: "The image of every people is not what it itself thinks of itself within time but what God thinks of it within eternity." [66] Humility which ends with self-deification, he argued, results in the justification and acceptance of reality, in the triumph and perpetuation of the State in its worst chauvinist manifestations.[67] "Holy Russia" is an ideal, rather than a reality; an ideal which is to be achieved not through self-glorification, but through self-denial in the service of God.[68] The main task that Russia could and should perform is the re-establishment of Christian unity, the healing of the schism between East and West in a spirit of brotherly love. But in all of its actions, Soloviev wrote, Russia must know that "Holy Russia demands holy deeds." [69] The implication of this requirement was that Russia may not live up to the ideal, and in his *Tale of Antichrist* Soloviev expressed his pessimism. Russia, as all other countries, fell under the spell of the false messiah, and salvation came to the world finally through the union of all the Christian faiths, all

66. In A. V. Soloviev, *Sbornik*, 109.

67. V. Soloviev, "Natsional'nyi Vopros v Rossii," *Sobranie Sochinenii*, 5 (St. Petersburg, 1901–7), 8ff. and *passim*.

68. Soloviev, 5, 51, 336f., 379f.

69. Soloviev, 5, 50.

acting as equal partners.[70] But the *Tale* also allows a symbolic interpretation: the power of the Antichrist, the Earthly God, was exactly due to the fact that he did not know he was Antichrist, that he was convinced of being the true Messiah. Soloviev obliterated the line dividing Dostoevsky's "every people has its own god" from Luther's "every people has its own devil." Yet, describing Russian national character, he wrote:

"Usually a people, when trying to praise its own nationality, expresses in this praise its national ideal, that which is best in it, that which it desires most of all. Thus a Frenchman speaks of . . . *la Belle France, la gloire du nom français;* an Englishman says with love . . . *Old England;* A German rises higher and, giving an ethical character to his national ideal, with pride speaks of *die deutsche Treue.* What does the Russian people say in similar circumstances, how does it praise Russia? Does it call it beautiful or old, does it speak of Russian glory (the glory of the Russian name is sometimes found in the newspapers, but it is a translation from the French) or of Russian honesty and loyalty? . . . it speaks only of *Holy* Russia. That is the ideal: not a liberal one, not a political one, not an esthetic one, even not a formal-ethical one, but a moral-religious ideal." [71]

In spite of all his warnings and injunctions, Soloviev was caught up in the logic of the myth, in the fact that the conclusion implied the premise. If the Russian people had such a unique ideal, such an extraordinary and particular purpose, then they must be different in their essence, which is "Holy Russia." [72] Repudiating Russian reality and also the self-deification of the individual rebel against God, Soloviev nevertheless remained within the aura of the myth. He denied the false "Holy Russia" in the present, but in order to achieve it in the future.

70. "Kratkaia Povest' o Antikhriste," *8,* 556–83.
71. Soloviev, *5,* 50.
72. Cf. Soloviev *5,* 30f., 51–52, 342f.

Thus Dostoevsky and Soloviev indicated the full scope of possibilities within Russian mythmaking: The individualist "Russian" rebellion against God; the acceptance of reality imbued with the Russian God; and the repudiation of a false reality for the sake of the same reality transcendent. Neither of the two men created these conceptions. Both were reflecting the solutions offered by the myth in an age of constantly increasing tension. By the reign of Nicholas II (1894–1917) this tension had reached intolerable proportions. Its nature and cause were best described by Count Witte in the discussions which preceded the constitution of 1905: the government should either crush ruthlessly all opposition, or it should respond favorably to the public clamor for reforms.[73] In a society of growing political and social contradictions, however, the government had pursued and continued to pursue a policy of programless, haphazard and hence meaningless oppression. Within this context the intelligentsia sought desperately for solutions, and the Russian myth was sufficiently broad to offer escape to many.

The myth continued its existence, even in its official, "Uvarov" form.[74] But Dostoevsky, who had formulated the greatest justification of the myth by making Russian suffering and misery its main feature, had released the demons of the myth by reflecting too clearly its human origin. Ivan Aksakov hit out at the "liberals" who argued that the qualities of "Holy Russia"—"holy patience," "holy humility"—were descriptive not of a great people but of "holy cattle," [75] but the demons could not be exor-

73. N. I. Vuich and Prince N. D. Obolensky, "K Istorii Manifesta 17-go Oktiabria," *Arkhiv Russkoi Revolutsii*, 2 (1922), 9–10.

74. Cf. A. Gratieux, *Le Mouvement Slavophile à la veille de la Révolution* (Paris, 1953), 130ff. Gratieux himself reflects the monstrous racist features of late slavophilism.

75. Cf. I. Aksakov's tirade against the liberal *Otechestvennyi Zapiski*, *Sochineniia*, 5, 42.

cised very easily. The novelist Dimitry Merezhkovsky, one
of the leaders in the religious revival among the intelligentsia, founder of the Religious-Philosophical Society,
discussed the monument to Alexander III in an article entitled "Mother Pig" (*Svinia Matushka*): [76]

> "Yes, little mother Russia is erected with her tsar.
> —Well, what kind of a horse is Russia,—a pig, not a
> horse . . . She won't dance well . . . But what a be-
> hind, mainly what a behind that horse has! You must
> have noticed the esthetic taste of Russians, of the most
> aristocratic ones . . . to make for their coachmen, for
> some reason, monstrous behinds, by placing a whole
> pillow under their coats! What kind of an idea is that,
> tell me! But it must be some kind of historical tendency,
> a 'cosmic' taste, perhaps? . . . Russia is 'mother,' and
> Russia is 'pig.' The pig is mother. The song of tri-
> umphant love is the song of the triumphant pig." [77]

Merezhkovsky felt that this image would amuse particu-
larly Feodor Karamazov: "Oh, you, little children, piglets!
All of you are the children of one and the same Mother
Pig. We don't need another kind of Russia. Long live
Mother Pig!" [78]

The bitterness is shocking and illuminating. It is the
bitterness of a man who, to continue his image, is profoundly and personally outraged that the horse is a pig
rather than a beautiful, dancing charger, that the dream of
"Holy Russia" has become the nightmare of the lecher
and cynic Feodor Karamazov. This same fury of a betrayed
man, of a man who would have wanted so desperately to
believe, Merezhkovsky directed against the myth of the

76. Cf. note 7.

77. The first part of this statement is Merezhkovsky quoting from an
article by Varvarin in *Russkoe Slovo* (unavailable to me). Varvarin was a
pseudonym which, Merezhovsky felt, was penetrated by everyone, for *"ex
ungue leonem,* only one man in Russia wrote this way" Merezhkovsky, *12*,
156, and note. Professor Vernadsky has informed me that Varvarin was
V. V. Rozanov.

78. Merezhkovsky, *12*, 157.

ruler who ruled over a Karamazov reality. Dostoevsky, their common teacher, was wrong, he proclaimed to the intelligentsia. The Russian State, the dream of the Third Rome, Autocracy itself, were the ideas of Antichrist.[79] In the years following the revolution of 1905, the status of the ruler-myth, for the intelligentsia at least, was symbolized by Merezhkovsky when he wrote: "After all, what is autocracy raised to the level of religion, except the greatest insanity of them all?"[80]

Yet, though the intelligentsia anathemized the "Holy Russia" of the "Blessed Tsar," the false "Holy Russia" of present-day reality, the myth of a simple, popular, shabby, pious "Holy Russia" of the present, and of a more glorious "Holy Russia" in the future, continued to exist. Vladimir Korolenko ended his story "At an eclipse" ("Na Zatmenii") with the verse of N. Berg, an early nineteenth-century poet: "Soon, in Holy Russia, the cocks will crow,/ Soon in Holy Russia the day will dawn," and the sentiment was echoed by a revolutionary populist in Gorky's *The Life of Klim Samgin*.[81] Another character in the novel declaimed with enthusiasm on the Russian God: "Yes, exactly: the hovels [referring to the little churches of Moscow] of the Russian, Moscovite, most national God! We have a marvellous God,—simple! Not in jewels, not in a mantle, but in a simple shirt, yes, yes!"[82] Valery Briusov's image of Russia, in his poem "On the Boundary" ("Po Mezhe") was: "How clear, how tender is the sky!/How gaily the martlets swoop/Around the church of Boris and Gleb!" evoking the gentle saintly brothers as

79. Merezhkovsky, *11*, 210; *12*, 60f, 269. Cf. Gorky, *Zhizn' Klima Samgina*, where one of the characters calls Nicholas II a nihilist. *Sobranie Sochinenii, 20*, 471.

80. Merezhkovsky, *12*, 161.

81. V. G. Korolenko, *Polnoe Sobranie Sochinenii, 3* (St. Petersburg, 1914) 217; Gorky, *Zhizn' Klima Samgina, 20*, 92.

82. Gorky, *19, 392*.

the personification of the Russian countryside.[83] And
Alexander Blok wrote, with pain and longing, about
"Beggarly Russia," *Nishchiia Rossiia,* standing in her
"beautiful rags," regretting nothing in the past and caring
nothing for the future; [84] about a mysterious Russia, full
of magic and legends; [85] about:

"Russia, my life! are we tied to one fate for us?
Tsar! yes, Siberia! Ermak! and jail!
Does no repentance, no parting await for us?
To my free soul can your darkness avail?

What do you know? Faith in God were you treasuring?
What do you wait for your singing to say?

· · · · · · · · ·

Why do you charm me so, mirage of dreaming, then?
Why do you play with my free spirit so?" [86]

"Beggarly Russia" is also "Holy Russia," but only if it
takes a magic jump, if it becomes "Holy Russia" in actual-
ity. So Blok, who wrote that: "Perhaps Russia is the
triumph of the 'inner' man, a permanent reproach to the
'outer' man," also wrote: "I am not with those who are for
the old Russia . . . nor with those who are for Europeani-
zation . . . but I am for a *New* Russia . . . or for *no*

83. *Izbrannye Stikh.,* 231.

84. A. A. Blok, *Zapisnye Knizhki,* ed. P. N. Medvedev (Leningrad, 1930),
91.

85. "Rus'," *Sochineniia, 1* (Moscow, 1955), 181–82.

86. *Sochineniia, 1,* 348; transl. by Bowra in *Book of Russ. Verse,* 108–09.
Blok's mystical feeling for Russia reached its highest expression in his
correspondence with the peasant poet Kliuev. The latter, to describe
Blok's relation to Russia and the people wrote about the "marriage of
God's servant Alexander to God's servant Russia." The poet had replaced
the tsar. Cf. *Sud'ba Bloka,* eds. O. Nemerovskaia and Ts. Vol'pe (Leningrad, 1930), 171. In 1907 Blok wrote: "I insist further that, if there is a
real conception of "Russia" or better, of "Rus'" beyond the idea of ter-
ritory, state power, state church, classes, etc. . . . it is that great, infinite,
spacious, sad and promising [something] that we are accustomed to sub-
sume under the name of Rus'. . . ."; "O Realistakh," *Aleksander Blok o
Literature,* ed. V. V. Gol'tsev (Moscow, 1931), 55.

Russia." [87] And the poet Andrei Belyi, despairing, pleaded: "Vanish, vanish in space, Russia, my Russia!" [88]

Blok and Belyi reflected the feeling of the liberal and radical intelligentsia that an eschatological jump was necessary to justify the existing "Holy Russia," a jump forward into something utterly new. The events of the early twentieth century and particularly the revolution of 1905 drove many, however, to seek refuge with the more familiar aspects of the Russian myth. Reviewing Belyi's *Ashes,* a book of poems on shabby and poor Russia, Sergei Soloviev, nephew of Vladimir Soloviev and himself a poet, wrote: "It is characteristic that the poet sees in Russia everything that was seen by Nekrasov, everything except the *church,* on the stones of which the poet [Nekrasov] of popular misery beat his head . . . His [Belyi's] next book can only be about the 'God of the oppressed, God of the saddened, God of the generations standing in front of this poor altar.' Without this God, Russia, nationality and our own personality can be only a heap of *Ashes.*" [89] Belyi was silent, but the poet Viacheslav Ivanov, esthete and student of Greek philosophy, responded to Soloviev's appeal: "The mystics of both East

87. *Zapis. Knizhki,* 122, 127.

88.   *Dovol'no: ne zhdi, ne nadeisia—*
          Rasseisia, moi bednyi narod!

          .   .   .   .

          Izchezni v prostranstve, izchesni,
          Rossiia, Rossiia moia!

Stikhotvoreniia (Berlin, 1923), 137. For the denigrating epithet which was, at the same time, an expression of love and hope, in the same rhythm as "Holy" Russia and appearing as the other side of the coin of "Holy Russia," see, e.g., Belyi's cycle of poems called "Deaf Russia," *Glukhaia Rossiia,* ibid.; L. Andreev's "Ubogaia Rus'" (Shabby Russia), *Polnoe Sobranie Sochinenii,* 6 (St. Petersburg, 1913), 204f.; A. Amfiteatrov, *Oderzhimaia Rus'* (Possessed Russia), (Berlin, 1926); A. Remizov, *Vzvikhrennaia Rus'* (Stirred-up Russia), (Paris, 1927).

89. Sergei Soloviev in *Vesy,* 1909, no. 1, 86 (unavailable to me), quoted in Belyi, *Mezhdu Dvukh Revolutsii* (Leningrad, 1934), xix.

and West are agreed that, at the present time . . . the
torch has been given to Russia." In contrast to the Western European desire for ascending, the Russian Idea is
expressed in the urge to descend, which is related "to the
mystery of the Second Hypostasis, the mystery of the Son."
That is why the Russian people are the "Christ-bearer." It
dies in Christ and is resurrected in the Holy Spirit, he
wrote in 1909.[90] A poem written in the medieval epic style
began with the line: "Shine out, our mother, the Holy-
Russian Land!" and went on to describe the Russia of
saints, ascetics, miracle-workers and churches.[91] And in his
poem "The Mercy of the World," Ivanov wrote: "To Him
Who took on the aspect of a slave/And, Blessed, walks over
our fields,/Go to the dark stirring of our heart,/ And the
prophetic stirring of the spirit!/ . . . No, my people, You/
Oh, Sower, will not abandon!/You will not deny the God-
bearer:/Who wishes for Your yoke!" [92]

The same desperate need to revivify *the* Russian myth
is reflected in the work of the painter Michael Nesterov;
most strikingly in his painting entitled "Holy Russia,"
done in 1906 (Fig. 19). Russia is represented by children, by
old men, particularly by women, struggling over the snow-
covered fields, and finding the one they sought, Christ, who
waits for them with a group of Russian saints. The Russian
people seeking and finding Christ—Nesterov's vision was
similar to that of the poets; yet the painting reveals, more
clearly than the poetry, the bankruptcy of the idea. Most
of the critics thought that the painting, though a brave

90. V. Ivanov, *Po zvezdam* (St. Petersburg, 1909), unavailable to me,
quoted by Merezhkovsky, *12*, 178–79.
91. "Stikh o Sviatoi Gore," V. Ivanov, *Kormchie Zvezdy* (St. Petersburg,
1903), 79.
92. "Milost' Mira," *Zvezdy*, 76. Cf. the other poems of the cycle
Raiskaia Mat', particularly the one on the "Russian Mind," which "thinks
realistically about the world/While swimming in a mystical gloom," 77.

effort, failed in its intent; that the cold and artificial de-
piction of Christ and the saints contradicted the warmth
and humanity of the right side of the canvas which showed
the Russian people. Tolstoy, while admiring Nesterov's
idea, called the painting a "Funeral mass" of Russian
orthodoxy, for the Russian people "Cannot see Christ as
an Italian singer." [93]

More and more, however, Dostoevsky's devil was emerging into the open. The same Viacheslav Ivanov accused
Russia that she stood "dumbly,/At the cross-roads cross,/
Daring neither to bear the sceptre of the Beast,/Nor the
light yoke of Christ." [94] Blok, in his article "Nature and
Culture," wrote of the "orthodox people, sung to sleep
by government vodka . . . with drunken priests." A people capable of singing, "You love, you are love,/You are
holy love/Persecuted always,/Washed by blood." and who
also sing, "We have sharp little knives,/Heavy weights/We
are free fellows,/Practiced ones." [95] Briusov appealed to
"Our Demon": "Appear in radiance like God's angel/Or
rise, a phantom from the grave,/But give us sign that not
in vain/Were our fatal century-old deeds!" [96] Dostoevsky
was as wrong about the people as he was about autocracy,
insisted Merezhkovsky; he had confused a religious ideal
of "Holy Russia" with the reality.[97] Observing the Russian
people Merezhkovsky felt "as if the Russian 'people-God-
bearer' had become the most godless of all the peoples; as

93. Cf. A. Mikhailov, *Mikhail Vasilievich Nesterov* (Moscow, 1958), 214
and n. 1; Tolstoy's diaries, *56*, 542, n. 532.

94. In Merezhkovsky, *12*, 182.

95. *Sochineniia*, 2, 100–01.

96. *Iavis' v luchakh, kak strazh gospoden',*
    Il' vstan', kak prizrak grobovoi,
    No dai nam znak, chto ne bezploden
    Stoletnii podvig rokovoi!
"Nash Demon," *Izbrannye Stikh.*, 214–15.

97. Merezhkovsky, *11*, 175ff.

if the peasants [*krestianstvo*] had stopped being Christians [*khristianstvo*]." [98] They seem to be holy only when they are slaves, and, once free, become utterly sinful. "Holy slaves. Holy Russia, the land of holy slaves." [99] The question, for Merezhkovsky, is obvious: "Is the Russian idea, Russian insanity?" [100]

The poets and writers were not reacting primarily to Dostoevsky's devil, of course. This last was itself a reflection of a reality within which it became more and more difficult to force the increasingly restless Russian people into the procrustean image of "Holy Russia" which the intelligentsia was imposing on them. That the crisis was felt is shown by innumerable discussions, pamphlets, and articles on one theme: The People and the Intelligentsia.[101] There were two alternatives: to accept what the Russian people were according to their own words and actions, or to reject them for not fitting properly into the conception of "Holy Russia." [102] The danger was great, however, no matter what choice one made. Gogol' had compared Russia to a madly galloping troika; "What if that troika," wrote Blok, *"is flying right at us?"* [103] There was a third possibility of becoming the truly alienated rebel against God, symbolized by the talkative bums of Gorky and by the demonic and Christlike *Savva* of Leonid Andreev; but

98. Merezhkovsky, *11*, 208.

99. Merezhkovsky, *12*, 183.

100. Merezhkovsky, *12*, 187. Still, the insanity persisted. Rather nastily Belyi reports Merezhkovsky's boasting to Jaurés, in Paris: "We Russians are not men; we are gods or beasts," *Mezhdu Dvukh Rev.*, 164.

101. See a listing of such discussions in Blok, *Zap. Knizhki*, 99–100; also see for example, Merezhkovsky, *11*, 129; M. Gershenzon, *Istoricheskie Zapiski* (Moscow, 1910), 172f.

102. This last was represented by the famous *Vekhi*, a collection of articles by seven Russian writers and philosophers, published in 1907, warning the intelligentsia that they are wrong in seeking an ideal in the Russian people who are only prevented from massacring the intelligentsia by the bayonets of the tsar's army.

103. "Narod i Intelligentsia," *Sochineniia, 2*, 90.

this was not very promising in a time of social and political crisis.

The crisis was resolved, in a way, by the First World War in 1914. That it should have become the occasion for a new and vital expression of national myths was to have been expected. But the myths re-emerged in a very pure and concentrated form, thrown back, in a certain sense, to their historical origin. Of the ruler only the person remained, and though the French ambassador, Maurice Paléologue, wrote that the Russian people thought of the Tsar as Christ, probably a more accurate popular image of Nicholas was that of the "Unlucky Tsar." [104] As a person, Nicholas II could not live up to the image of the Tsar, and the Russian myth of the ruler as we have known it, died very quietly in February 1917. Yet it received a fitting and striking epitaph. In his reminiscences, Gorky wrote of one Breef, a monarchist, who visited him after the revolution had begun. Breef had not changed his mind:

"I know the people. They don't care a cent who is sitting on the throne—it might be a Tartar or a Kirgiz for all they care—so long as there's someone, something, on which to hitch their dreams . . . The people need a hero, a saint—General Skobelev, Feodor Kuzmich, Ivan the Terrible—they are all alike to them. And the more remote, the more vague, the less accessible the hero, the more freedom for the imagination . . . There must be a 'Once upon a time there lived' about it—something of the fairy tale. Not a God in heaven, but here, on our dismal earth. Someone of great wisdom and monstrous power . . .

The R-russian Tsar must be Terr-r-rible and fierce! Terrible even to look at, not only by nature. Or else he must

104. Maurice Paléologue, *La Russie des Tsars pendant la Grande Guerre*, *1* (Paris, 1921), 273–74; *2*, 55. Cf. S. Mel'gunov, *Na Putiakh k Dvortsovomu Perevorotu* (Paris, 1931), 116; cf. the words of Lev Tikhomirov after the revolution of 1905, that the tsar was a "sacrificial victim," 205.

be a beautiful fairy-tale prince, or just an improbable
monster; but—a R-russian Tsar must be terr-r-rible and
fierce . . .
    Do you know the picture of the Tsar Ivan the Terrible
by Vasnetzov? [105] Do you remember how one of his eyes
squints ever so slightly? That's a tsar's eye for you! An
all-seeing eye. A tsar like that sees everything and believes
in nothing . . . The tsar of the tsardom, the lord of the
realm." [106]

Breef had woven in all the Dostoevskian strands of the
ruler-myth in one mad outpour. A last one can be suggested, for the image of the tsar presented by Vasnetsov
evokes another image of a "ruler," the fourteenth-century
icon "The Saviour of the furious Eye," *Spas Iaroe Oko*
(Fig. 16). Whether Vasnetsov meant it or not, the image of
the Christian ruler returned to its origin, even though in
a rather strange way.
    The myth of the people also appeared, during the war,
in its primitive form. "Holy Russia" was rediscovered and
evoked by many and various members of the intelligent-

    105. See Fig. 14.
    106. "Monarkhist," Gorky, *15*, 303–09; the translation is from M. Gorky,
Fragments from My Diary (Penguin Books Ltd., London, 1940), 213–18.
    107. All the poets discussed here reacted to the war in terms of "Holy
Russia" and frequently in more jingoist terms. The exception was Blok,
who apparently distrusted the new wartime patriotism; cf. *Sochineniia*,
2, 467. A. Remizov wrote a small book entitled *For Holy Russia, Za
Sviatuiu Rus'* (Petrograd, 1914 [?]). The epithet appeared in a soldiers'
song: "Bravely into battle we shall go/For Holy Russia. . . ." (My smelo
v boi poidem/Za Rus' sviatuiu.) (A. Argunov, "Bez Svobody," *Golos
Minuvshogo Na Chuzhoi Storone, 13* [1925] 116) and, at the same time, in
a letter by Grand Duke Andrei Vladimirovich (Mel'gunov, 136) and in a
letter by Prince A. A. Orlov to the Minister of War, A. A. Polivanov (A. A.
Polivanov, *Memuary, 1* [Moscow, 1924], 233), and in a speech of M. A.
Rodzianko before the Duma (*Arkhiv. Russkoi Rev.*, *17* [1926], 81). These,
of course, are but a few examples out of the mass that is available. The
emperor, too, spoke of the faithful sons of "Holy Russia." (Order of the
Day, December 12, 1916, in General A. S. Lukomsky, *Vospominaniia, 1*
[Berlin, 1922], 116).

sia.[107] And as the war went on, for many, the Russia of the common people, "Holy Russia," offered the only hope. The philosopher F. Stepun, serving as an artillery sub-officer at the front, wrote that Russia could not accept war, that she was "either above or below it, and therefore Russia should not have accepted the challenge to war, but should have lifted up her holy and miracle-working icons and gone, without arms, against the enemy. No matter how mad these words may sound, I cannot see any serious objections to them." [108]

For the painter Nesterov, too, the war served as an impetus to solve the problem of portraying Russia. For years he had worked on a painting which was to be, in effect, a logical consequence of his "Holy Russia"; in 1916 he finished his *"Na Rusi,"* best translated as "Russia" (Fig. 20). Again the Russian people, this time led by a small boy, are seeking Christ; but, in this painting, an unseen Christ. Rather than risking a portrait of Christ, Nesterov tried to convey, in detail, his image of "Russia," against the background of *the* Russian river, the Volga. The crowd is huge, but carefully chosen to present the Russian essence. On the left, a little ahead of the crowd, comes a *iurodivyi,* a holy fool, arms high in ecstasy. To the right of him, in the front row, we see a seventeenth-century patriarch, bishops and *boiare,* and a Moscovite Tsar in full regalia. Equally ahead of the crowd on the right is a blinded soldier, tapping his way to Christ, and behind him, in the mass of medieval costumes and paintings we see Dostoevsky, Vladimir Soloviev, and Tolstoy. A more explicit statement of the Russian myth would be difficult to find, even to the exclusion of the emperor; yet, except for the three writers, the symbols of Russia appear curiously anachronistic.

The myth did continue for a time, in fact with renewed

108. F. A. Stepun, *Iz pisem praporshchika artillerii* (Prague, 1926), 98.

vitality, and the revolution of 1917, rather than destroying it immediately, provided an occasion for an outburst of mythologizing. The true face of the Russian people which emerged after the revolution, the new reality, was not accepted by very many of the intelligentsia. Even those who rejected it, however, like the poet and writer Ivan Bunin, did so in mythical terms. Instead of 150 million "holy" Russians, one now had the same number of beasts, Dostoevsky's possessed, murderers and sadists one and all.[109]

For the peasant poets, Sergei Esenin and Nikolai Kliuev, the revolution meant a return to the "Holy Russia" of old, of peasant life but in a new freedom.[110] For the poet A. Remizov, revolutionary Russia is a land punished by God and visited by God, Christlike in her suffering and expiation of all sins, but Remizov saw no resurrection.[111] Andrei Belyi felt the revolution as the eschatological leap promised by "Holy Russia" and achieved through the culmination of suffering in the revolution:

> Wail, element tossed by the tempest
> In pillars of thunderous fire:

109. Ivan Bunin, "Okaiannye Dni," *Sobranie Sochinenii, 9* (Berlin, 1935), 104f. and *passim*. Emigré literature is full of discovery that there was no Russia, that the Russian people had not developed far enough to form a nation. In this connection, see the conversation between the White officer, Roshchin and his former orderly, Aleksei, in Alexis Tolstoy's *Khozhdenie po mukam, 1* (Moscow, 1950), 319. The orderly tells Roshchin: "You don't know our people. 'How's that?' Just so, and you have never known them. You were always cheated. 'Who cheated me?' We did, we, the soldiers, the peasants. . . . Oh, Vadim Petrovich! Bravery, love for the tsar, for the fatherland,—the gentry have thought it all up and we had to memorize it."
110. Particularly for Kliuev with his Old Believers connections, cf. his cycle of poems "Krasnyi Ryk," *Polnoe Sobranie Sochinenii*, ed. B. Filippov, *1* (New York, 1954), 379f. Less so for Esenin who, nevertheless, still saw the salvation of revolutionary Russia in a peasant Christ. Cf. his poems "Mikola," "Tovarishch," "Prishestvie," "Inoniia," *Sobranie Stikhotvorenii, 2* (Moscow-Leningrad, 1926), 9, 32, 46, 64.
111. A. Remizov, *Vzvikhrennaia Rus'*, 52f., 180ff., 479.

O Russia, my Russia, my Russia,
Rage, rage, burn me up in thy pyre!

For into thy fated destruction,
Thy shrouded abysses, is borne
A host of winged spirits like angels
Whose dreams are as bright as the morn.

Then weep not, but kneel in devotion
And play in the hurricane's blaze,
The thundering chorus of seraphs,
The torrent of cosmical days.

The dry, barren wastes of dishonour,
The seas of unquenchable tears,
From light in His look, though He speak not,
Will sparkle when Christ's face appears.

Leave Heaven its girdle of Saturn,
Its milky and silvery ways;
And seethe, blaze like light in the tempest,
Earth-ball, with thy fiery rays!

O element, fiery, blazing,
Rage, rage, let thy flames feed on me,
O Russia, my Russia, my Russia,
Messiah of days soon to be! [112]

While Belyi left the origin of Russia's suffering cosmic and vague, the dialectic of the Russian myth was expressed clearly and bluntly by Blok in his poem *The Twelve*. The twelve revolutionaries who march through the dark and stormy winter night have to destroy "Holy Russia":

Don't shrink, comrade. Get your rifle out;
Give Holy Russia a taste of shot,
The wooden land,
Where the poor huts stand,
And her rump so grand!

Aha, but no Cross!

112. Belyi, *Stikhotvoreniia*, 463; transl. Bowra, *Second Book of Russ. Verse*, 88–89; cf. other poems, 370, 437.

The symbolic twelve have to destroy the "Holy Russia"
of the Blessed Tsar, of poverty and oppression, of misery
and suffering, so that, at the end of the poem:

> On they march with sovereign tread,
> With a starving dog behind,
> With a blood-red flag ahead—
> In the storm where none can see,
> From the rifle bullets free,
> Gently walking on the snow,
> Where like pearls the snowflakes glow,
> Marches rose-crowned in the van
> Jesus Christ, the Son of Man.[113]

"Holy Russia" appeared to survive the revolution by
having accomplished the eschatological leap forward that
Blok and Belyi had desired. Whatever was left of the "Russian God" was, after all, in the myth of the people rather
than in the myth of the ruler. Both myths, however, were
essentially Christian in origin and eschatology. "Holy Russia" could be transformed, apocalyptically, into the earthly
paradise, but in that paradise Christ would have to be
manifest in the flesh. If not that, then "Holy Russia," as
Blok had said, would have to become nothing. Despite the
dreams of Blok and Belyi, Kliuev and Esenin, the overthrow of the old order meant neither a return to a peasant,
Old-Believer past, nor a mystical search for the living
Christ. The mood of the new society was suggested by the
poet of the revolution, Vladimir Maiakovsky, in "Our
March":

> Do not look to the stars or bother;
> Without them our singing shall blow.
> Oh, ask, Great Bear, our mother,
> That alive to the stars we go!
>
> Drink of delight. Drink! Shout!
> Veins with spring-flood thrumming.

113. Transl. Bowra, *Second Book of Russ. Verse*, 78–79, 87.

Hearts up! Strike out!
Our breasts are brass cymbals drumming.[114]

The myth of the people, however, did not fail primarily because it had become so exalted that no reality could possibly live up to it. "Holy Russia" had been the myth of the peasant masses attempting to express their collective personality against the overpowering image of the centralized State through the only common and obvious quality they possessed—their faith. But while the gentry, and the centralized state itself, appropriated this myth, the peasants, seeking to express their own particular common denominator, found it in the idea of land and labor. "Holy Russia," with its implicit transcendental eschatology could not, for long, answer their needs. "Holy Russia" was also the myth of an alienated class, the intelligentsia. Through it the gentry intelligentsia expressed not so much its aspirations as its need for identity and its guilt over its alienation. The revolution of 1917 meant the social, political, and economic (if not the physical) end of such a group. And it also meant, for the intelligentsia, the disappearance of the familiar forms for the myths; the tsar was gone and the "Russian People" as one had been accustomed to think of them, no longer existed either.

"Holy Russia," "Russian God," "Russian Soul," and "Russian Tsar" were myths to justify a pretty intolerable reality, but, as myths, they were premised upon it. Also, as myths, they lived longer than the reality which they justified and reflected. As such, they died when the Russian people, whatever they were, passed from justification to change.

114. The last two verses of Maiakovsky's "Our March," trans. C. M. Bowra, *Book of Russian Verse*, 125.

Epilogue

THE need for personal and collective identity and for a justification of reality continued in Russia after 1917, and with it continued the process of mythmaking. But Russian reality and its mythological premises had changed. The myths we have been observing through centuries of Russian history, derived from a specific context. The Christlike Tsar and "Holy Russia" were myths not only Christian in terminology but in content as well. Both justified and explained reality in terms of an overarching and transcendental purpose—salvation. Hence, they were time-bound, beginning when Russia was Christianized and ending when, more and more, the purpose of Russian society was secularized until salvation was sought for, and justified, on earth.

Within their lifetime, however, the Russian myths seem to have been particularly vital. All societies have a need to worship power and to provide an exalted image of themselves. And, with the history of the last thirty or forty years in mind, the plethora of Führers and father-images, it would be very wrong to assign the Russians a unique propensity for the "cult of personality" and for self-worship. Yet the power and radical expressions of the Russian myths strike one as unusual. A likely component of this radicalism was the more immediate and intense religiosity of a comparatively primitive society which shared the Eastern, Greco-Byzantine predilection for an epiphanic God; one who came down to men rather than requiring their ascent to him. But this element in Russian culture could form only a small part of any explanation.

It has been observed by many that myths, rather than approximating reality, tend to be in direct contradiction to it. And Russian reality was "unholy" enough to have produced the "holiest" myths of them all. The greater the power of the government, the more extreme was the myth required to justify it and excuse submission to it; the greater the misery of the Russian people, the more extreme was the eschatological jump the myth had to provide so as to justify the misery and transcend it. But while myths are born of reality, they have a dynamism and logic of their own. The overwhelming completeness of the ruler-myth imposed itself on both Russian society and its ruler. Distinct from the police power of the tsar, the myth precluded, in effect, any theory of opposition to, or limitation of the ruler within the context of traditional Russia. Any challenge, no matter how slight, was by definition revolutionary, and the eventual answer, even on the part of the intelligentsia ruling class, was revolution. The power of the myth was sufficient to make the most intelligent and sophisticated Russians, well aware of the bureaucratic nature of modern society, assign all power and all responsibility to the person of the tsar.

The logic of the myth of the people was even more complex. Among the masses, "Holy Russia" retained its anti-state flavor and continued to exist as a rather vague

image of self-identity and of a promise for the future implied in the epithet. But the dynamism of this myth, inherent in the fact that it was created in order to balance
the image of the ruler and the state, was expressed by the
alienated ruling class of the gentry-intelligentsia. The desire for identity, the feeling of guilt towards the peasants,
and the need for support against the overpowering myth
of the ruler, led it to appropriate and develop, more and
more radically, the myth of the people. Though this development took place in the period of general European
romantic nationalism, significantly it received its great
impetus during the reign of Nicholas I, the apogee of the
ruler-myth in practice. While Garibaldi Italy could rally
to the cry of *Dio e popolo* without much fear of contradiction within Italy at least, and while Germans could
rally around Klopstock or Schiller and the myth of an inherent German love for Freedom (with slightly more fear
of contradiction), the problem of the Russian intelligentsia
was more difficult. Each step in the exaltation of the people was assimilated by the ruler-myth, requiring yet another transcendental leap forward: from "Holy Russia"
to the "Russian God," and then to the "God-bearer" and
beyond. And each step in the dialectic of the myth increased the tension between it and Russian reality until
the contradiction became intolerable and the myth began
to lose its meaning. In his struggle against this fact,
Dostoevsky revealed its existence, and the mythologizing
of the subsequent fifty years only confirmed it. Only because the Russian God was dead could the myth take on
such fantastic forms, fulfilling individual yearnings and
insecurities rather than a social function. Yet its power
was such that the intelligentsia still clung to it, constantly
attempting to resuscitate it so that it could again carry
the burden of Russian reality and dreams. The important
aspect of the myth is not that great humanists and realists

such as Lermontov, Turgenev, Chekhov, were immune to its appeal, but, rather, that so very many Russian thinkers, poets, musicians and writers were bound by it. And the three men named above were constantly criticized for their inability to deal with the "great issues." The majority of the intelligentsia sought for salvation in the Russian myth up to 1917 and beyond.

Ideas which are expressed by a society with such profound feeling and for so long are certainly part of its history. While they reflect this history, taken by themselves they provide a distorted image, a caricature seen in a crooked mirror; properly, they should be viewed as a facet of a multi-faceted whole. Caricatures, however, have long been honored for their ability to provide unexpected insights. Hence the history of the myths of the Tsar and the People, exiguous though it is in relation to the whole of the Russian past, may suggest some insights into it and thus gain a measure of historical validity.

Bibliography

Adrianova-Perets, V. P., "Slovo o zhitii i o predstavlenii velikogo kniazia Dmitriia Ivanovicha, tsaria Russkago," *T.O.D.R.L., 5* (1947), 73–96.

———, "Zadonshchina," *T.O.D.R.L., 5* (1947), 194–224.

Agapetus, Migne, *Patrologia Graeca, 86,* i, col. 1163–86.

Aksakov, I. S., *Polnoe Sobranie Sochinenii,* 7 vols. (Moscow, 1886).

Aksakov, K., *Polnoe Sobranie Sochinenii,* 3 vols. (Moscow, 1861–80).

Akty Istoricheskie, Sobrannye i izdannye Arkheografischeskoi Kommissiei A.N., 5 vols. (1841–72).

Akty Sobrannye v bibliotekakh i Arkhivakh, Arkheograficheskoi Ekspeditsiei, 4 vols. (St. Petersburg, 1836–38).

Alföldi, A., "Die Geburt der kaiserlichen Bildsymbolik," *Museum Helveticum, 9* (1952), 204–43; *10* (1953), 103–24; *11* (1954), 133–69.

———, "Insignien und Tracht der römischen Kaiser," *Mitteilungen des deutschen archäologischen Instituts: Römische Abteilung, 50* (1935).

Andreev, V. V., *Raskol i ego znachenie v narodnoi russkoi zhizni* (St. Petersburg, 1870).

Argunov, A., "Bes Svobody," *Golos Minuvzhogo Na Chuzhoi Storone, 13* (1925), 80–130.

Arkhiv Kniasia Vorontsova, ed. P. Bartenev, 40 vols. (Moscow, 1870–95).

Bakunin, M., *Narodnoe delo: Romanov, Pugachev ili Pestel'* (Moscow, 1917).

Barsov, E. V., "Drevne-russkie pamiatniki Sviashchennago Venchaniia Tsarei na Tsarstvo," *Chteniia* (1883:1).

Barsukov, N., *Istochniki Russkoi Agiografii*, ed. by Obshchestvo Liubitelei Drevnei Pis'mennosti, *P.D.P.I., 82* (St. Petersburg, 1882).

———, *Zhizn' i trudy M. P. Pogodina*, 22 vols. (St. Petersburg, 1888–1910).

Batiushkov, K. N., *Sochineniia*, 5th ed. (St. Petersburg, 1887).

Belinsky, V., *Pis'ma*, ed. E. A. Liatsky, 3 vols. (St. Petersburg, 1914).

Belyi, A. [Bugaev, B.], *Mezhdu Dvukh Revolutsii* (Leningrad, 1934).

Benediktov, V. G., *Sochineniia,* ed. I. P. Polonsky (St. Petersburg-Moscow, 1902).

Benz, E., *Russische Heiligenlegenden* (Zurich, 1953).

Berdiaev, N., *Russkaia Ideia* (Paris, 1946).

Billington, J. H., *Mikhailovsky and Russian Populism* (Oxford, 1958).

Bloch, M., *Les rois thaumaturges* (Strasbourg, 1924).

Blok, A. A., *Zapisnye Knizhki,* ed. P. N. Medvedev (Leningrad, 1930).

———, *Aleksander Blok o Literature,* ed. V. V. Gol'tsev (Moscow, 1931).

———, *Sud'ba Bloka,* eds. O. Nemerovskaia and Ts. Vol'pe (Leningrad, 1930).

Boborykin, P. A., *Le culte du peuple dans la Russie contemporaine* (Paris, 1883).

Bowra, C. M., "Pushkin," *Oxford Slavonic Papers, 1* (1950), 1–15.

Briusov, I., *Izbrannye Stikhotvoreniia* (Moscow, 1945).

Brodsky, L., *Rannie slavianofily* (Moscow, 1910).

Budovnits, I. U., *Russkaia Publitsistika XVI Veka* (ANSSSR, 1947).

Bunin, I., "Okaiannye Dni," *Sobranie Sochinenii, 9; 11* vols. (Berlin, 1934–36).

Byliny Severa, ed. A. M. Astakhova (Moscow, 1938).

Chaadaev, P., *Sochineniia i pis'ma,* ed. M. Gershenzon (Moscow, 1913).

Cherniavsky, M., "Holy Russia: A Study in the History of an Idea," *American Historical Review, 63* (April 1958), 617–37.

———, "Khan or Basileus: An Aspect of Russian Medieval Political Theory," *Journal of the History of Ideas, 20* (1959), 459–76.

———, "The Reception of the Council of Florence in Moscow," *Church History, 24* (1955), 347–60.

Chulkov, G., *Imperatory* (Moscow-Leningrad, 1928).

Cyril II, Metropolitan, *Slovo o sudiakh i vlastiteliakh, Pravoslavnyi Sobesednik, 1* (1864), 305–74.

[Daniil, Abbot], "Zhitie i khozhdenie Daniila russkia zemli igumena," ed. Mikhail Venevitinov, *Pravoslavnyi Palestinskii Sbornik* (St. Petersburg, 1883–85), nos. 3, 9.

Danilov, Kirsha, *Drevniie Rossiiskiie Stikhotvoreniie*, 2d ed. (Moscow, 1818).

Delo Petrashevtsev, Pam. Obshch. Mysli (Moscow-Leningrad, 1941).

Del'vig, A. I., *Polveka Russkoi Zhizni*, 2 vols., ed. S. Ia. Straikh (Moscow-Leningrad, 1930).

Derzhavin, G. R., *Sobranie Sochinenii*, 7 vols. (Akademicheskoe Izdanie, St. Petersburg, 1864–78).

Diakonov, M. A., *Vlast' Moskovskikh Gosudarei* (St. Petersburg, 1889).

Dimitrieva, R. P., *Skazanie O Kniasiakh Vladimirskikh* (ANSSSR, 1955).

Dolger, F., "Die Entwicklung der Bysantinischen Kaiser titulatur," *Bysantinische Diplomatik* (Munich, 1956).

Doré, G., *Histoire pittoresque, dramatique et caricaturele de la Sainte Russie* (Paris, 1854).

Dostoevsky, F., *Dnevnik Pisatelia za 1873 god* (Paris, YMCA Press, n.d.).

———, *Dnevnik Pisatelia za 1876 god* (Paris, YMCA Press, n.d.).

———, *Dnevnik Pisatelia za 1877 god* (Paris, YMCA Press, n.d.).

———, *Sobranie Sochinenii*, 10 vols. (Moscow, 1956–58).

Dragomanov, M., *Istoricheskie pesni malorusskago naroda* (Kiev, 1877).

Dubrovin, N., *Pugachov e ego Soobshchiniki*, 3 vols. (St. Petersburg, 1884).

Dukhovnye i Dogovornye Gramoty Velikikh i Udel'nykh Kniazei XIV–XVI vv., ed. L. V. Cherepnin (ANSSSR, 1950).

Erdmann, C., *Die Entstehung des Kreuzzungsgedankens* (Stuttgart, 1935).

Esenin, S., *Sobranie Stikhotvorenii* (Moscow-Leningrad, 1926).

Evgen'eva, A. P., "O nekotorykh poeticheskikh osobenostiakh russkago ustnago eposa XVII–XIX vv.," *T.O.D.R.L.*, 6 (1948), 154–92.

Exempliarsky, A. V., *Velikie i Udel'nye Kniazia Severnoi Rusi*, 2 vols. (St. Petersburg, 1889).

Fedotov, G. P., *Sviatoi Filipp Mitropolit Moskovskii* (Paris, 1928).

———, *Sviatye Drevnei Rusi* (Paris, 1931).

Fet, A. A., *Polnoe Sobranie Stikhotvorenii*, ed. N. N. Strakhov, B. V. Nikol'sky (St. Petersburg, 1912).

Filaret, Metropolitan, *Slova i Rechi*, 3 vols. (Moscow, 1845).

Folz, R., "Zur Frage der heiligen Könige: Heiligkeit und nachleben in der Geschichte des Burgundischen Königtums," *Deutsches Archiv, 14* (1958), 317–45.

Fonvizin, D. I., *Polnoe Sobranie Sochinenii* (St. Petersburg-Moscow, 1888).

Frolenko, M., "Chaikovsky i Ego Bogochelovechestvo," *Katorga i Ssylka* (1926), no. 5.

Gershenzon, M., *Istoricheskie Zapiski* (Moscow, 1910).

Gipiius, Z., *Siniia Kniga* (Belgrade, 1929).

Gogol' N. V., *Polnoe Sobranie Sochinenii, 1–7, 10–11* (Moscow-Leningrad, 1951–52).

Golikov, I. I., *Deianiia Petra Velikago, 30* vols. (Moscow, 1778–98).

Golikova, N. B., *Politicheskie protsesy pri Petre I* (Moscow, 1957).

Golubinsky, E. E., "Istoriia kanonizatsii sviatykh v Russkoi tserkvi," *Chteniia* (1903:1).

Gorky, M., *Sobranie Sochinenii, 30* vols. (Moscow, 1949–55).

Granjard, H., "Du Romantisme Politique: Slavophiles et Populistes," *Revue des Études Slaves, 24* (1957), 73–80.

Gratieux, A., *Le Mouvement Slavophile à la veille de la Révolution* (Paris, 1953).

Gregoras, Nicephorus, *Historia Byzantina, Corpus Scriptorum Historiae Byzantinae, 3* vols. (Bonn, 1829–55).

Grigoriev, A. D., *Arkhangel'skie byliny i istoricheskie pesni, 3* vols. (St. Petersburg, 1904–10).

Guilland, R., "Οἱ Βυζαντινοι αὐτοκράτορες καὶ τὸ θέλγητρον τοῦ μοναστηρίον," Ἐπετηρὶς Ἑταιρεις Βυζαντινῶν Σπονδῶν, *21* (1951), 215–234.

Herberstein, Baron Sigismund, *Zapiski o moskovitskikh delakh*, A. I. Malein, trans. (St. Petersburg, 1908).

Herzen, A. I., *Polnoe Sobranie Sochinenii i Pisem*, ed. M. Lemke, *22* vols. (Petrograd, 1913–25).

Iazykov, N. M., *Polnoe Sobranie Stikhotvorenii*, ed. M. K. Azadovsky (Moscow-Leningrad, 1934).

"Istoriia Pechatnaia," *Chteniia* (1863:1).

Istrin, V., *Otkroveniia Mefodia Patarskago i apokrificheskie videniia Daniila v vizantiiskoi i slaviano-russkoi literature, Chteniia* (1897:2).

Ivanov, V., *Kormchie Zvezdy* (St. Petersburg, 1903).

——, *Po zvezdam* (St. Petersburg, 1909).

——, *Die Russische Idee* (Tubingen, 1930).

Ivanov, Vsevolod N., *My: Kul'turno-istoricheskie osnovy russkoi gosudarstvennosti* (Harbin, 1926).

Iz Pisem i Pokazanii Dekabristov, ed. A. K. Borozdin (St. Petersburg, 1906).

"Iz vospominanii raznykh lits o Nikolae Pavloviche i ego vremeni," *Russkii Arkhiv* (1895:2), 179–87.

Jakobson, R. O., "Izuchenie 'Slova o polku Igoreve' v S.Sh.A.," *T.O.D.R.L., 14* (1958), 102–21.

"Kak Vasplakalas' Rossia o svoem Belom Tsare," *Russkaia Starina, 68* (1890), 689–90.

Kallash, V. V., *Dvenadsatyi God* (Moscow, 1912).

Kampf, H., *Das Reich im Mittelalter* (Stuttgart, 1950).

Kantorowicz, E. H., *The King's Two Bodies* (Princeton, 1957).

——, *"Pro Patria Mori* in Medieval Political Thought," *American Historical Review, 56* (1951), 472–92.

Kapterev, N. F., *Kharakter otnoshenii Rossii k pravoslavnomu vostoku v XVI i XVII stoletiakh* (St. Petersburg, 1914).

——, *Patriarkh Nikon i Tsar Aleksei Mikhailovich*, 2 vols. (Moscow, 1909).

Karamzin, N. M., *Istoriia Gosudarstva Rossiiskago,* 12 vols. in 6 (St. Petersburg, 1892).

Kartashev, A. V., "Sud'by 'Sviatoi Rusi,'" *Pravoslavnaia Mysl', Trudy Prav. Bogos. Inst. v Parizhe, 1* (Paris, 1928).

Kheraskov, M. M., *Rossiada* (St. Petersburg, 1895).

Khomiakov, A. S., *Polnoe Sobranie Sochinenii,* 8 vols. (Moscow, 1900–04).

——, *Stikhotvoreniia*, ed. and comment by V. A. Frantsev (Prague, 1934).

Kireevsky, I. V., *Polnoe Sobranie Sochinenii,* ed. M. Gershenzon, 2 vols. (Moscow, 1911).

Kliuchevsky, V. O., *Boiarskaia Duma Drevnei Rusi* (Moscow, 1883).

——, *Kurs Russkoi Istorii,* 5 vols. (Moscow, 1957).

Kliuev, N., *Polnoe Sobranie Sochinenii,* ed. B. Filipov, 2 vols. (New York, 1954).

"Kniga glagolemaia opisanie o Rossiiskikh sviatykh," ed. M. V. Tolstoy, *Chteniia* (1887:4).

Koht, H., "The Dawn of Nationalism in Europe," *American Historical Review, 52* (1947), 265–80.

Kologrivov, I., *Essai sur La Sainteté en Russie* (Bruges, 1953).

Korf, M., *Materialy i Cherty k Biografii Imperatora Nikolaia I, S.R.I.O., 98* (1896).

Korolenko, V. G., *Polnoe Sobranie Sochinenii,* 9 vols. (St. Petersburg, 1914).

Kotoshikhin, G., *O Rossii v Tsarstvovanie Alekseia Mikhailovicha* (St. Petersburg, 1884).

Kots, E., "Volneniia krepostnykh v Nikolaevskuiu epokhu," *Russkoe Proshloe*, 2 (1923), 74–88.

"Kratkoe Opisanie Blazhennykh Del Velikago Gosudaria, Imperatora Petra Velikago, Samoderzhtstsa Vserosiiskago," *Zapiski Russkikh Liudei. Sobytiia Vremen Petra Velikago*, ed. N. Sakharov (St. Petersburg, 1841).

Krause, H., *Kaiserrecht und Rezeption* (Abh.d. Heidelberg Akad., 1952).

Krestianskaia Voina pod predvoditel'stvom Stepana Razina, Sbornik Dokumentov (ANSSSR, 1957).

Küppers, L., *Göttliche Ikone* (Dusseldorf, 1949).

[Kurbsky, M.], *Sochineniia Kniazia Kurbskago, R.I.B., 31* (1914).

Lampert, E., *Studies in Rebellion* (London, 1957).

Latkin, V., *Uchebnik istorii russkago prava perioda imperii* (St. Petersburg, 1909).

Lednicki, W., *Pushkin's Bronze Horseman*, Univ. of California Publ. Slavic Studies, *1* (Berkeley, 1955).

Lemke, M., *Nikolaevskie Zhandarmy i literatura 1826–55* (St. Petersburg, 1909).

Leonid, Archimandrite, *Sviataia Rus, ili svedeniia o vsekh sviatykh i podvizhnikakh blagochestiia na Rusi*, ed. Obshchestvo Liubitelei Drevnei Pis'mennosti, in *P.D.P.I., 97* (St. Petersburg, 1891).

Leontiev, K., *Vostok, Rossia i Slavianstvo* (Moscow, 1885).

Leontovitsch, V., *Die Rechtsumwälzung unter Ivan dem Schreklichen und die Ideologie der Russischen Selbstherrschaft* (Stuttgart, 1947).

Likhachev, D. S., "Poslanie Groznogo v Kirillo-Belozerskii monastyr, 1573g.," *T.O.D.R.L., 8* (1951), 247–86.

Liubimov, L., *Taina Imperatora Aleksandra I* (Paris, 1938).

Liwoff, G., *Michel Katkoff et son Epoque* (Paris, 1897).

L'Orange, H. P., "Sol Invictus Imperator," *Symbolae Osloensis 14* (1935), 86–114.

Lossky, N. O., *Kharakter Russkogo Naroda* (Frankfurt, 1957).

Lukomsky, A. S., *Vospominaniia*, 2 vols. (Berlin, 1922).

[L'vov, N. A.], "Neizdannye stikhi N. A. L'vova," ed. Z. Artomonova, *Literaturnoe Nasledstvo, 9/10* (1933), 264–86.

Maikov, A. N., *Polnoe Sobranie Sochinenii*, ed. P. V. Bykov (St. Petersburg, 1914).

Malia, M. E., "Herzen and the Peasant Commune," *Continuity and Change in Russian and Soviet Thought*, ed. E. J. Simmons (Cambridge, Massachusetts, Harvard University Press), 197–217.

Malinin, V., *Starets Eleasarova monastyria Filofei i ego poslaniia* (Kiev, 1901).

Mansikka, V., *Zhitie Aleksandra Nevskago* (St. Petersburg, 1913).

Medalliony v Pamiat' voennykh sobytii 1812, 1813, i 1815 godov, izobretennye grafom F. Tolstym, Arkheograficheskaia Kommissiia (St. Petersburg, 1838).

Mel'gunov, S., *Na Putiakh k Dvortsovomu Perevorotu* (Paris, 1931).

Mel'nikov-Pechersky, P. I., *Polnoe Sobranie Sochinenii,* 7 vols. (St. Petersburg, 1909).

Merezhkovsky, D. S., *Polnoe Sobranie Sochinenii,* 17 vols. (St. Petersburg-Moscow, 1911).

Mikhailov, A., *Mikhail Vasilievich Nesterov* (Moscow, 1958).

Mikhailovich, A. (Grand Duke Alexander Mikhailovich Romanov), *Kniga Vospominanii* (Paris, 1933).

Mikhailovsky-Danilevsky, A. I., "Zapiski," *Russkaia Starina, 68* (1890), 489–534.

Miller, V. F., *Istoricheskie pesni russkago naroda, XVI–XVII vv., Sbornik Otdeleniia Russkago Iazyka i Slovesnosti, 93* (1915).

Mouratow, P., *L'Ancienne Peinture Russe* (Rome, 1925).

[Nartov], *Raszkazy Nartova o Petre Velikom,* ed. L. N. Maikov (St. Petersburg, 1891).

Nekrasov, N. A., *Polnoe Sobranie Sochinenii i Pisem,* ed. V. E. Evgenev-Maksimov, A. M. Egolin, K. I. Chukovsky, 12 vols. (Moscow, 1948).

[Nepluiev, I. I.], *Zapiski Ivana Ivanovicha Nepluieva* (St. Petersburg, 1893).

Nifontov, A. S., *Rossiia v 1848 godu* (Moscow, 1949).

Nikitenko, A. V., *Zapiski i Dnevnik,* 3 vols. (St. Petersburg, 1893).

[Nikon, Patriarch], "Vozrazhenie sviateishago Nikona patriarkha," *Zapiski Imperatorskago Russkago Arkheologicheskago Obshchestva,* 2 (1861), 423–98.

Novgorodskaia Pervaia Letopis', ed. A. N. Nasonov (ANSSSR, 1950).

Novikov, N., comp. *Drevneiia Rossiiskaia Vivliofeka,* 2d. ed., 20 vols. (Moscow, 1788–91).

Odoevsky, A. I., *Polnoe Sobranie Stikhotvorenii i Pisem,* ed. I. A. Kubasov and D. D. Blagoi (Moscow-Leningrad, 1934).

Oreshnikov, A., *Materialy k russkoi sfragistike* (Moscow, 1903).

———, *Russkie monety do 1547 goda* (St. Petersburg, 1910).

Paleologue, M., *La Russie des Tsars pendant la Grande Guerre,* 3 vols. (Paris, 1921).

[Palitsyn, Avraam], *Skazanie Avraama Palitsyna,* Arkheograficheskaia Kommissiia (St. Petersburg, 1909).

Palmer, W., *The Patriarch and the Tsar*, 6 vols. (London, 1871–76).

Pamiatniki Diplomaticheskikh Snoshenii Rossii s Derzhavami Inostrannymi, S.R.I.O., 35.

Pamiatniki Drevnei Russkoi Pismennosti otnosiashchiesia k Smutnomu Vremeni, R.I.B., 13.

Pamiatniki Istorii Staroobriadchestva XVII v., R.I.B., 39 (1927).

Paul of Aleppo, "Puteshestvie Antiokhskago patriarkha Makariia v Rossiiu v polovine XVII veka, opisannoe ego synom, arkhidiakonom Pavlom Aleppskim," trans. G. Murkos, *Chteniia* (1896:4, 1897:4, 1898:4).

Pesni sobrannye P. V. Kireevskim, 8 vols. (Moscow, 1863–79).

Pierling, P., S. J., *La Russie et le Saint-Siège* (Paris, 1890).

Platonov, S. F., *Drevnerusskiia Skazaniia i Povesti o Smutnom Vremeni* (St. Petersburg, 1888).

——, *Ocherki po Istorii Smuty* (St. Petersburg, 1899).

Pobedonostsev, K. P., *Moskovskii Sbornik* (Moscow, 1896).

[Pobedonostsev, K. P.], *K. P. Pobedonostsev i ego korrespondenty*, intro. M. Pokrovsky (Moscow-Leningrad, 1923).

Polivanov, A. A., *Memuary* (Moscow, 1924).

Polne Sobranie Russkikh Letopisei, 26 vols. (St. Petersburg, 1841–1959).

Polnoe Sobranie Zakonov Rossiiskoi Imperii (St. Petersburg, 1825–1916).

Portrety Gerby i Pechati Bol'shoi Gosudarstvennoi Knigi 1672g., ed. St. Petersburgskii Arkheologicheskii Institut (1903).

Poslaniia Ivana Groznogo, ed. D. S. Likhachev, Ia. S. Lur'ie, V. P. Adrianova-Perets (ANSSSR, 1951).

Post, G., "Blessed Lady Spain—Vincentius Hispanus and Spanish National Imperialism in the 13th Century," *Speculum, 29* (1954), 198–210.

Povesti o Kulikovskoi Bitve, ed. M. N. Tikhomirov, V. F. Rzhiga, L. A. Dmitriev (ANSSSR, 1959).

Presniakov, A. E., *Obrazovanie veliko-russkago gosudarstva* (Petrograd, 1918).

——, "Samoderzhavie Aleksandra II," *Russkoe Proshloe, 4* (1923), 3–20.

——, "Samoderzhavie Nikolaia I," *Russkoe Proshloe, 2* (1923), 1–21.

Prokhorov, V., *Khristianskie i russkie drevnosti i arkheologia* (St. Petersburg, 1872).

Propp, V. I., *Russkii Geroicheskii Epos* (Leningrad, 1955).

Prozorovsky, D. I., "Ob utvariakh pripisyvaemykh Vladimiru Monomakhu," *Zapiski Imperatorskago Russkago Arkheologicheskago Obshchestva, 3* (1882), 1–64.

———, "O znachenii tsarskago titula do priniatiia russkimi gosudariami titula imperatorskago," *Izvestiia Imperatorskago Arkheologicheskago Obshchestva, 8,* 192–218; 449–77.

Prutkov, K. (The brothers Zhemchuzhnikov and A. Tolstoy) *Polnoe Sobranie Sochinenii,* ed. I. Iampol'sky (Moscow, 1933).

Pskovskie Letopisi, ed. A. N. Nasonov, *1, 2* (ANSSSR, 1955).

Pugachevshchina, ed. S. A. Golobtsov, 2 vols. (Tsentrarkhiv, 1929).

[Pushkin, A. S.], *Dnevnik A. S. Pushkina,* Trudy Gos. Rumian. Museia, *1* (Moscow-Petrograd, 1923).

Pypin, A. N., *Istoriia Russkoi Literatury,* 4 vols. (St. Petersburg, 1902).

Raskol'nichie Dela XVIII Stoletiia, ed. G. Esipov (St. Petersburg, 1861).

Remizov, A., *Za Sviatuiu Rus'* (Petrograd, 1914).

Rerum Moscoviticarum Auctores Varii: Unum in Corpus Nunc Primum Congesti (Frankfurt, A. Wechelus, 1600).

Reutsky, N. V., *Liudi Bozhii i Skoptsy* (Moscow, 1872).

Riazanovsky, N., "Khomiakov on Sobornost'," *Continuity and Change in Russian and Soviet Thought,* ed. E. J. Simmons (Cambridge, Mass., Harvard University Press, 1955), 183–96.

———, *Nicholas I and Official Nationality in Russia 1825–1855* (Berkeley and Los Angeles, 1959).

———, *Russia and the West in the Teaching of the Slavophiles,* (Cambridge, Mass., Harvard University Press, 1952).

Rogger, H., "The 'Nationalism' of Ivan Nikitič Boltin," *For Roman Jakobson,* ed. M. Halle, H. C. Lunt, H. McLean, C. H. Van Schooneveld (The Hague, 1956), 423–29.

———, *National Consciousness in 18th Century Russia* (Cambridge, 1960).

———, "The Russian National Character: Some Eighteenth-Century Views," *Harvard Slavic Studies, 4,* 17–34.

Rostopchinskie Afishi 1812 goda, ed. A. S. Suvorin (St. Petersburg, 1889).

Rovinsky, D. A., *Podrobnyi Slovar' Russkikh Gravirovannykh Portretov,* 3 vols. (St. Petersburg, 1886–88).

Salaville, R., "Pour un repertoire des neo-saints de l'eglise Orientale," *Byzantion, 20* (1950), 223–37.

Samarin, Iu. and F. Dmitrev, *Revoliutsionnyi Konservatism* (Berlin, 1875).

(Sanin, Iosif), *Poslaniia Iosifa Volotskogo*, ed. A. A. Zimin and Ia. S. Lur'ie (ANSSSR, 1959).

Sarkisyanz, E., *Russland und der Messianismus des Orients* (Tübingen, 1955).

Sbornik Istoricheskikh Materialov izvlechennykh iz Arkiva Perv. Otd. Sobst. E. I. V. Kantseliarii (St. Petersburg, 1876).

Schaeder, H., *Moscau das Dritte Rom* (Hamburg, 1929).

Schilder, N. K., *Imperator Nikolai Pervyi*, 2 vols. (St. Petersburg, 1903).

Schramm, P. E., *Der König von Frankreich* (Weimar, 1939).

Sedel'nikov, A. D., "Drevneia Kievskaia legenda ob apostole Andree," *Slavia, 3* (1924–25), 316–35.

Semevsky, M. E., *Slovo i Delo! 1700–1725* (St. Petersburg, 1884).

Semevsky, V., *Krestianskii vopros v Rossii* (St. Petersburg, 1888).

Serebriansky, N. I., *Drevnerusskiia Kniazheskiia zhitiia, Chteniia* (1915:3).

Ševčenko, I., "A Byzantine Source of Muscovite Ideology," *Harvard Slavic Studies, 2* (1954), 141–80.

(Shishkov, A. S.), *Zapiski, Mneniia i Perepiska Admirala A. S. Shishkova*, ed., N. Kiselev and Iu. Samarin (Berlin, 1870).

Shmurlo, E. F., "Petr Velikii v otsenke sovremennikov i potomstva," *Zhurnal Ministerstva Narodnago Prosveshcheniia, 35* (1911), 315–40; *36* (1911), 1–37, 201–73; *39* (1912), 1–40, 193–259.

Simoni, P. K., "Velikorusskie pesni zapisannye v 1619–20 gg. dlia Richarda Dzheimsa," *Sbornik Otdeleniia Russkago Iazyka i Slovesnosti, 82* (1907).

Slovo o pogibeli Russkiia zemli, ed. Kh. Loparev, *P.D.P.I., 84* (St. Petersburg, 1892).

Slovo o Polku Igoreve, ed. V. P. Adrianova-Perets (ANSSSR, 1950).

Smolitsch, I., "Die Stellung des russischer Kaisers zur Orthodoxen Kirche in Russland vom 18, bis 20 Jh.," *Forschungen zur Osteuropäischen Geschichte* (Ost Europa Institut an der Freien Univ. Berlin), II (1955), 139–164.

Sobranie Gosudarstvennykh Gramot i Dogovorov, khraniashchikhsia v gosudarstvennoi kollegii inostrannykh del, ed. N. N. Bantysh-Kamensky, A. F. Malinovsky, et al., 5 vols. (Moscow, 1813–94).

Sokol'sky, V. *Uchastie russkago dukhovenstva i monashestva v razvitii edinoderzhaviia i samoderzhaviia* (Kiev, 1902).

Soloviev, A. V., "Der Begriff 'Russland' in Mittelalter," *Studien zur Alteren Geschichte Osteuropas* (Wiener Archiv für Geschichte des Slawentums und Osteuropa), 2 (1956), 143–68.

Soloviev, A. V., "Le dit de la ruine de la terre russe," *Byzantion*, 22 (1952) 105–28.

——, "Helles Russland—Heiliges Russland," *Festchrift für Dmytro Čyževskii zum 60. Geburtstag, Veröffentlichungen der Abteilung für slavische Sprachen und Literatur des Osteuropa-Instituts* (Slavisches Seminar), an der Freien Universität Berlin, 6 (Berlin, 1954), 282–89.

——, *Holy Russia, The History of a Religious-Social Idea* (The Hague, 1959).

——, Le Nom Byzantin de la Russie (The Hague, 1957).

——, "Sviataia Rus' (ocherk razvitiia religiozno-obshchestvennoi idei)." *Sbornik Russkago Arkheologicheskago Obshchestva v korolevstve S. Kh. S., 1* (Belgrade, 1927), 77–112.

——, "Weiss-, Schwarz- und Rotreussen," *Jahrbücher für Geschichte Osteuropas*, 7 (1959), 1–33.

Soloviev, V., *Sobranie Sochinenii*, 10 vols. (St. Petersburg, 1901–07).

Spassky, I. G., "Denezhnoe obrashchenie v Moskovskom Gosudarstve," *Materialy i Issledovaniia po Arkheologii SSSR, 44* (1955), 214–354.

Stepun, F. A., *Iz pisem praporshchika artillerii* (Prague, 1926).

Stief, C., *Studies in the Russian Historical Song* (Copenhagen, 1953).

Subbotin, N., *Materialy dlia istorii raskola*, 8 vols. (St. Petersburg, 1875–87).

[Timofeev, Ivan], *Vremennik Ivana Timofeeva*, ed. O. A. Derzhavina and V. P. Adrianova-Perets (ANSSSR, 1951).

Tiutchev, F. I., *Polnoe Sobranie Sochinenii*, ed. P. V. Bykov (St. Petersburg, 1913).

Tiutcheva, A. F., *Pri Dvore Dvukh Imperatorov*, ed. S. V. Bakhrushin and E. V. Ger'e (Moscow, 1929).

Tkhorzhevsky, S., "Donskoe voisko v pervoi polovine semnadtsatogo veka," *Russkoe Proshloe, 3* (1923), 9–28.

Tolstoy, A. K., count, *Polnoe Sobranie Sochinenii*, ed. I. Iampol'sky (Moscow [?], 1937).

Tolstoy, Lev N., *Polnoe Sobranie Sochinenii*, ed. V. G. Chertkov, 90 vols. (Moscow-Leningrad, 1928–56).

Treitinger, O., *Die Oströmische Kaiser-und Reichsidee* (Jena, 1938).

Troitskaia Letopis', ed. M. D. Priselkov, (ANSSSR, 1950).

Troyat, H., *Souvenirs et réflexions* (Paris, 1956).

Trubetskoy, Prince N. S., *K Probleme Russkogo Samopoznaniia* (Paris, 1927).

"Tsenzura v tsarstvovanie imperatora Nikolaia I," VI, *Russkaia Starina, 113* (1903), 305–28, 571–91.

Turgenev, I. S., "Letter to P. V. Annenkov," *Krasnyi Arkhiv, 32* (1929), 196.

Unbegaun, B., "Les relations vieux-russes de la prise de Constantinople," *Revue des Études Slaves, 9* (1929), 13–38.

Uspensky, G. *Polnoe Sobranie Sochinenii,* 12 vols. (St. Petersburg, 1908–09).

Ustrialov, N. G., *Istoriia tsarstvovaniia Petra Velikago,* 5 vols. (St. Petersburg, 1858–63).

Uvarov, S. S. "Desiatiletie Ministerstva Narodnago Prosveshcheniia 1833–1843 gg.," *Epokha Nikolaia, 1,* ed. M. O. Gershenzon (Moscow, 1911).

Val'denberg, V. E., *Drevnerusskie ucheniia o predelakh tsarskoi vlasti* (Petrograd, 1916).

———, "Nastavlenie pisatelia VI veka, Agapita v russkoi pis'mennosti," *Vizantiiskii Vremennik, 24* (1923–26), 27–34.

Varadinov, N., *Istoriia Ministerstva Vnutrennikh del* (St. Petersburg, 1862).

Venturi, F., *Il Populismo Russo, 2* vols. (Turin, 1952).

Vernadsky, G., "Die Kirchlich-Politische Lehre der Epanogoge und Einfluss auf das Russische Leben in XVII Jahrhundert," *Byz.-Neugriechische Jahrbücher, 6* (1928), 119–42.

———, "Vizantiiskie ucheniia o vlasti tsaria i patriarkha," *Recueil d'etudes dediées à la memoire de N. P. Kondakov* (Prague, 1926), 143–54.

Viazemsky, P. A., *Polnoe Sobranie Sochinenii,* 10 vols. (St. Petersburg, 1880).

———, *Staraia Zapisnaia Knizhka,* ed. L. Ginzburg (Leningrad, 1929).

Voinskie povesti drevnei Rusi, ed. Adrianova-Perets (Moscow, 1949).

Weidle, V., *Zadacha Rossii* (New York, 1956).

Zabelin, I. E., *Domashnyi Byt Russkago Naroda, 2* vols. (Moscow, 1872).

Zhmakin, V. I., "Koronatsii Russkikh Imperatorov i Imperatrits 1724–1856gg.," *Russkaia Starina, 37* (1883), 499–538, *38* (1883), 1–36.

Zhukovsky, V. A., *Sochineniia,* 6 vols. (St. Petersburg, 1878).

Zimin, A. A., "O politicheskoi doktrine Iosifa Volotskogo," *T.O.D.R.L., 9* (ANSSSR, 1953), 159–77.

Index

THE SELECTION of subjects for the index always presents great difficulties; in the case of this book made greater by the fact that the main subjects are indicated and stated in the general title and in the chapter titles. In the event, while the index presents various nuances and definitions of such subjects as "Holy Russia" or the "Russian God," the subjects which form part of the general or chapter titles are not indexed. The reader can assume that the bulk of the relevant references can be found in the chapter dealing with the subject in question.